I Make Mark

I Make Mark

Dee Tze

Copyright © 2019~Dee Erica

Apart from any fair dealing for the purpose of private study, research, criticism or review, as permitted under the Copyright Act, no part may be reproduced by any process without permission from the author. Every effort to comply with copyright requirements has been made by seeking permission and acknowledging owners of source material used in the text.

Disclaimer:

i) This book is a collection of memories. Information gathered has come from a wide variety of sources. The personal stories and memories by individuals recorded here are their version of events and have been both provided and reproduced in good faith with no disrespect or defamation intended. Every effort has been made to ensure the researched information is correct. No liability for incorrect information or factual errors will be accepted by the author.

ii) The views and opinions expressed in this work are solely those of the author. Some names may have been changed to protect privacy however they reflect real people and events.

Writing style: Every intention has been kept to retain the authors voice in this biography. Her writing style, a combination of idiotypical usage of syntax, diction, punctuation, dialogue, etc., within the body of text is unique and raw and conveys the author's attitude, personality, and character. No editing occurred, no changes were made. The content is the important message and we encourage you to peruse accordingly.

A catalogue record for this book is available from the National Library of Australia

ISBN: 978-0-6484500-0-9 paperback
ISBN: 978-0-6484500-1-6 hardback
ISBN: 978-0-6484500-2-3 ebook

Cover and interior:
Pickawoowoo Publishing Group www.pickawoowoo.com

Printing and distribution:
Lightning Source (USA, UK, AUS, EUR).

For Fabian

My Son was and continues to be my greatest teacher, even from beyond the veil.

Contents

Introduction	1
CHAPTER ONE	8
CHAPTER TWO	16
CHAPTER THREE	36
CHAPTER FOUR	42
CHAPTER FIVE	51
CHAPTER SIX	62
CHAPTER SEVEN	68
CHAPTER EIGHT	75
CHAPTER NINE	85
CHAPTER TEN	92
CHAPTER ELEVEN	101
CHAPTER TWELVE	115
CHAPTER THIRTEEN	128
CHAPTER FOURTEEN	137
CHAPTER FIFTEEN	149
CHAPTER SIXTEEN	155
CHAPTER SEVENTEEN	167
CHAPTER EIGHTEEN	175

CHAPTER NINETEEN	193
CHAPTER TWENTY	202
CHAPTER TWENTY ONE	213
CHAPTER TWENTY TWO	237
CHAPTER TWENTY THREE	244
CHAPTER TWENTY FOUR	258
CHAPTER TWENTY FIVE	270
CHAPTER TWENTY SIX	292
About the Author	300
Acknowledgement	302

Introduction

'Behind the Scenes' of I MAKE MARK

Writing this book came as a surprise at first, certainly not something I had planned. A Psychic Medium advised me during a reading in 2000 that I would write two books (with help from "*the other side*"). I didn't realize at the time this was to become a passion, a passion which was to be ignited following a counselling session.

All my life, from a very young age (like Primary school age), I would have a particular dream … always the same …it would fade for a time … then it would be back … loud and clear … I would always remember it next day and know I had experienced this dream previously. A huge pencil would appear and I would try ever so hard to balance it and try to use it to write … but the pencil was so large, how could one who was so small balance the sheer size and write at the same time? I was always on the 'small' side, my hands so tiny, this huge pencil was a challenge, even in my dreams. It wasn't until many years after I commenced our story that I realized I hadn't had 'that' dream for quite some time….since I started writing in fact! To this day I am unsure of the true meaning of that dream. Maybe it was a sign that writing was to be an important component of my complicated life. Maybe I would not achieve my dream until I was old enough to 'balance' and hold the huge responsibility which came with it. Since that first dream I have certainly been waiting a long time to reach this point and 'master that pencil'!

It has taken years for me to get to this point, as it is now July 2018. The framework was completed by January 2006. After that point it was a case of edit, add, edit - repeat! Each and every time I thought it was complete

I would hear from 'someone' read 'something' and know it needed to be included. It felt like a never ending process.

Little did I know how true that prediction was to become. I listened to those words at the time, recalled occasionally then would forget until the next time they made a fleeting appearance.

There were times I would hear "Go and write your book". I would think to myself, "But I am sitting quite comfortably on the lounge thank you, with no desire to move". Then I would hear those thoughts again "Go and write your book" more insistent this time. I had my very own conscious issuing orders. I would venture to the computer - three hours or more later I would realize I was either cold, hungry or if I didn't get to bed I sure wasn't going to make it to work next day.

I was literally taken over, words coming easily, next time I sat down to write I would occasionally re-read the last written pages. To my constant surprise it would make perfect sense, other times the words and spelling an indication of how very tired I was, but at least the details were sufficient to build upon.

I would be lying in bed and I would hear the words "You have to put this in your book." Lo and behold, two or three past events would be taking turns running through my mind, acting out in detail as if they occurred yesterday. Pad and pen were constant companions beside my bed for those *you have to* moments.

"You have to elaborate on your feelings," so ok, now I needed to edit the book from scratch, this time elaborating as per my instructions. Bossy and unrelenting, you had better believe it! Is this what the medium meant when she said "With help from *the other side*?" To say with "*insistence* from the other side" may have been a more correct statement!

I soon learned there was no point in arguing. It was easier to take notice and follow the instructions as they came to mind, or at least make notes until I had the time to undertake the next three hour session.

One night, in bed, I was feeling so very sick, in came the now familiar words "You have to put this in your book", I remember saying "Oh

Fabian, can't it wait, I feel so bad tonight?" Thankfully the events outlined remained in my mind until I was well enough to put to print.

My aim is to encourage discussion regardless of the topic, to seek understanding, guidance and expert advice, to encourage readers to learn the lesson the experience is trying to teach them. To marvel and be thankful for the qualities gained and friendships which flourish as a result of the experience.

I have been given many challenges. At first I did not understand why. Then I began to study numerology and realized I was here on Earth to master certain lessons and to learn from them. I assumed I was given the challenges for a reason. and if, by writing this book, even one person no longer feels alone, then my experiences have been worthwhile.

My counsellor tells me there are two ways in which to learn: to experience or to hear of another person's experience. The majority of my learning has definitely emanated from the 'to experience' category.

A challenge does not have to be viewed as 'punishment' it is a 'lesson', a lesson which can be navigated, conquered and learned.

I am hopeful that by reading my book you will realize it is possible to get through trying periods, that it is possible to remain sane even under the most trying circumstances and that laughter and tears bring us back to the 'position of truth'. To live in the moment, no matter how difficult it may appear, it is not getting from A to B which is important, but the journey itself. To live, learn and appreciate each individual experience, to appreciate the people who come into our lives when we most need them, people who assist us to learn, grow and appreciate life. To understand that people leave our lives when they are ready and in their own time and for reasons which may not be known or understood at the time. If we can no longer grow from an experience or friendship it will leave us at the appropriate time.

I have written this book by combining both the past and the present simultaneously. What I hope to illustrate is the fact that the book was written under difficult circumstances. I am a mother. I was working full time, have serious health issues, housework has to be done, lawns mowed, spend time with friends and family and the list goes on. Above all I want to continue writing my book … and the biggest challenge of all - come to terms with the death of my son.

I have been on a 'slow trail of learning' spanning many years, each experience adding to my list. My aim is to take you on my journey so although I could explain the meaning of certain challenges I choose to impart that information in the year I learned of it. In most cases the learning and understanding came many years after the original event. So my original feelings and thoughts on particular incidents have modified and transformed with the years. With age comes wisdom and understanding. Hopefully by reading my books your understanding will come far sooner and your life richer as a result. I have outlined certain books or authors from whom I have gained insight and I hope you avail yourself of their work and the work of others. There is a wealth of knowledge sitting on the shelves of bookshops. The books will 'choose' you, they will make themselves known to you and you will have difficulty leaving the store without them. These are the books you are meant to read to assist you in your journey. Whilst the books I outline have helped me immensely they may not be the books for you, use your intuition, listen to your inner voice and choose the books for you.

For years I was in a *'happy'* place and could not bring myself to continue with our story. Then in mid 2008 I became so ill I had to admit defeat and resign from work completely. My usual experience was - have three months off work and my health would return, not this time, it didn't work! I became more and more ill. By December 2008 I knew I had to take steps to seek additional assistance. Therein began my quest to seek holistic treatments which would work in unison to help restore my body to working condition.

I put my intuition to work and came up with Kinesiology, Reflexology and Massage (lymph drainage massage, with the aim of jump starting my immune system). It has taken hours of therapy, vitamins and supplements to get me to the stage where I now have 'some' quality of life once again. I shall elaborate more fully in my next book 'Beyond Description'.

I have used my 'good' days to continue writing, editing and crying. At long last the end is in sight. Hmmm end of the book that is, not end of me!

The lesson I hope you take from this: 'you can achieve anything' if it is important to you, that you can keep going even under adverse conditions, if you have the correct recipe!

My Recipe for Dealing with Life's Challenges

Ingredients: Open mind, love yourself, support, encouragement, laughter, tears, anger, self pity, physical exercise, listen to your own intuition, gratitude for all that is good in your life, sleep, time to meditate or contemplate the proverbial navel, reduce stress levels, spend quality time with friends and above all keep that sense of humour and strong belief in yourself.

Method: Mix well and use each ingredient as and when required. If all else fails throw a minor teary tantrum and then begin again. Don't dwell on the past, don't worry about the future, one is too late, the other too early, the 'here and now' is the important factor.

Allow *self pity* in moderation only. A stipulated time period clause may be beneficial, then extend if required.

Anger is acceptable, even mandatory under certain circumstances, be mindful of where or to whom the anger is being directed - might be more appropriate to aim it constructively and combine with physical exercise - I can guarantee squash is excellent for that purpose, especially if one has just been raided by the police - works wonders! When you understand more about your own behaviour and that of others, anger may even become redundant. Whatever feeling you 'feel' love and appreciate that feeling even if it is negative, love every part of you and move past it with love and gratitude.

Ballroom Dancing is like a 'happy drug'. Age, sex, marital status has no bearing on this particular form of exercise. It is for anyone who wants to have fun, forget problems for three hours and get fit in the process.

Meditation can help to heal emotional wounds by bringing you to a state of peace. Delve into numerology. Read Spiritual books. Forgive yourself and forgive others. Love yourself and love others. Learn and grow. When you realize what your lessons are in this life, previous or current challenges will make sense to you. You will no longer hate those who hurt you, instead you will thank them for giving you a chance to grow and learn. It may sound a difficult concept to grasp but have faith when I say it is true!

Put your own recipe together, a recipe which suits *your* needs.

Thank you to my 'proof reader' who, years ago, devoted and volunteered hours of his free time for proof reading purposes. I appreciate his efforts and am truly grateful for his comments. His brief was to allow me to use my everyday 'Denise-isms', I wanted readers to feel as if I was sitting on a lounge talking with them as friends. I wanted the reader to relax and gain from my experiences if at all possible. He explained where I needed to expand on a topic in order for the reader to understand. I know what I am talking about but I sometimes tend to forget others don't and I need to elaborate. I am not a professional nor do I profess to be. I am a regular person trying to assist others in navigating their way through their life challenges. He kept me on the right path, grammatically speaking. Thank you! Thank you so very much.

Thank you to those friends who supported me at different times throughout this very long process, know that friends come and go as do our thoughts, as in all things….it too shall pass. If we are no longer growing from a relationship we move on when the time is right. People come into our lives other leave. Life is a learning process with many paths.

Thank you also to my daughter Laura, who has put up with me, my diseases, my moods and for all the times I said: *"What is it? I am trying to work on my book!"* Thanks Smidge for being the beautiful individual free spirit you are, for believing in me and for your never ending unconditional love, I love you with all my heart.

I also need to make mention and thank the revered Lao Tze who has graciously channeled to me for a number of years. Lao Tze is my 'Spiritual Father'. I give thanks for his input and guidance and for allowing me the privilege of channeling his Holistic Wheel Theory incorporated at the end of I MAKE MARK. Thank you my 'Cherished One'.

Please enjoy our story. I would like to think it may help you in some small way…now for me it is back to the drawing board 'BEYOND DESCRIPTION' awaits.

CHAPTER ONE

Over the years friends, acquaintances, psychic mediums even my chiropractor have said "You should write a book, you will write a book, or when are you going to write your book" my reply, where on earth would I start? I really believed it was figments of their imaginations. I had had so many challenges I couldn't even comprehend where I might begin, even if I wanted to. Those very thoughts would be dismissed within minutes of hearing the words, put aside as a 'maybe if I ever get the time or inclination'. The idea did have merit but lay dormant for many years.

I believe that everything happens for a reason. I learned many things through my son Fabian, *I MAKE MARK* appeared at the bottom of what I can only describe as a *'statement of feelings'* he wrote when he first began to experience the symptoms of schizophrenia. Grappling with the onset of this condition must have been horrendous. His words give a minute insight into the confused state of his tormented mind and the solution he saw and sought. A scanned copy of the original words are inserted at the appropriate location, you can read and understand firsthand what he was experiencing and how he viewed life at that moment in time. It wasn't pretty!

Writing was probably the furthest thing from my mind until December 2003; I didn't even realize I wanted to write. A visit to my Dr Counsellor took on new meaning one particular day. My diseases were out of control, all the usual methods of repair not working, I didn't understand why. I was doing everything humanly possible to repair me and failing miserably. He asked what it was I was trying to get out and wasn't achieving. I thought for a while. After a few "I don't knows" and him saying, "Yes you do, think about it" I realized what it was he was helping me to understand. A few weeks prior I had cut out an article from a magazine; it was a competition for a short story. It hadn't eventuated into anything material, merely an idea. I had filed the article and hadn't had time to get back to it. I wanted to enter this competition, *what I wanted to get out was a short story!*

Prior to the visit to Dr Counsellor I had attended a Mind, Body and Soul Expo. I didn't have anything definite in mind; I was merely guided to attend. One of the psychic mediums had a coat of many colours; reminded me of the story in the Bible. I wanted to see this particular person, no other would suffice. I waited my turn. I said to him "You have something to tell me that I need to hear, I don't know what it is, I just know that it will come from you". Amongst other things, he said these words to me "Does air going through a bird's wings mean anything to you?" He looked puzzled. I smiled, it sure did. He said "You want to be *like* the bird, but not *be* the bird". Prior to this, a friend, Laura and I had been on a short holiday to Scamander on Tasmania's east coast. I was sitting on a balcony early one morning and a pelican had flown so close I could hear the rush of air through its wings as it made its way back to the beach for the day. I thanked the Universe for that beautiful, memorable experience, it was truly magic, I felt so grateful to that bird, the Universe was trying to tell me something, I just didn't know what. No one but a friend and I knew how meaningful that experience was for me.

I exited the psychic expo feeling satisfied I had received information I required but confused as to what it meant.

As I left my Dr Counsellor's office my now overworked and confused brain had a 'light bulb moment' and the pieces fell into place. I found myself feeling elated, overwhelmed, grateful; excited to the point you could not even begin to imagine.

Thanks to two amazingly, beautiful souls, I realized I wanted to not only enter the competition with my short story but I wanted to win. I was hoping a publisher would see the story, view it as a stepping stone and realize there was sufficient depth and content for a book. The majority of funds raised would then be channelled to organizations which assist others to make sense of their mangled, often trauma filled lives. To guide them in taking responsibility to make their lives once again work for them, instead of against them.

Dr Counsellor knew very early in life what it was he wanted to achieve and set out to accomplish his vision. When I met him *'the world according to Denise'* finally began to make sense for the first time in my life. I wanted this scenario to be experienced by many who would benefit from understanding their emotions and be able to apply it to their lives. I wanted understanding for all those who seek a more positive outcome for themselves. Understanding is Power! Personal Power!

At one time he had a safe house where he allowed the most vulnerable he was assisting to live (clients who needed to have a 'time out' period from society), in return they worked on the daffodil farm, they were making a contribution by producing award winning daffodil bulbs. They were given a wage for their contribution to the farm; this wage in turn paid their rent. This plot of land housed 250,000 daffodils so I imagine they well and truly earned their keep by taking care of the precious bulbs. This environment was established with the aim of teaching them skills they hadn't learned growing up. They were treated as guests, not locked up, so their cooperation was purely on trust and based on the belief they wanted the knowledge which would enable them to lead a normal life, free of trauma and pain. Counselling was part of the package; they were assisted in every way possible.

If only we could foster more of the same it would make the world a far better and safer place to be. How much those chosen few gained from this experience we can only imagine, I know I was extremely grateful to know a man who would do this for the emotionally disadvantaged, I imagine their gratitude was way more than I could surmise.

This particular humanitarian also had a dream of setting up a suicide clinic whereby acutely suicidal people could attend and talk through their problems. This clinic would operate twenty four hours per day, seven days a week. Again it would operate on a purely voluntary basis, clients would be free to enter and leave as they desired. It would be based on a belief that it is not possible to 'save' everyone, for some it is their time to leave and as such should be allowed to follow their particular path. For others it would be part of a 'process' they were going through and once help was sought could see their way through their problems and come out the other side, more self aware as a result.

Suicidal thoughts can be a catalyst for change if handled correctly. This clinic would work with them to help them understand what *part* of their life they wanted to kill. What part of their life did they want to change? Give them strategies for dealing with the more pressing problem, whether it be financial, relationship, health or addiction. Hopefully they would leave the clinic armed with a more positive attitude, a coping mechanism and hope for a more productive and positive future. A future where they knew society cares for them and about them and where counselling and support is available for those who seek same.

I wanted so much for this type of work to continue: this brand of counselling isn't for everyone but for people like me and for others who have been challenged beyond comprehension it provides an invaluable insight into the reasons why our lives are what they are.

This type of counseling/education forces clients to take a look at their behavior: thoughts and actions. Confronting it is, which is why I say, it is not for everyone. It is for those who want to change and are willing to work toward that end. He taught me to trust my intuition more, to listen to my own counsel. He told me I had always managed to get to the correct point even though I had not understood how I got there. He gave me the skills and insight which enabled me to make sense of my life, helped me to understand where I had been and where I was going.

So, having discovered what it was I was trying to get out, the next major questions were: how, when and did I have the talent, time and ability to pull it off?

Following this realization it took me a time to acknowledge I wanted to write two or three books. *One evening I had to sit up in bed and write the beginnings and titles of three books, am guessing this was the onset of the 'with help from the other side' comment.* It awakened something in me I didn't even know existed; it was the beginning of my new life. Hmmm, maybe I should say a 'new' ambition or addition to my life, bearing in mind I had a child to raise solo, a fulltime working life, still had a normal household to run and my ever growing collection of diseases to keep in check.

Was there more to life than I could see? Was there a connection between the body and mind? Could our diseases really be connected to, caused by or influenced by our thinking patterns? It certainly gave me something to think about.

During the year 2000 *normal* people went to work, me, I attended the Coroners' Hearing into Deaths in Custody almost every day for over two months. I took notes each and every day not even knowing the reason why. My feelings, significant events which took place in and out of the court room all written down in detail. I knew one day the reason would be revealed to me. At the time it was merely something I knew I had to do, I placed my trust in that belief and allowed myself to go with it.

My life has been filled with many and varied learning experiences, not always pleasant but events which taught me lessons one could not hope to learn from a text book. I hope by reading of my experiences you may realize that events do not have to be categorized into bad or good but merely as 'learning experiences'. Experiences appreciated for what they are. We gain strength, confidence, grace, humility, understanding, a range of qualities from living and navigating our way through life challenges. Embrace and celebrate the strong *you* who emerges at the end. Remember, you are very special; there is no other person on earth like you, so love and above all, accept *you* for who *you* are.

On occasions I have felt as though I am standing outside of *my* life watching it unfold, unable to change or guide it to a conclusion of my choosing. I did not knowingly encourage all of my experiences, some were choices other people made in their lives and I was merely an *unwilling* participant. Either way, I learned a considerable amount as a result and met some amazing people, thus making each experience one to cherish and be thankful for. Please note: not that I wish to relive any of these experiences, once was sufficient, thank you. But still I am grateful.

I have always felt like I was abandoned in a foreign land without a 'how to do it' manual. I have never felt like I belonged anywhere or to anyone. I have always felt like an outsider even in my own family. No one has spoken the same language or thought the same thoughts; I would know things without understanding how I knew them. I have managed to collect a series of symptoms all of which still remain a mystery to the medical profession, some I had never heard of or knew anyone who had. Of late I have learned and come so far spiritually that I am finally beginning to understand. This understanding I shall impart in my next book, who knows it may even help you to make sense of your life.

I have learned one really important lesson; we have incarnated on Earth in order to fulfil our '*Life Purpose*', we have chosen our beautiful body for a reason, small, large, short, tall, regardless, it is *still* beautiful and up to us to look after and maintain to the best of our knowledge and ability. At the end of this book I shall introduce the '*Holistic Wheel*' theory and explain how this will help to support the body so the body is able to support us thru 'Life's Journey'.

I MAKE MARK seemed to be an appropriate title for my first book, a dedication to Fabian's short tormented life and testament to the fact that he did indeed make a positive mark on those who knew him. Unfortunately, I never realized how much of a mark he made until after his death. Words of support and individuals with their own stories began to flood into my life, stories of how polite, friendly and considerate he was in his dealings with others. People and professionals went out of their way to assist him through various stages of the worst years of his very short life, to quote one professional "what wasn't to like" he may have been extremely mentally ill but still very loveable. That was my boy!

To say life for Fabian was difficult is something of an understatement, right from birth he endured problem after problem but still he continued to see good in people, friends he treasured, everyone was his friend. One night whilst watching a documentary on a third world country he turned to me and said "We don't realize how lucky we are, do we? He informed me at one stage "Nan won't be going to a nursing home she will come to live with us won't she?" He couldn't bear to think of his grandmother in a home for the aged.

He would not tolerate anyone denigrating his friends in any way, shape or form; he would help anyone who asked him even if it meant leaving him without. Watching him spiral downhill was heartbreaking, soul destroying, but somehow he managed to give me strength and inspiration to carry on and to write this book. I know this book is written with his guidance, insistence, blessing and love.

There are omissions in my story, it does not mean that these people are less important, that the events were less important, this couldn't be further from the truth, I have Fabian's permission to discuss **his** journey. This does not imply I have the right to discuss the journey of 'others' so please understand there are reasons for omissions. Others have a right to their privacy. Some relationships are also off the radar but will be incorporated in my third book *IMAGINE*.

Having only this minute (September 2108) acquainted myself with invasion of privacy lawsuit and libel issues I now find it necessary to protect not only myself but others who were previously named (with pride and gratitude in most cases) throughout my story. Sooooooo unfortunately I now find myself obliged to either omit or change names. The only positive I can glean from this, is for those who read our story to recognize themselves and know they contributed in a positive way to our lives, our soul development and know I appreciated them so very, very much. I wish with all my heart I could use your rightful given names but unfortunately this is no longer an option. Thank you for being a positive part of my life. … A few days later … I tried in vain to substitute names … but it seemed too false and I found I was unable to action, it felt like

I was out of integrity with myself in doing so. I apologise in advance for how many instances I found it necessary to write …my husband … my girlfriend … my daughter … Fabian's dad etc. Substitution felt like I was diminishing their role in my life and I was unable to do that. I thank you in advance for your understanding.

I hope you gain something from reading our story and I thank you for taking the time to do so.

CHAPTER TWO

Now as to where to start, I guess I had best take it from the beginning, my arrival on planet Earth.

I was born Sunday March 2 1952 at 2.10pm and named Denise Erica Filbia Harris. I have a sister and a brother, eleven and eight years older than me. People ask "Where are you from" I reply "Crabtree" their shocked response is invariably "Where?", that's how small it is, I found it easier to say near Huonville, this explanation means a little more and most people appear happy with that response. Huonville is a small country town in southern Tasmania once renowned for apple growing. Even now if I had to choose somewhere in Australia to live, Tasmania would be my preference, the air maybe cool on most occasions but it is so clean and beautiful refreshing. A five minute drive from pretty much anywhere can guarantee the air intake is *'officially unpolluted'*.

Life seemed simple, go to school, under take allotted tasks after school and on weekends. Pick small fruit during the summer school holidays. Little did I know what life and the Man Upstairs had in store for me! My life was to be full, from the perspective of experience, learning and content. I certainly came with a full agenda.

Boring was a word I wasn't to become familiar with. There are times I would love to know boring, but it still remains an elusive state for me.

In those days children were 'seen and not heard', the 'speak when spoken to' attitude prevailed, consequently life's problems eluded me over the years, life was relatively carefree and happy, I was naïve enough to believe that is how it would remain. I had no other yard stick on which to measure life, only this one. I have never applied that measure to my children; I have always discussed events with them and answered any questions as honestly as I could. I didn't believe they should be brought up under an 'illusion', I don't believe illusions help in the real world. Life may not always be pretty but it is life and should still be celebrated faults and all, how would we ever know and appreciate true happiness and peace if we do not know grief and stress. How will our children learn how to cope with problems if we do not give them examples? There is a positive in most situations, find it and focus on it and it only. You are the model upon which children base their behaviour. Be a positive role model.

Only balance can put us on the true path to peace and bring us back to the position of truth. Balance and moderation in all things is the key, easy to say, not so easy to achieve!

My earliest memory was one of waking to find myself alone, I couldn't find anyone, I remember walking into the kitchen, one bucket of water between me and the doorway, (well at least that meant someone was home) I managed to land in it somehow. Found my dad outside talking to my great uncle, think I may have uttered some kind of (*what I obviously felt was warranted*) abuse. Turned out I would have only be about 18 months old, mum was in hospital at the time, my brother and sister at school, I was speechless when I discovered my age associated with that memory. I remember the kitchen floor seemed to go on for an eternity, quite ironic when I consider how small the whole house was, let alone that particular room.

When I close my eyes I can see it as if it were yesterday, so why can't I remember what I went into the bedroom for five minutes ago. Memory is a funny thing. Sometimes there, other times nowhere to be seen when you most need it. I would dearly love to understand why some memories are so vivid and remain with us as if placed there by a branding iron. Other events which occurred around that same time appear gone forever and can only be recalled with external prompting and extended periods of concentration.

My dad worked for the Public Works Department, repairing bridges, roads and culverts; quite often he would be away for the whole week, dependent upon which remote location he may be working at the time. Not such a bad thing I learned. Friday nights on these occasions, dad would be at the hotel with his mates, when he finished, he and I would go into the newsagency and I would be allowed to choose a book, always elves, fairies and gnomes - I cherished those books, I still wonder what became of them. I still like David the gnome stories to this day and wish for the return of children's programs full of beautiful stories, stories which help to teach valuable life lessons in lieu of stories which promote and condone violent behaviour as the norm.

My uncles and aunts on my dad's side of the family all lived in the Hobart area, one family used to visit on the occasional Sunday, I longed for those visits, my uncle used to play with me tossing me around his shoulders. Those visits meant fresh town bread, such an important commodity, bread we received in the country just didn't cut it, I still remember how fresh the town bread (as we termed it) used to taste - unreal.

I attended infant, primary and high schools at Huonville. Still have mostly fond memories of those days. Some not so fond like the mathematics teacher who used to put his finger on his chin, then when I least expected it, there it was pointing right at me, if only I hadn't been daydreaming, listening would have been a distinct advantage at those moments. Maths? He may have been speaking a foreign language for all the good it did, the lesson would usually sail right on past without even giving a hint of stopping or slowing long enough for me to take any of it onboard! It just wasn't my thing and there wasn't anything I could do about it. Be that as it may, it didn't seem to deter this particular teacher from trying and trying.

Memories like lining up to make the long walk to the bus stop, long, well these days it is more like a hop, step and jump but when one is in primary school the walk seemed so long.

Black and white television, I was in grade 3 at the time, one neighbour bought the first television I had ever seen. It was a case of, off the school bus, get changed into old clothes, race out the door, up the hill and be running in their door just in time to hear "Clutch Cargo and his Pal

Spinner and Paddlefoot", yes made it, just in time for the episode for that day. I think I was in grade 4 before we had such an important addition to *our* family home.

Winter in the Huon is a story in itself. Wake to fog, fog clears by lunch time, 3pm it is back. My friends and I used to buy hot chips of a morning, not really for the hunger aspect, more to keep the hands warm. Fog would engulf the whole quadrangle, cold unbelievable. In those days to work in the school kiosk was something every one vied for, the kiosk was warm.

I remember the floods in 1960 which took out most of the bridges, remember having to walk across a plank over the river (still remember how scared I was, wishing I didn't have to make that walk to my nan's house) the memory is hazy, it probably wasn't as dangerous as I remember, but at the time it was a positive nightmare and courage required with each crossing. I absolutely hated and dreaded that crossing.

The one thing that can make a person feel very insignificant is a huge flood, to stand by the river's edge and watch as large logs thunder along with the surging water, listening to the thud as the logs hit other logs rushing in the same direction and crash over rocks. It is as if they are all competing and in a hurry to reach their distant destination. Lying in bed at night listening to the distant rumble as the logs continued on their course. It is a truly awesome feeling, leaving one feeling very insignificant and weak in comparison but wondering at the marvel of nature and the force by which she can strike.

> *I look back now and I think – wow, a flood mimics life in a way. The corporate world is like that, everyone rushing and trampling each other in a race to get to where they want to go. Whether it be the next promotion, to keep in favour with the boss, all rushing to get to the top of the pile, regardless of who they trample in the process. If only relationships at work could sail along in tranquil waters with the focus being on the big picture in lieu of individual achievement and recognition. The one thing that has fascinated me*

since my very early working days was watching the expressions of people as they made their way to work for the day. Not many expressions said "I can't wait to get to work, I love what I do" most said "oh geez I wish I was on my way to anywhere but work" no hint of a smile, satisfaction or anticipation. If we were not in 'flood' mode would workplace stress be less prevalent? Do we need to be in 'flood' mode?

In contrast to the flood, I remember vividly, peaceful moments spent sitting by the river's edge at dusk, watching the fish jump for insects, sense of wonder as the ripples danced on the surface, the splashing sound as their bodies made contact with the water upon reentry, insects meeting their demise as they performed their part in nature's food chain. I never tired of this sight nor the peace of mind which came with it. I wasn't very old yet I felt extremely privileged to be part of that amazing scene.

Hours spent swimming in the river during the summer months; the water was always cool, clean and invigorating, pollution wasn't part of the scene during those years. Mind you, I could have done without one child holding me underwater by my foot. I struggled and struggled to break free, to this day I still need my feet to be touching ground, I never venture further than I can feel under foot. That memory remains with me, she was so much bigger and stronger, I was released, gasping for air and vowing never to put myself in that position ever again. She was an early version of the school yard bully, she just didn't contain it to the school yard, so if you think it is a more recent phenomena, it isn't! It was alive and well in the 50s and 60s. She would punch me, pull my hair and generally harass me, at school, on the school bus and on the home front.

One year I stepped back and put my foot down on a broken bottle (what did I say about pollution not being part of the scene in those days) hmmm. Dad piggy backed me all the way home. I wasn't taken to the doctor until days later, by this time he was unable to stitch me back together, he did make a point of saying it was a 'clean wound' my reply to that "Of course it was, I did it in the water". I wasn't very old and the idea of 'clean' to me was the obvious, wish I could recall the look on his face, exasperation or a hint of a smile? I have paid for that little episode for many years. That poor foot has been damaged once too often and now lets me know if I do not wear shoes with the correct support. I believe we take too many of our bodily parts for granted; correct fitting shoes should be the norm regardless of the medical situation. Like all parts of our body they should be given due respect and gratitude, after all they have to last us a long time.

Potatoes, row after row, grown and stored. This necessitated plowing the paddock, first we had a small Ransom tractor - that was easy to drive, couldn't really go wrong. This small piece of machinery was later replaced by a Massey Ferguson. I remember my first lesson, dad standing beside me on the tractor, standing … hmmm that was almost head first off when I first applied the brakes and applied pressure to the accelerator, not sure which or how dad managed to hang on but to his credit he did. Unable to recall whether or not I was permitted to drive after that, if I did you can probably surmise dad wasn't standing beside me, he was probably taking precautionary measures by supervising from a distance.

Organic vegetables, milk, cream and butter compliments of our resident cow; free range eggs and poultry thanks to our ladies from the hen house, rabbit meat caught and cleaned by dad. Haven't we come a long way since then, in order to have organic items we now need to travel kilometers in order to secure same. I firmly believe the ultimate will be a return to this type of lifestyle, our bodies no longer able to cope with years of abuse from toxins caused by pesticides, herbicides, preservatives, additives and genetic intervention of whole foods. How much has changed in 60+ years. I don't believe our bodies were ever designed with the intention to eat anything other than whole foods and it certainly wasn't designed with the intention of ingesting, or being exposed to the many, many toxic chemicals which have come into existence at an alarming rate and quantity.

Picking small fruit during the summer wasn't something to think about it was a fact of life. Raspberries, blackcurrants, loganberries, red currants, black currants. Still gives me goose bumps when I think of lifting a branch of the raspberry bush only to find a snake curled up sound asleep, the preferred option was to let him sleep and move on to the next bush quickly and quietly. Money from this exercise paid for our school books and clothes for the coming year. We learned at an early age money wasn't something to be taken for granted, it had to be earned.

Blackberries came at another time, all added to the family bank balance in some way. I had my own jam tin with string weaved through it tied around my small waist, I even looked at fruit picking as a challenge and set myself certain goals to reach. The fact I had a jam tin gives an idea of how young I would have been - or is that how small I must have been! Hmmm, when I come to think about it, some things haven't changed much, except that piece of string would need to be much longer these days!

Strawberry picking was another item on the Christmas calendar; dad had planted about 2,000 strawberry plants. I used to hoe the rows for six pence a row, I was too young to understand multiplication so I'm told I used to place lines in a row and add them to gain a total. A stroke through the line meant I only hoed half a row. I'm willing to bet those rows were well worth six pence. My very first bike was earned from strawberry picking (or at least I thought it was). I suppose only mum and dad could answer that question truthfully.

Strawberry picking did have other advantages. One year my sister and I were picking together (summer time, hot weather - light clothing was the order of the day), she hated frogs, and me, well I quite liked them. Frogs were plentiful, they enjoyed the ambient temperature and regular watering conditions under the strawberry plants, encountering yet another under the leaves I couldn't help myself. Goal, six points, target reached. It landed with an ungainly thump inside her top; boy did she jump and shout. Well I thought it was worth the scolding I got for my trouble. Can't say I had seen her move that fast before, it's a wonder we didn't end up with rain after the dance she performed. It also alleviated the monotony of strawberry picking, at least for that day anyway. For the record, the frog lived to jump another day; I only tossed him/her lightly from a short distance, no animals were harmed in accumulating tales for this story!

It didn't end there, whether it was boredom or the sheer joy of 'because I could factor' I don't really know but I couldn't help myself…. our toilet was external to the main house, unfortunately for my sister it also had an external lock, she went in and I locked the door. She shouted and shouted for me to let her out. Remember I said I was only quite small. I had managed to lock the door but when it came to reverse the process I wasn't tall enough to reach or I was so stressed by the shouting, either way I couldn't manage the unlock stage … Yes she did eventually get out but for the life of me I can't remember how. You can expect I wasn't too popular when she finally emerged. I am willing to bet I started running really fast.

One not so good memory was the spraying of the apple orchards, we lived at the bottom of a hill, the apple orchard not far away, if spraying was undertaken on a windy day - the smell was foul to say the least, the film of spray would cover everything in its path, not a healthy place to be. A situation reluctantly accepted without question in those days. Don't imagine it did much for the soil either. I shudder to think of the damage the spraying of chemicals caused either directly or indirectly to numerous innocent people. Safety precautions were not high on the agenda in those days; work place safety remained somewhere in the future. Makes me wonder how many of those men lived to a wise old age or were they taken from cancers, heart disease or a myriad of medical problems caused indirectly or directly by the toxic chemicals.

> *I know I have pesticides in my body which amazed my holistic doctor when tests indicated their presence in 1997. She asked me how I managed to accumulate pesticides in my body: my reply "Easy" I outlined the location of our house in relation to an apple orchard. Given the location I probably would have been more surprised not to have accumulated pesticides in my system.*

> *Years later I heard of some research which had been undertaken by one particular holistic doctor, seems many of us chemically intolerant bods hailed from the Huon Valley. Not surprising I suppose. I only 'heard' about this research so I have do not have evidence of validity. All I can say is that it is definitely logical that this could be the case.*

My mum loved her garden, flowers everywhere, my poor nose seemed to be constantly red, my dad used to say "I have never seen a kid with so many colds" my reply "It goes when I get on the school bus, I don't have it as school" unfortunately for me, allergies were not even on the radar in those days, let alone anyone contemplating I could be allergic to my own surroundings.

A walk to the river to swim and lo and behold, everywhere the grass seeds touched my skin I sported red welts, bumper to bumper. If I wanted a challenge early in life, I certainly got my monies worth. Whilst I loved growing up in the country my body certainly wasn't all that thrilled with the experience.

Dad used to say they should put me in a glass case as it would be the only way I would be safe from the world (*if only I had known how true those words were to become!*) At the time no one seemed to know any different, it was like I arrived with this package and it was mine to keep.

Milk - my body was unable to tolerate raw bottled milk. During my early school days milk was provided free, as in mandatory free. If mum failed to write a note to the teacher which would exclude me from drinking that much feared little bottle of milk, I would have to drink it. Believe me when I say it would come back up way faster than it went down. Mum tried various ways to assist, flavoured drinking straws, flavouring - didn't help. So it was best for everyone if we ensured the 'note' was in place at the beginning of a new school year. Why? I don't know, I can tolerate milk if incorporated in a meal but unable to drink straight. Like I said - I arrived with this package; I was, in effect a total contradiction to country living.

My health didn't actually improve until I went to live in the city after I finished high school and was able to take responsibility for my own health and surroundings. But I have to say I enjoyed my time in the country growing up and I wouldn't want to change a thing - except for my allergies that is!

Life wasn't easy financially for my parents, I am guessing. Mum worked at the apple factory during winter. I think she quite enjoyed it. I don't remember how old I was when mum first started working at the factory. I do remember being most indignant at the suggestion I should go to the bus driver and his wife after school. I voiced my disapproval loud and clear, I explained that if the stork had wanted me to be at their house he would have deposited me there and not where I currently was. As such I thought I had every right to remain in situ, even after school. I do believe dad made it perfectly clear that if I wasn't happy then mum had to stay home. Bribery was obviously called into play here, seems mum wanted to go to work by foul means or fair - a doll worked a treat it seems, her name Rosemary (Rosie*)*.

Mind you by the time I finally parted with her, she was looking a little like me, tired, worn, hair thinning and a bit ragged around the edges! Still lovable even in that condition, I only parted with her whilst cleaning out in preparation to move house in 2017. I knew it was time to leave many items behind, leave many memories in the past where they belonged. I needed to press the refresh button and begin the next chapter of my life.

In high school during 'winter apple factory times' I used to get home from school then go at break neck speed to get all my required chores done before night fall. Yep, scared of the dark I was. Guilty as charged on that count.

Mind you, I did have good reason, when I was really young my brother used to wait somewhere between the chook shed and the wood pile at night then jump out at me, got me every time. Then there was the night one of the neighbours dressed up, black all over her face, I answered the door, a move I was to regret. Halloween has a lot to answer for. When I opened the door she scared me silly with her noise, costume and blackened face. Although I was only quite young the 'afraid in the dark' remained with me for quite some years following those events. I do wonder how many children have had traumatic experiences all in the name of Halloween.

I said previously, dad used to work away from home, mum would drive him to the Public Works yard early, like very early of a morning, this meant I was again alone in the dark during winter months. One time whilst I was still quite young (thought I should remind you of that fact so I don't look quite so stupid) three men had escaped from prison. Shortly after mum and dad's early morning departure a knock on the back door scared me, could it be the three men were here, saw mum and dad go and thought it a safe haven. Oh boy is all I can say, the thoughts that raced through my mind. Did I feel stupid when I learned it was one of dad's mates; he was going to offer to drive him to work that morning. I didn't answer the door, I learned this later on. Why he didn't call out and explain is beyond me. Hence I decided I had valid reason to be scared in the dark.

Fresh water is also a memory which remains with me, the water used to be so fresh, so naturally clear and cold. The catchment area for the Crabtree water supply was further up the river from where we lived but not too far. When I started work and moved to Hobart I just couldn't come to grips with the town water supply, it just wasn't the same, always tasted as though it had been in the old pipes for an eternity. Childhood memories and a wish I could turn on my tap and still achieve the same beautiful, cold, fresh, revitalizing, pure water. These days one has to have a filter or filtered bottled water to achieve even a similar quality. In this day and age we take many things for granted - for me, water isn't one of them, I long to return to the days when fresh, clear, chemical free cold water ran from the tap naturally.

Another wonderful memory of country living … The grocery man used to call in his truck weekly, the owner would walk on ahead take the orders, return to the van, pack and deliver, even put some groceries in the fridge if required. Can you imagine that happening today, I think not! Pity when trust in society is replaced by suspicion and projection of our own paranoid thoughts as to what the ulterior motive of someone may or may not be. Innocence is something to be cherished. If only we could return to trust and innocence, I would dearly love the world to return to this state in my life time.

One man who worked on the grocery van, would swap a kiss for an icy pole during the school holidays, I would give him a kiss on the cheek and my reward was my icy pole. I thought that was a pretty good deal. Can you imagine the flack that would cause these days if some kind man undertook that mission … he would be in court before the icy pole melted. By the way, we are talking a very young age here before your mind goes off on a tangent. Nothing sinister in his motives, he was a beautiful, wonderful man with children of his own, he probably knew I would not have otherwise had my prize of an icy pole had it not been for his generosity and the make believe cost.

Mum reminded me of another incident which had my family confused for awhile. I would hear a motor bike coming down the road, I would shout "Here comes Wow" and take off at lightning speed. The gentleman in question, apparently as he sped past he would throw me sweets and I would be on hand to collect my prize. My family finally twigged to what caused my excitement and haste at the sound of that beloved motor bike. Fond memories of a man who found the time in his life and heart to make me feel 'special' and deserving of his attention. Again this incident illustrates how much has changed over the years; children these days would not be able to experience this beautiful gesture, as the motives, however innocent, would be in question and would not be condoned. Stranger danger has taken over and unfortunately, it is our children who suffer as a result.

I was somewhere around 3 years old when I insisted on being a boy. Mum made me short boy pants and cut my brother's golf socks down (but not before he had worn them out of course) to my size. No way would I give them up for the mere sake of a wash and clean, the only time mum had access was night time whilst I slept.

I played with trucks and cars, my icy pole benefactor named me Sammy seeing as though I kept insisting I was a boy. Not sure how long Sammy prevailed, just a memory I now smile about when it comes to mind. I remember vividly, sitting in our back porch playing with the trucks and my benefactor happening by as he did, I still don't understand why some of these memories are so very vivid when I can't remember so many others.

> *I learned a few years ago of the reason for my fervent desire to change sex and wear boy's pants, I shall outline the events in my next book and how these events would go on to adversely impact my life for many, many years. It is amazing to think as a 3 year old I would think boy's pants would afford me the safety I craved and deserved.*

Grade 1, I was in the same class as my icy pole benefactor's son. His son used to walk up the aisle beside our desks and kiss each of the girls in his path as he went. Seems I came home from school quite excited because I had found the man I would marry. Turned out he wasn't that unlucky, he was saved from that fate.

I asked dad why fathers walked up the aisle with the daughter's at weddings, he explained they were giving them away. Well I took exception to that! I mean what self respecting father would give his daughter away? I made dad promise he would never ever give ME away. So now can you see what comes next … my wedding day, nah he wouldn't give me away, my brother gave me away instead …dad sure took that promise extremely seriously.

I was walking to the toilet one day during lessons at school, infant school I should add. Coming from a class room was the sound of children spelling in unison, their chorus of voices music to my ears. I remember feeling so grown up and thinking very soon, I will be grown up enough to spell like that and thinking I couldn't wait to get to that grade. Pity we grow up and face reality isn't it. I was in awe at the level attained by the grade two spelling group; the world seemed full of wonder and valuable experiences to be had.

If only we could retain that same sense of enthusiasm for some of the life lessons we are dealt as adults. Learn to handle them with the same amount of childhood accomplishment and wonder, instead of believing we have been dealt an unfair hand and then feel resentful and depressed as a result. Life would take on a whole new meaning. The next time something happens to you, think about what you may have had to learn from that experience, thank the Universe for that treasured moment, then leave it exactly where you found it, in the past! If we didn't carry around so much resentment would illness become a thing of the past? Would life as we know it improve?

When you become ill, think about what may be causing the ailment, Louise Hay's book, 'You Can Heal Your Life' is a valuable tool for this purpose, as is "The Secret Language of your Body" by Inna Segal. Think about it, change your thinking and the results will speak for themselves. Think about the lesson you may have had to learn by getting this problem in the first instance. Food for thought! Take a leap of faith, after all, what have you got to lose? It isn't like the health problem you are experiencing is a pleasant experience, free yourself, if all else fails seek assistance from holistic practitioners and combine that treatment with positive thought patterns and affirmations.

I remember going to sleep night after night to the sound of the sewing machine. Mum used to sew bridal dresses, you name it, mum sewed it. I am here to tell you that gene definitely skipped a generation, my sewing machine cringes whenever I get close. I swear I can hear its teeth shudder. I undertake minor repairs only and that keeps us friends and the sewing machine reluctantly surrenders when required for these short bursts.

Mum taught me lots of life lessons, like sit up straight, my daughter Laura must now be sick of hearing me say these very words over and over. You would have to laugh, Laura, a girlfriend and I would be at a shopping centre having coffee, I see Laura slouching and I say "sit up straight" both her and my girlfriend immediately straighten. Never ceases to amuse me watching them both simultaneously correct their posture.

Another favourite of mum's was "Don't care was made to care", as sure as eggs, if I said I don't care, you knew straight away what was coming next. Yes, I pass that one on as well; every time someone says to me I don't care. I tell them "My mum said……."

The third major statement was "If a job is worth doing, it is worth doing well", so if we undertook a task, mum ensured it was in accordance with the above statement. It may have taken 'take two' or 'take three' but you can be sure it complied. Mum wasn't someone to be argued with.

I grew up attending the Salvation Army Sunday school, I was a junior soldier and a corps cadet, I loved the Salvation Army it was a major part of my life. One time I had to go to Sunday school with a friend with whom I was spending the weekend. That day I learned the difference between formal shoving down your throat type religious teaching and the fun, loving way in which the same information was imparted through the Salvation Army officers. No prizes for guessing which I preferred or how grateful I was to be me and not her. Tuesday nights were nights to look forward to also, on these occasions we played games as well as undertaking positive lessons. I used to watch out the window for ages before time, scared they might forget to come and collect me for youth group.

> *I read an article where it stated … Tuesday, May 7, 1929 – the church hall committee had put the first coat of paint on the new hall. I was so pleased when I read this and discovered the associated date.*
>
> *I never knew when it was built, only that it was destroyed by fire. It is like pieces of a jigsaw coming together, at least I now know it*

had a beginning and an end – it wasn't merely there, somehow it makes it seem more personal.

My sister was often tasked with my care, so much so in my mind she was as much a mum to be as mum was. We even had to share the same bed. I wasn't impressed when she went out on a date and didn't even think of taking me with her. I mean how could she be so remiss, wasn't I an important part of her life? Mum used to make us dresses that were similar so I would put my dress on too in the hope I would fool the boy friend – ok you have to remember I wasn't very old and I thought it would work. I wouldn't talk to her by the time she left, but I still had her night dress wrapped around the hot water bottle for when she came home. I guess from that she managed to deduce that I wasn't really angry and did in fact still love her with all my heart. She would make me the most beautiful birthday cakes, cakes made with pride and love. I think when my sister left so did any chance of future birthday cakes; mum's forte definitely wasn't stored in the kitchen.

On one occasion during the school holidays my sister was again in charge of my care, I am uncertain as to where mum may have been at the time. In those days a van came around country areas to test residents for tuberculosis, sister dearest left me home alone whilst she walked the long distance to the van. I became so scared (after being left for what seemed like an eternity) I started off walking to find her, hoping and praying I would meet her coming back home. I didn't! She was nowhere to be found, I found the van ok but not my sister. Rattles coming from the thick scrub on either side of the road scared me; snakes were a part of country life, today wasn't a day I wanted to meet up with one. I got back home, even more scared by now, where was my sister? Had something happened to her? I later learned she had stopped off to have a coffee with one of our cousins who lived between us and the van! When I learned this I bet I was more than a tad miffed but am unable to recall if anything happened as a result. I only remember feeling very let down once again, she was tasked with my care and in my very young opinion, leaving me home alone to fend for myself did not fall into the 'care' category.

She left for the bright lights of Melbourne when she turned 21, me all of 11 years old, just wished I could stay in bed for the rest of my life, here was this very important person walking right out on me, little was I to know she would never return to Tasmania except to visit occasionally. In retrospect maybe I did know; I pined so badly I ended up sick as a result; a trip to the local GP confirmed I was run down; I was fretting for my sister.

I think there began my learned pattern of 'don't trust anyone to take care of me except me theory'. Between waking up to find no one home at 18 months, being left home alone at a young age for hours and my sister leaving home when I was still quite young, I stopped trusting others to take care of me. Comes under the heading of 'abandonment' and could explain a few things! I will explain more of the consequences of this in my next book.

Living in the country meant birds, birds and more birds. One day dad was cleaning the gutters and removing any bird nests he came across. Squirt came into my life that day. A baby sparrow devoid of feathers, dad reluctantly allowed me to keep him. He slept in a box on the pillow beside me until he was old enough to live in a bird cage in the bathroom on top of the hot water cylinder. He would wake me early for his morning feed. He was so cute, watching him grow was amazing, I gave this little bird all the love I could muster.

The day came when he was sufficiently grown to be able to take to the skies and fend for himself. He didn't go far, one morning I heard a thump against the fly screen door (back door). I went to investigate; it was Squirt letting me know he wanted his breakfast. He may have been grown up but he still believed me to be his provider, guess I was still his mum after all (I was the only mum he knew).

He would fly with me as I walked up the quiet country road, he would fly on ahead, land on a fence post and wait for me to catch up, then fly on to the next post.

One day he came no more, I would like to think and believe he found a family of his own, as in 'of the feathered variety' the other option of maybe falling foul of a sling shot, well I just didn't want to go there. So my prayer for Squirt was one of a happy life filled with Mrs Squirt, baby squirts and freedom.

February 7 1967 - first day of the school year. My final year of high school! A day that was to become known as Black Tuesday and go into history books as the fire causing the largest loss of life and property in the history of Australia (to that date). Sixty two lives lost; approximately 1,300 homes destroyed, more than 4,000 people left homeless.

The state was experiencing its driest summer for seventy years. A high pressure system over coastal Queensland moved southwards over inland Australia and, at a point on the western side of Tasmania, it collided with a low pressure system. The collision produced a vortex of winds and small whirlwinds of up to 100mph. Small fires merged creating a huge bush fire moving on a ninety mile front.

At school we were unable to see anything for smoke, smoke engulfed the area like a thick winter's fog but with a more menacing atmosphere. The gravity of the smoke didn't hit us until over the PA system; specific areas were announced as bus drivers phoned into say those areas were impassable. All children from those areas were to report to the gymnasium. If the buses couldn't get through it must be bad. The realization we would have to sleep at school was daunting. How bad was it? We had no way of knowing, our emotions mixed, ranging from excitement, ignorance, fear and everything in between, imaginations unable to comprehend the sheer magnitude of the problem, we had not experienced a fire of this magnitude previously.

Then I heard my name called out of the PA system, report to the office, a neighbour had come to collect me along with his children. The drive home was surreal; everywhere we looked everything was either black or still smoldering; houses, bushes, power poles. We were in a state of shock and disbelief.

When I got home, houses around us had been burned to the ground, smoldering ashes all that remained. I don't remember how many neighbours slept at our house that night. The men taking it in turns hosing down the house, the wood pile; sheds and all areas around the house, most of which kept re-igniting as if intent on destroying everything that was still standing, complacency was not on the agenda for the next few days at least. Respect was called for on this occasion and a lot of common sense.

The night before I had woken saturated with perspiration, I was surrounded by fire, flames everywhere, I was surrounded yet I was safe, didn't make a lot of sense, a dream…make that a nightmare, one I was pleased to wake from. Next morning all that could be seen was smoke behind the distant hills - turned out there was a fire at Lachlan near New Norfolk. Not in my wildest dreams would I have imagined that that distant smoke would end up on my own doorstep. Little did I realize that dream was a warning for me, a message from above, a sign of what was to come, at the age of 14 I wasn't to know or understand either the significance or realization of the psychic connection.

No school on February 8, the day was spent pouring water over anything and everything still burning, stumps in nearby paddocks included. Mum had been home alone, dad in hospital in Hobart, mum had tried to save our house and that of our neighbour. We had a huge willow tree on the lawn beside the house, the poor willow tree wasn't particularly healthy after taking the brunt of the fire storm, it had most likely saved the house in some weird way - at least that is what we chose to believe.

You hear people say how selective a fire storm can be; one house remains relatively unscathed whilst others around it are burnt to cinders. I believe there is a reason, a definite reason known only to the Universe and to our Higher Selves, all in accordance with the lessons we are here to learn and the Divine Plan. Diana Cooper explains the meaning of these events in her book 'Angel Answers', it is extremely informative and interesting for those searching for deeper spiritual meanings behind events both small and large.

It took some time for life to return to normal. Some families rebuilt others chose to move on and put the past behind them.

I did successfully complete School's Board and emerged with an 'A', it took hard work and long hours of study to achieve that valued 'A'rating!

And for the record … my allergies continued to worsen that summer. I was picking raspberries on my uncle's property. Those dreaded grass seeds were out in full force, my height didn't help as my nose and those seeds were often on the same level. I sneezed and sneezed my way through that season until I found I was unable to walk without gasping for air and in danger of collapsing with any exertion. Therein began my experience with asthma.

The asthma continued for quite some time following its takeover bid on my little body.

CHAPTER THREE

I commenced work in 1968 at the ripe old age of not quite sixteen. I remember my dad saying it was going to be hard to get work because work was scarce. I set off to Hobart alone on the bus. I visited banks, department after department, any business which would listen to me. By lunch time I had secured a temporary position as a shorthand/typist. Don't even remember being nervous when required to sit for a shorthand and typing test. Looking back I realize how much confidence and courage would have been required to undertake that journey, you see we usually only went into the city a couple of times a year so I was quite unfamiliar with the whole scene. To virtually door knock until I located a vacancy, well that certainly took courage. To set off unaccompanied on that mission was quite something, my only landmark in the city was the 'Greengate' (the Greengate was one of the local cafes). I had to gain my bearings from that point when asking for directions.

Work secured, I needed to board in Hobart, travelling that distance each day wasn't something I relished, so with that thought in mind I walked to my grandmother's house, secured board and set off for the bus trip back home. I was only aware of one way to get to my grandmother's house (that was the long way which was quite a walk). My salary $45 a fortnight, don't laugh, I thought it was a small fortune at the time.

Tired and excited I alighted from the bus with nan's front door key held proudly in my hand. That moment signified a major change in my life, guess mum and dad realized that also, probably tinged with a little sadness as I was the last of the litter, or not, maybe they could see peace on the horizon and were looking forward to that state at long last.

I was never one to take things lying down, I fought for what I believed, dad used to say: "The other kids swear at me behind my back, you do it to my face". Hmmm I will never know whether that earned me respect or punishment as I received both at different times. I know I did myself out of many trips to the cinema because I couldn't help but argue back when I thought I was being unduly punished.

Dad used to start an argument, it would often result in a smack across my face as my punishment, from this I deduced dad didn't like me very much. It was years and years later after dad's death before it was explained to me. Dad believed he was 'toughening me up' ready for my launch into the big world. I was so small he believed I would need to stand up for myself more than most if I was to survive, he was undertaking the mission he believed would assist me. Kind but cruel and it certainly didn't do anything to strengthen my self esteem!

Words of advice from my dad "Always be a member of the union at work", something I will always remember and have adhered to. There have been times I did not believe unions have the power to fight for us anymore, but for some reason I cannot go against those words of wisdom I received in preparation for my very first job. Unions have an extremely important role, a role which should be used for the Greater Good and not abused. Think how much better the world would be if employers, unions and employees could work together in unison to create optimum working and safety conditions. It shouldn't be a case of them against us perception, so much more could be accomplished by working collaboratively.

I remember buying my very own coat, it was yellow, I was so proud of that coat. I think it signified independence, it wasn't merely a coat. It was a coat which was shop bought not home made. When one has homemade clothes for fifteen years, shop bought takes on a whole new meaning, it was exciting, I felt like a *real* person. Occasionally I was given clothes which one of my cousins had outgrown. It was an exciting time sorting through shop bought clothing. The fact that it was second hand meant absolutely nothing, shop bought was a far more important criteria. Funny when I look back now, these days I have the most fun in secondhand shops, in particular Lifeline's Chosen Pieces, seems for me these clothes have a 'past' a 'history' they have been loved and like me, not quite perfect. We are compatible.

Don't think for one minute I didn't appreciate clothes which were made with love, I certainly did, it was just that I didn't know what it was like to go shopping for clothes, other than items for school. Consequently shop bought was such a novelty and seemed like total luxury to me.

Soon after I commenced work, I received word I had been successful in gaining a two year secretarial scholarship. My science teacher had completed all necessary paperwork on my behalf. I thank him for his support, belief in me and his encouragement. I agonized for a time, work, scholarship, work, scholarship. The deciding factor, during my whole time in high school each time I required money for school fees, dad exploded and would say he would refuse to pay. I now deduce he most likely didn't have the money, I suspect a pension wasn't a whole lot of money in those days. Each time it was a fight for days. I could no longer endure two years of squabbling over spending money or money for any other reason. I could not even contemplate the idea, let alone the reality of same. As much as I wanted to be a court reporter, I was not prepared to continue in the same vain; consequently I chose to continue working. At this time I was totally unaware of dad's 'toughening me up policy' and this explosion over money may have been just another tick in a box of that very same document.

I should probably explain, dad had had an operation on his knee in Palestine during World War II, an operation on his other knee meant in could no longer work and as such was granted a Repatriation Pension. TPI, totally and permanently incapacitated to be precise. I believe dad found that rather difficult to deal with, at least initially anyway.

My teacher informed the class one day he wanted to 'frame' me as the only student who ever listened to him in class. He would undertake the lesson for the day, follow up with an impromptu test, I loved science so

I paid attention (which is more than I can say for my maths classes). I suppose because of my diligence he decided I was a worthy cause to support. This very kind, considerate man will always have my sincere gratitude.

Whilst I was growing up my great uncle would always say "You are so ugly, you must be a Harris", so yes I grew up believing I was really ugly. During 1968 I worked in a temporary position at the Commonwealth Employment Service, there I accidentally found my employment history card written by the officer who interviewed me in high school. Imagine my surprise and disbelief when I read the words 'quite attractive' I read those words over and over. I kept thinking this can't be true, every so often, I would return to the drawer of files and find myself re-reading that card and those words which meant the world to me. Maybe I wasn't so ugly after all, maybe I was ok. I was so grateful to the person who wrote those two precious words, words which helped to restore some of my belief in me.

I don't believe people realize how much damage they impose on a person's life with a few careless words repeated over and over. I don't believe for one minute my great uncle meant me to take them seriously but I am here to tell you they certainly had a major impact on my self esteem. Words he obviously meant in jest but being so young I took so seriously. Reading those words lifted quite a burden, a burden I had carried for quite a few years. So I ask: before you choose to speak to someone, regardless of their age, please consider your words carefully and remember that words do have impact, a huge impact, make your words count, make them meaningful for the Greater Good of all concerned. Remember what Thumper's mother told him "If you can't say something nice, don't say anything at all"…in "Thumper's own words "If you can't say sumfin nice, don't say nuffin at all" as he shuffled his little paw on the ground. Good advice from a baby rabbit. So before you speak, think of Thumper, before you know it you will be smiling and thinking positive happy thoughts. You will be living the Tao.

Maybe I should explain something else at this point. I am 4'11" in *shoes* (149cm) at the time of writing this I weigh in at approx 47 kilo so I am not exactly a giant, in those days I weighed far, far less, unfortunately my self esteem was also a tad on the small side and this certainly didn't help the 'ugly' perception.

Living in the country was different in those days, for instance, one could start at the top of Crabtree and undertake a family inventory. It was a real family affair with close relatives living further down the road, others not so close but living in the same district. Not something one is likely to encounter these days.

Years later, early one morning I was sitting in a coffee shop in Hobart, awaiting a trip to the dentist. Imagine my surprise when a total Crabtree catch up ensued. Think the people at a nearby table mentioned everyone in sequence from one end to the other, just goes to show, one shouldn't gossip in public with names included, Tasmania is just too small. Just like Days of Our Lives, didn't seem like much had changed since my departure twenty something years previous. Maybe if they had watched or read 'Bambi' they may have thought twice before gossiping in public, they could have made Thumper proud by taking a leaf out of his book.

I am convinced I always had my 'independent streak' plus a mouth to match. When I first commenced work, I would board in the city all week then go home of a Friday night, so scared in winter I would fall asleep on the bus and not wake up until I was at Geeveston or somewhere else south of Huonville. No phone in those days so should I have landed somewhere way past the Grove I was in trouble with a capital T. (Grove was the location on the Huon highway where mum met the bus – Geeveston, well that was many, many kilometers further on and the end of the bus route). Sunday afternoons it was back to the bus stop for the return journey. On occasions my parents would ask if I needed money. Well, red flag to a bull here. My interpretation …. I obviously couldn't manage my money and therefore needed them to supplement my income … their kind offer was refused with a less than kind response. For this I ask forgiveness!

I had always been brought up with the concept that everything had to be earned, I didn't understand the concept of 'generous donation', it just hadn't happened in our family. A concept which seems to have reversed with the years! I know my children certainly believed in the 'generous donation' theory.

During my first working year, my health would be ok during my week at work, then it would be time to go home of a weekend. My allergies would worsen so I would go back to the city with asthma threatening to halt any notion of me going to work for a few days. I remember nan not understanding how bad I felt, I would have to walk to the doctor's office which was all uphill. I would want to phone for a taxi but nan always insisted on walking. Alright for her, she was in better condition physically than me with asthma! Injection to help me breathe again and we would set off back to home, me a little worse for wear by this time.

I managed to survive those attacks and my health gradually improved with city living. I imagine my state of mind contributed to that - I absolutely loved working, meeting new people both at work and on to way to work. I walked to and from work each day, make that almost danced, skipped my way to and fro. Smiling and saying hello to those beautiful souls I passed each day.

Those people became more like friends, one Christmas I received a small gift from two of them as we met at different locations on this daily ritual. I was overjoyed and humbled that they would think me worthy of this kindness. I think smiling and being so happy helped them start off their day in a truly magical way. I know they certainly did that for me.

> *These days I have a verse displayed on my lounge room wall, it is titled 'JUST SMILE'. I smile whenever I read it....how could I not?*

CHAPTER FOUR

STILL holding on to the happy ever after theory I married in 1972, I don't remember that heady romantic feeling (maybe time has stolen that memory); it just seemed the right thing to do, sad when I reflect upon that theory now. Don't get me wrong, I was in love and truly believed we would be together forever. That is how life is supposed to be, or I thought it should be, I didn't know any different.

Fourteen or so months following our marriage I became quite ill, every time I stood up I almost fainted, am unsure as to all the finer details, but I think my doctor believed I was pregnant (ectopic pregnancy suspected), I was referred to a gynaecologist. The whole fainting thing went on for a short time before I was put in hospital; he undertook a curette. I was sitting in the shower/bath (children's size) when the gynaecologist happened by with his report. Nothing found of interest, must have been a hormone imbalance. Yeah right, like a curette would cure a hormone imbalance. Maybe he believed in the placebo effect, if so he was the only one, I sure didn't. I am sure there must have been a little more to this story; maybe I lost some important detail in the translation. I am giving him the benefit of the doubt here as you may have surmised.

When I look back, this is the point where my learning really began, life seemed to sail along quite nicely with only the odd hiccup, after this it was almost a case of 'fasten your seatbelt' and 'duck for cover'. Knowing what I know now, sitting life out in a bomb shelter may have been the preferable option; sure would have been safer.

I look at my life as a series of learning experiences, I don't believe we have failures, we have experiences! If, when something goes wrong, we take a lesson from that experience then we haven't failed we have learned and grown as a result.

No, I haven't always been this positive or wise; I have experienced a few melt downs in my sixty plus years. I have not always understood why things have happened, or the fact those events may have occurred for a reason, nor have I understood my reaction to them. Melt downs are frightening to a person who believes they are in control of their life. It is akin to being sucked up into a whirlwind, going around and around, losing total control of where you will eventually touchdown and in what condition.

I have searched for answers in a variety of places, my peace of mind these days attributed to learning, reading and understanding my emotions and subsequent reactions to them. Without that understanding this book may not have been possible or probable. It has given me the confidence to pursue my ultimate ambition. Assisted me in locating the real me hidden deep inside, the Me I was born to Be. Helped me put aside the vertically challenged, insecure person and concentrate instead on what I wanted to do, as opposed to what I had to do.

Right now I have a sink and bench full of dirty dishes; a week's ironing awaits me, the housework taunting me at every turn. Yesterday was Saturday, I was sick all day, an all too frequent occurrence these days. Instead of undertaking the previously outlined list of chores, here I am at my precious computer, where time and pain evaporate into a continuous stream of words, flowing on the screen, as the computer takes me on a journey through time.

Freedom comes in many forms; I was to learn that freedom for me; came in the form of a modern computer with a wonderful word processing package. Freedom which allowed me to free my mind as opposed to physical freedom one would normally relate to. To be free like the bird, but not be the bird….this was MY freedom, this was the meaning of those words from the medium with a coat of many colours. Thank you for passing on that very important message, it was appreciated and received with love.

I sit in my family room; I am looking out onto my fern garden, the fern fronds dancing to an ever so slight breeze. The sun is shining and from here the world looks happy and peaceful, so with this thought, I continue to unfold the 'Days of My Life'.

Married life seemed normal, at least for awhile anyway. Not long after we were married one of husband's friends called in, his wife was in hospital with their first baby. My size lent me to people thinking it was ok to treat me like I was a toy or a rag doll. He lifted me up; my arms pinned by my sides, turned me upside down, then accidentally dropped me on my head, so you think this explains a few things….hmmm very funny. My head thumped with the pain, from memory I told him what I thought of him and went to bed to try to ease the pain. That winter I woke one morning, unable to move, it was akin to being paralyzed, I was so very scared, I hadn't experienced anything like this before. No telephone, I finally got myself up and organized, walked the few kilometers into work and phoned the doctor, weeks and hours spent on heat pads at the doctor's surgery. I still have back and sciatic problems to this very day. *The reason I included this seemingly innocent experience will become clearer in my next book.*

Events happen to us, at the time they seem innocent enough, we deal with them and we think we have put them behind us. It is only recently I learned it is not that simple, our body remembers even if our mind doesn't. At some point we need to deal with them if we are to heal and move forward with ease and not dis-ease. Stay tuned as Beyond Description will explain in more detail.

I was working at the time when I came down with a virus (or at least that is what the doctor called it). Funny but the virus didn't clear up, nausea all day, even the thought of coffee (let alone the smell of it) churned my stomach to the point where I would have to make a hasty dash to the little girls room. The virus turned out to be a beautiful baby girl born on the 23 December1974.

My grandmother died prior to her birth, I remember wondering if this is how life goes, someone dies, a baby is born. My grandmother was my father's mother, as far as I was concerned she was *my* grandmother, mum's mother was my sister's grandmother, but nan was *mine*. Although we had had our differences she came into work to see me one day prior to her death, I guessed that was her way of saying sorry for our past differences and let's be friends again. From memory she died on her way shopping, that was my 'town' nan. These days I proudly wear her wedding ring, I rarely leave the house without it, I don't quite understand why but I figure we had a lot in common, we both had to raise our children alone albeit for different reasons, she worked tirelessly she was still cleaning offices of an evening whilst I was living with her. A mouthful of uncooked rice, a few Bex and off she would go night after night on her cleaning mission.

My grandmother on my mother's side (my country nan) always made me feel as if I was second best, probably didn't mean to, probably didn't even know that was how it came across, but unfortunately for me that is how she made me feel. But I had my town nan and that was important to me. Presents would arrive - lined writing pads, biros - stationery - she may have lived in the city and I didn't see her often but despite that she seemed to know or understand what I liked best.

Both my grandfathers departed this life prior to my entry, *inconsiderate on their behalf I thought, one of them could have stayed a little longer, hmmmm*). I felt like I had been 'robbed'. I was never to know or understand the beautiful experience of being loved and cherished by a grandfather. I choose to think they are with me now, assisting me with my greatest challenge.

My water broke whilst we were attending a Christmas dinner party at a neighbour's house. Time to go home, now that was getting more obvious by the minute; the house was in the next street, so we had to negotiate cross country in the dark. We lived in a relatively new area so fences were still some way off. The fastest route was definitely cross country. I stumbled and fell into our vegetable patch, so by the time we arrived inside the house; it was a fast track to the shower for more reasons than one.

The night of labour seemed to stretch forever, I had been given an injection of something, no idea what, just knew the pain came through loud and clear whilst my ability to deal with it was significantly diminished. I remember saying to the nursing staff "If you let me go home, I *will* come back tomorrow", yeah like that was going to happen. I wanted out, like right out! What I thought I was going to do with the unborn baby is anyone's guess; at that point it wasn't high on my 'wanting to think about list'. I desperately wanted to be free of pain, blame the state of my mind on the medication ok! A rational mind would have been just that, I was way short of rational at that point.

….I had to sneak out of bed and down to the nursery to take a peek every so often. In those days the babies were whisked away straight after birth, a forceps delivery necessitated a mandatory time out period in the nursery under observation. I had to keep checking and pinching myself. Was this tiny baby really mine? Could life get any better?

I woke on day two or three, tried to sit but couldn't. I couldn't get off my back, sometime during the night my milk had come in and for the life of me, my breasts were too heavy to allow me to move, embarrassed I buzzed for help. Never would I have imagined in all my twenty two years that I would have breasts so huge that I would be held captive, trapped under the weight.

Christmas Day or Eve I can't quite remember, either way the shops were shut which meant, no fitting for a super large bra was about to occur in the immediate future. So the trusty nursing staff got busy and fitted me up with baby nappies and nappy pins and were on hand to hoist me to sitting position when needed. I figured this could only happen to me, but I suspect not, I suspect this scenario in reality, isn't all that rare.

My milk glands had blocked causing the huge backlog of milk and the resultant 'not being able to get to sitting position problem'. Now I know what it feels like to mimic a dam. A hydro engineer could probably learn from this experience, not even a drop was escaping.

It took a couple of days of persuasion, pumping and squeezing and cracked nipples before this problem was rectified. Pity we can't report 'design flaws' to the Man Upstairs so he could think about improvements along the way. Two ends both sore at the same time seemed a little unfair and a raw deal after so many hours of pain and fog.

Cyclone Tracy wreaked havoc on Darwin, the Tasman Bridge collapsed compliments of a ship slightly off course (doesn't pay to turn your back on the world) all of this happened within a week or so of me giving birth, maybe this was an omen of things to come.

My life was to take a turn into the fast lane of what I can only describe as a complex maze. A maze which I negotiate as situations arise; a maze where dead ends are aplenty, where I muddle through and get to the correct point but not always understanding how I arrived at that location. Times I am left feeling totally out of my depth and helpless. Other times so proud of myself because of what I achieved or learned as a result.

Following the birth of my daughter, life seemed to return to a 'different' type of normal. My husband appeared to become more and more stressed re money (or lack thereof) his work with Telstra necessitated a considerable amount of travel. Weekends I would have loved to go for a drive but because he had been on the road all week he would prefer to stay home. Life settled into a rut of sorts.

We would go to bed exhausted, whilst bub would still be in full throttle, some nights we would let her cry, change her soggy clothes, when exhausted from crying she would finally fall asleep. Five o'clock and she would be firing up ready to commence another day of input. What can I say, the housework would be all under control quite early in those days, no wonder her and I had time for lots of walking and discovery tours.

One day a neighbor said "You always beat me hanging the washing out, it doesn't matter how early I have mine out, yours is always out first", clever, I managed to win a competition I never even knew I had entered. I deduced she obviously didn't have enough to do. What do you do with a comment such as that one? My little girl was my competitive edge, my trade secret, my secret weapon. I shake my head even contemplating why one would even consider wanting to 'win' the game of 'get your washing on the line first'.

I should have sensed something; she would practice for hours and hours to roll over, determination evident on her baby face. Five months old she was trying to walk. She couldn't but this didn't deter this mini dynamo from trying. Imagine my surprise one evening, I left her in the lounge room on the floor, she came rolling out to me in the kitchen. At that stage she was too young to comprehend direction, let alone have sufficient understanding which would enable her to follow the same route.

This wasn't how babies were supposed to behave, was it? Other babies didn't do these things, at least not this early. At least none of the babies I knew.

We would go walking through the bush near our home of a day with our German shorthaired pointer, Stella. Stella was liver and white. We would pack a small lunch and head up the track; here we found native orchids, small insects, all of which became a source of amazement and wonder. She was like a mini sponge soaking up all available information which came into her world; she was like a mini Harry Butler. We would walk to the nearest shopping centre, to the beach, never once would she complain about the walking distance. She took it all in her tiny stride.

One day we were walking back for the shopping centre, a passing lady, stopped and scooped her up from the footpath. The startled look on her face said it all, *'who on earth was this strange lady and why in the world has she picked me up without my permission'*. The lady apologized but explained she just couldn't help herself; she looked so tiny and beautiful. My beautiful miniature daughter searched my face for some kind of sign that this action had been sanctioned and that she was in safe hands.

On other outings, people would stop us and ask how old she was, she mastered and grasped words and their meanings at a very early age, strangers would hear her speaking and because she was so tiny, start up a conversation, amazed at the continuous stream of words from such a tiny subject.

I look at the size of her little dresses now and can understand perfectly why people were amazed; the dresses are the size similar to a baby doll's dress. I have a photo of her eating a strawberry; the strawberry looks absolutely enormous in her little hand. I don't think the strawberry was on steroids; she was so tiny and beautiful.

Once on a bus, I could see the look of confusion on her face, could see the words forming, scared at what might be coming next I knew quick thinking was going to be in order. Then it came "What is that?" there it was, I replied "No darling, we say who is that when it is a person", knowing full well she had meant exactly what she had said. The difficulty you see is that the person in question didn't look like either a male or female, not something she was used to on a day to day basis. Yes the day was saved; no offence taken, luckily, her size had been a bonus on this occasion.

My little daughter continued on her course, learning everything possible, each day or days I would introduce her to a new word and respective meaning. There were times I did believe this may not have been the best plan. Adults would be speaking (grammatically incorrect) and she would feel the need to correct them and advise them of the correct way to speak those words. Embarrassing, you had better believe it. Still I had to be proud of her, the fact she was correcting adults meant absolutely nothing to her in her quest for a grammatically correct world.

School took on a whole new meaning where she was concerned. First we had a mutiny in kindergarten. She indignantly informed me she had come to school to learn, if she wanted to play, well she could do that at home, and if, they weren't prepared to teach her something new, to teach her to read and write, then she wouldn't bother at all. Oh dear, where to from here? And this was only kindergarten!

Grade one wasn't much better; I explained to her that if she chose not to learn and listen to the teacher she would be left behind when the other children went into grade two. Her reply "Well I will be able to help with the younger children", so that didn't work. Now what?

I don't know how or when it happened but all of a sudden she decided that it was time to call a truce and start paying attention. Learning now accelerated, she was in her element. By the time she was in grade three she was complaining about the 'lack of suitable material in the library' and the fact that she had read every book contained therein. Did I receive flack from other parents, friends, you guessed it. I was told we were pushing her, pushing her! She was pushing us!

In life, don't compare your child's progress to that of another, each are 'unique' in their own special way, love them equally regardless of their achievements or imperfections. My little girl was just being her 'true self', let your child be who they are, let him or her follow their own path, free of judgment, competition or comparisons.

One day the teacher asked her to read her story she had written to the class, she was once again in her element, when the teacher tuned back in, not only had she finished reading, she was asking them questions to ensure they had been paying attention. She was the teacher. Other children were writing half a page, her stories were four pages plus. Must have had something to do with all the hours she didn't sleep for the first four years ...

CHAPTER FIVE

My little daughter would have been about two years old when the second child would have been born, this was not to happen. I had a miscarriage around thirteen weeks. I wasn't feeling too well, lethargic, not sick but not healthy. We had invited friends for dinner; I was lying on the floor in front of the heater, wishing I was in bed instead of entertaining guests. One of our supposed friends (of the male variety), kicked me and told me not to be so lazy (yes, the very same guy who years previously dropped me on my head). Like I said earlier, he was my husband's friend, fast turning out not to be one I wanted on my Christmas card list. The words formulating in my mind as his foot made contact with my body I won't put to print, I am sure you can adequately surmise the form my thoughts may have taken. The kick wasn't hard but it was still disrespectful and unwarranted.

During the night I felt like I needed to go to the toilet, I lost the baby. I tried to wake my husband, I explained I thought I had just had a miscarriage, he mumbled something inaudible and went back to sleep, alcohol has a lot to answer for. To say I stressed during the night was something of an understatement. Please don't think this was a 'normal' state for him, nothing could be further from the truth. Any other night and the situation would have been so totally different – I hope!

I seem to have had to experience many of my most trying moments 'alone', whether this was to further my training in independence, whether it was to make me stronger, I am still unsure. Did it go back to the moment in my life where I decided to trust me and only me to take care of me? Had that thought pattern created the 'alone' phenomenon I was continuing to experience?

When the first problem pregnancy arose my husband was on Three Hummock Island with Telstra, I don't even remember how I got to the hospital at the time, I think he was there to collect me from hospital but not take me to. From here on in the majority of my problems were definitely in the 'deal with alone category'.

I got up a few times to look at this tiny white object at the bottom of the toilet bowl, wondering if I was seeing what I thought I was seeing or if it was part of a nightmare I wasn't quite waking from. Any female who has found themselves in this same situation will know exactly what emotional state I was in, it ranged from shock, nausea, lack of understanding, fear, through to one of sadness for this tiny life lost. I felt so alone at that moment. The night seemed to last forever.

Next morning I was as white as a sheet, stomach starting to hurt. I don't remember if I visited a doctor that day or the next, either way it wasn't a pretty scenario by the time I did. An infection already in progress, suppose that explained the very, very white face. I was so pale I almost convinced myself I could walk through doors. Casper could have been excused for thinking I was a distant relative.

I was whisked off to the hospital immediately; pethidine shot awaited me along with a wheel chair. The wheel chair was unnecessary as I was capable of walking under my own steam. The pethidine shot, now that was a different kettle of fish! My involuntary muscles went into spasm before the syringe left my body, insufficient to cause a major problem just enough to scare the nurse and for me to wonder what on earth was going on.

These days I am told the next shot may be my last, so from here on in I have to hope pethidine isn't on the hospital menu, at least not when I am visiting. Be good if we had an early warning system that would go 'no don't have that because…….' I had no idea I could have been allergic to pethidine….unless that is what I had been given when I had my first child, if so, it would certainly explain why it didn't stop the pain but had stopped my ability to meditate or to think logically.

Having overcome this miscarriage, I again became pregnant; this one was real bad news. Nausea was a constant companion along with the most horrendous stomach cramps you could imagine. I knew something was wrong, I just didn't know what. My gynaecologist had a puzzled expression each time he examined me.

The stomach cramps would leave me totally exhausted, lying on the lounge with a two year old doing her 'own thing' until some type of normality returned to my weary body.

By the time I was supposedly four months pregnant, cramps continuing, an ultra sound was ordered. The ultra sound did not detect any sign of a pregnancy. The gynaecologist telephoned me at home to announce a curette was in order due to the lack of findings on the ultra sound. He wanted me to go immediately to the hospital. I explained I was at home alone with a two year old; I would have to get to hospital on the bus with both the suitcase and the child in tow. "Could it wait until morning I asked?", when my husband would be available to drive me.

In retrospect, my doctor would have preferred the first scenario. As it was I had to telephone and chase him around Hobart to advise, you guessed it, I had started to haemorrhage. "What should I do?" I finally located him at his club, thanks to his very kind wife. Yes, you are probably correct in assuming I probably wasn't too popular with him at that very moment. I met him in hospital in record time, didn't think it prudent to keep him waiting on that occasion. If he was annoyed with me he certainly was professional and did not allow it to interfere with my treatment, for that I thank him.

Being four months pregnant meant my uterus was too large to undertake a normal curette; I had to be put on a drip which would induce labour. My doctor undertook a final examination prior to my trip to the operating theatre. The pain was excruciating to say the least, I grabbed his leg. When the examination was finished I explained that I wasn't trying to get fresh, merely needed something to hold, due to the high pain factor.

He explained; if I had wanted to 'get fresh' I would need to go just a little higher to achieve the desired result. So with that thought in mind I went off to the operating theatre laughing. He did look cute in his white operating overalls and his engaging smile.

My mind had been in a confused state since the ultra sound, I would lie down at night and I could feel movement so I couldn't understand why the ultra sound was supposedly clear. If it wasn't the baby's movements, what was it? Did they have it wrong?

I woke from the anaesthetic crying, crying because I had lost yet another baby, one I thought I could feel inside me. Official explanation: Hydatidform mole, this insidious growth overtakes and destroys the foetus; something like one in 20,000 pregnancies, I couldn't win a raffle but I could come up with something like this!

> *'Hydatidform mole': an uncommon benign tumour that develops from placental tissue early in a pregnancy in which the embryo has failed to develop normally. A hydatidform mole, which resembles a bunch of small grapes, is caused by degeneration of the chorionic villi, minute finger-like projections in the placenta. The cause of the degeneration is unknown.*
>
> *Vaginal bleeding and excessive morning sickness usually occur. (Think they definitely forgot to mention the stomach cramps – or maybe they were saved just for me because I am special!)*
>
> *A hydatidform tumour shows up on ultrasound scanning. Urine and blood tests detect excessive amounts of chorionic gonadotrophin which are produced by the tumour.*
>
> *The tumour can be removed either by suctioning out the contents of the uterus or by a D and C. A hysterectomy may be considered.*
>
> *There is a small risk that a malignant tumour may develop later; for this reason, tests are performed regularly for several years to*

determine the levels of human chorionic gonadotrophin in the blood and urine.

A woman should not become pregnant again until the levels have returned to normal for at least a year. There is a one in 75% risk of a recurrence of the condition in a future pregnancy.

So there was my official explanation, when I would lie down at night the bunch of grapes would move, confusion now cleared but even that didn't help very much.

Recently my gynaecologist retired so I had reason to obtain my medical records. I summoned up the courage to skim over these records. The words read:

Fragments of membranous and placental material. A pregnancy sac is evident which has been opened and a degenerate embryo measuring 1cm is evident in length is identifiable. The report went on to say, *this therefore represents a histologically benign HYDATIDFORM MOLE. There is no evidence of 'invasion' in the tissue received - dated 3/2/77.*

I suppose I was surprised at how deeply reading the above report cut into my very being, here it was, almost twenty seven years later and it still hurt reading those words, it felt like it was yesterday as the tears trickled down my cheeks. That embryo was a tiny life and I still felt as if it was a huge recent loss. As with most things, doctors at that time were not big on explanation, think we only ever received enough data to cover the very basics. As such, I am sure the fact that an embryo was discovered never rated a mention at the time.

My husband brought our daughter into hospital to visit me; I asked her how she was. She informed me "Daddy tried to kill me", how so I asked "He put shells in my egg at breakfast and left plastic on my cheese in a sandwich". Those words sure brightened the nurse's day and she exited the room laughing – my baby girl had been quite serious and indignant at her dad's seemingly lack of care and attention to detail - hard to imagine she was only just two years old.

Six weeks following my first hospital visit, I haemorrhaged in the lift on the way to the doctor's office. Blood was streaming down my legs, I can still remember that moment vividly, felt the colour in my face alternating between bright red, snow white, back to red, wishing that damned lift would hurry instead of what seemed like an eternity, we only had to get to the 5th floor. Goodness knows what the other occupants noticed or thought, I pray *nothing* is the reply to that one!

So it was back to hospital that very afternoon for another D & C.

Six weeks later, you guessed it, another hospital, this time, too many persistent symptoms which by now should have subsided at least marginally. Laparoscopy this time, the doc needed to see what was going on.

Prior to surgery I had had to sign a paper authorizing the doctor to remove 'whatever' he had to, dependent upon what was discovered during the surgery. I was beside myself, if the hydatidform mole had returned even slightly it meant a full hysterectomy. Hence I went into surgery not knowing in what condition I would wake. Would I have all my pieces intact? Had it turned to cancer? Would I be able to have more children? Not a nice way to go into surgery, I would rather know what was going to happen and what was going to be removed. The unknown is way more daunting!

I woke from surgery; my hand went straight to my stomach, hmmm no major cut evident; that had to be a good sign. I couldn't wait to get the official result.

Thankfully, no re-growth detected; no cancer evident. Internal pieces still intact!

The day came to leave the hospital, do you think the nurses could find a sharp implement to cut my stitches. Not a one in sight, so a rather blunt razor blade had to suffice. The fact that it was blunt meant the nurse had to saw through my stitches in lieu of one swift karate chop.

Rating on that one, pain plus. One of the stitches was inside my belly button so it had to be held high even before the sawing commenced.

By the time I arrived at the hospital check out, my legs were beginning to wobble beneath me, I knew if I fainted the game would be up and I would be returned to the bed I had just managed to escape from. If I didn't want to go back; it was imperative I hold it together, at least for the next ten minutes anyway.

My *beloved* husband (too busy to leave work to collect me) meant my mum turned up in a taxi in which to facilitate my escape. My *beloved* doctor had forgotten to leave me a prescription which I **had** to have, so it was taxi to his office to collect said prescription. I made it to his office and promptly burst into tears. He couldn't understand why, he was looking for some deep psychological reason. The fact that I had just been subjected to an attack by a blunt razor blade, tried to remain standing with legs of jelly, walk the distance from taxi to office in quite an emotional state, the fact my husband didn't think me sufficiently important to warrant time off work … If that isn't sufficient justification for a teary tirade … then what is I ask?

By now I was feeling very able in giving a critique as per the most proficient hospital in the Hobart metropolitan area. I could comment on staff, food quality, hospital efficiency, accounting practices.

I was informed I would not, under any circumstances, be permitted to become pregnant. Should this occur it would mean termination straight away. Again instructions were not specific or detailed, I did not learn until years later that it could have turned to cancer hence the 'not get pregnant' under any circumstances rule.

I had to undertake 24 hour urine specimens. First one was a major flop, official explanation: insufficient to undertake required tests. So it was back to the drawing board so to speak. DRINK MORE WATER, DRINK CONSTANTLY FOR THE WHOLE 24 HOURS. I am here to tell you that even today I cannot consume large quantities of water or any liquid, I would fail miserably if I tried to become an alcoholic. During the many months of these tests I swear I could hear myself squelching as I walked, the water threatening to come up instead of going down. Ugh.

If undertaking the tests weren't embarrassing enough, I then had to catch a bus; child in tow and get myself and the very large urine sample to the hospital before some ungodly time next morning. Reason: the tests had to be transferred to the Royal Women's Hospital in Melbourne. In order to achieve this, the sample had to land at the Royal Hobart Hospital quite early in the morning.

These tests went on for quite some time before a report finally came back saying I was again allowed to become pregnant as my 'whatever' levels were now at a reasonable and acceptable level.

I might add here that during this whole time, I would encounter friends, acquaintances they would ask 'where the baby was?' That was difficult. All around me other women were having their second babies, all seemingly without problems. Me? I was playing a waiting game, my future in the hands of professionals I had not even met. It was a difficult period of my life. One I had to endure alone.

Only one friend had even heard of hydatidform mole, her sister had experienced the same problem. Even now, when I have to volunteer my medical history, I say those two words, the reply is quite often "Oh and where did you have that?", like they are expecting I say "Oh on my face" or some other logical spot. There is something to be said for having 'common' medical problems.

Oh well, I knew which hospital I would prefer should the need ever arise; I was an expert on this subject after recent events.

To keep my mind off the possibility I would have to have a hysterectomy should all else fail, I telephoned the Employment Office for a position to tide me over. I had to get out of the house, at least for a short time. Saving my sanity was mandatory at that point. Sitting around worrying wasn't going to help me or my family; I needed to feel 'normal' at least for a short time.

Me and normal should never be used in the same sentence as you are probably beginning to surmise by now. So I shall rephrase: *as normal as I could be given the circumstances.*

I landed a position as an assistant for an opthalmic surgeon. Six week position which seemed to last an eternity. His sister was going on annual leave; he didn't want to pay the same wage so I was employed to undertake some of the same work, with absolutely no training whatsoever. Who needed a weight loss program, this guy could have run a secondary, quite successful business, wouldn't have required a money back guarantee, weight loss was assured.

Confusion came hand in hand with the introduction to the surgical instruments, I had to learn what they were used for, their respective names and which were required for specific surgeries. It was definitely like the ad on television: this goes with this, goes with this. I had to draw myself diagrams; it was the only way I could remember which instruments were required for which procedure. Then there were the drops, a different drop in each pocket. Left pocket first, right pocket for this reason, this pocket last. I was too stressed to eat before work, too tired after work. First day, went to lunch only to get blasted for daring to take a lunch break. I didn't know what I had encountered; it was one shock after another. Note I said shock, nor surprise. Surprise I could handle.

The day I lost a patient all hell broke loose. He screamed at me for all and sundry to hear. First person ever to lose one of his patients, how careless was I. Me, personally, I thought she was fortunate to be lost, who needed this guy! Once the eye drops had landed successfully, this particular lady had felt nauseous, the surgeon suggested she have a short break in the waiting room prior to the next step. The trouble was the silly woman sat herself in a chair behind the door, so when I tried to locate her, I couldn't. How did I know to look *behind* the door, what person would willingly take up a seat *behind* an open door out of sight - only one who didn't want to be found I suspect.

One time I had to assist with a minor operation in the surgery, my instructions, "You have to put drops in her eye every …… seconds, I don't care if you have to push my hand away to do it, the drops have to go in or she will be blind". Oh terrific I thought. At the end of the surgery, the opthalmic surgeon suggested the lady might light a cup of hot tea. By this time my legs were not in a great state, here I am thinking at least she was sitting, I'm the one who needs the hot drink right now before I faint! No, I didn't share my version with him; somehow I made it to the next patient.

Then there was the time I removed an old lady's handbag, she didn't want to part with that bag no matter what. I suspect her worldly possessions were in that bag, no way was she going to be parted. I finally convinced her to part with it, placed it in the required location and exited the room to set up the next patient. Doctor enters room, old lady sitting in front of machine handbag firmly back in her steely grip. Once again all building occupants heard the scream of frustration from an indignant surgeon, whose valuable (and expensive) time had been taken up trying to extricate the handbag. I will add: it made a thorough eye examination almost impossible if the eye cannot get close enough to the machine….sense of humour on his part would not have gone astray though.

The six weeks couldn't come fast enough. One small patient did bring me undone. This little mite was the same age as my daughter, all of three years. Diagnosis; a brain tumour, unfortunately it was inoperable. She was losing her sight and concentration, it was doubtful she would make it to Christmas that year.

I was so grateful to get home that evening. My little daughter was healthy and happy; I prayed she would remain so.

The experience made me grateful for what I did have, maybe that was my lesson, to teach me to be content with what I did have instead of regretting what I couldn't or may never have - another child. So as traumatic as it was, I was grateful for that experience although certainly not one I would ever wish to repeat.

Finally the medical report arrived to say I was again permitted to become pregnant. Mixed emotions also arrived with that letter, and hit in full force. Would the same thing happen? Would I have another miscarriage? Would the next baby be healthy? So many questions, unfortunately no visible answers appeared on the horizon. I didn't have anyone with whom to share my confusion and fear. I think at the time I would have given anything to know other people who had lived through and survived the emotions of this condition.

CHAPTER SIX

I knew the next morning after conception, how? I felt so different, so happy, I just knew, weird huh? Intuition was working on my behalf, a sign from the Universe. What was it about this child? Why had I been given such an early thumbs up signal?

The following nine months were extremely stressful, the above questions still surfacing to haunt me continuously, my husband telling me how fat and revolting I looked. Time after time he would reinforce those two horrid words. Happy or loving, where are those two words when one needs them? They should be mandatory I say!

It was during this period I knew my husband was having an affair with another woman, he couldn't stop talking about how wonderful she was (bit of a dead giveaway wouldn't you say?) Yes I asked, yes he denied it - must be my imagination he told me. Didn't know the truth until about eight or nine years later, yes, I had been correct in my assumption.

> *He was talking to my mother one day, years after we had separated; he was being honest with her. Mum asked him if he ever apologized to me for all the hurtful things he had said and done. His reply "No I never apologized".*

Come to think of it, I don't think he even had sorry in his vocabulary.

Be good if I could *imagine* a lottery win and be as correct as I had been about his affair!

Toward the end of the pregnancy I had a night from hell, I was in so much pain I had to get up periodically in order to gain some relief. My immediate reaction was one of: oh no, this baby is going to be early, too early. Next morning my dutiful husband went to Army (he liked to play Saturday Soldiers as they are termed). I should not be so disrespectful; Army Reserve is the correct title. Saturday the pains continued only stronger.

I telephoned my gynaecologist, located him in his office (what a stroke of luck), only problem was how to get to him when he suggested I come in for an examination. I telephoned around the street in the hope of finding a lift to the city; I didn't have sufficient money for a taxi. One kind neighbour offered to drive me, poor thing she was so flustered at the thought that I might deliver sooner than expected; I am surprised we made it to the city at all; we almost missed the major turn off. I know it wasn't funny but honest you have to see the funny side or cry at times, I hoped and prayed I wasn't about to go into labour, obviously she thought it a possibility, I am willing to bet she was saying a silent prayer all the way to the city as well. Thanks to this wonderful lady for being there for me when I most needed her. I shall never forget that kind deed.

Examination confirmed a bladder infection - phew that all. Never thought I would ever be grateful for a bladder infection.... I telephoned my husband and asked he come collect me from the doctor's office. He came ok, drove me home, said "You had better go to bed and rest", then left me home alone with a three year old and went back to the Army to cook for - wait for it - it was the Annual Army Fair the next day and he needed to cook. Not bad when a scone rates higher on the priority scale than a pregnant wife in pain - well you can't say I didn't know my place in life.... *It was somewhere lower than scones!*

Fabian was born on December 28, 1978, he was overdue, my gynaecologist decided two weeks was two weeks too long and arranged for me to go into hospital on December 27. Seemed Fabian was unimpressed by what the doctor had in mind and decided he would arrive under his own steam. Well as much as possible anyway.

I was sharing a room with another lady; she too was to be induced next day. The contractions commenced, I was lying in the dark trying to count the minutes between contractions, I didn't want to wake my roommate as she too had a huge day ahead of her next day. Finally I thought it was time I sought help. One way to get me out of room sharing I suppose. Labour went on all night and into the following day.

Fabian wasn't born without the doctor's help, stuck solidly for a while, slightly too large for my small body - 7lb 11oz, my body wasn't designed for that size. Given my experience with my daughter's birth I had refused injections for pain this time. My doctor arrived and he had different ideas. I remember him yelling "Oh God now she is hyperventilating - get a paper bag QUICK", what could he expect, he shoves an injection into my inner workings at a time when contractions are aplenty - bet he would hyperventilate too if someone did that to him! At that point I would have liked to test that theory.

Fabian was whisked away, no one said a word. Oh God, I'm thinking please tell me he is healthy, why isn't anyone saying anything. He was obviously off to a bad start. I couldn't bear to lose another child, not after all I had had to endure to get this far. After what seemed an eternity someone assured me he was *now* alright. I think I said a silent prayer of thanks at that point in time.

New Years Eve, I had fed my precious boy and the staff returned him to the nursery. Minutes later in comes another nurse, crying baby in her arms, wants to be fed she says. Fed, I'm thinking, just done that. As soon as he was put in my arms he fell asleep, he wasn't hungry, he wanted his mum. So it was just the two of us, sitting in our hospital room listening to the fireworks outside on the Derwent River. It was such a peaceful and beautiful experience. This is how it will always be I told him. ...I wasn't to know.

Home we went, my little daughter at the ripe old age of four, immediately settled in as the big sister, little mother figure for the new arrival. She was so precious, so grown up.

I did have to laugh. I had always explained as much to her as I thought she was capable of computing. I can't remember exactly why or how it came about but she knew I had to have an episiotomy to facilitate

Fabian's birth, she didn't know what it was but knew that was the correct terminology. Here I was this night running my bath bending slightly to feel the temperature of the water. I turned around to find her bending over behind me. I asked her what she was doing. Trying to look at your episiotomy mummy she explained. I suggested she wait until I have a bath and then I would show her the stitches. Ok, that went down without a hitch, mission accomplished. Should have seen the look on my father-on-law's face one night whilst they were visiting when this little person felt it necessary to impart her new found knowledge to him, four years old explaining to a male adult that mummy had to have an episiotomy and what it was. I wish you could have seen his face. Me? Well, I didn't quite know where to put mine at that point.

Fabian was somewhere between six and thirteen weeks old, I felt like I was sitting on a mountain. I was too scared to go to the doctor at first; I had lumps swelling up in my groin as well as my mini mountain. Poor gynaecologist I was forever getting him 'out of somewhere'. This time it was a National Gynaecological Conference (luckily for me it was held in Hobart) he must have dreaded hearing my name. Seems I had developed this habit of giving any doctor assigned to me medical challenges they never entertained.

Bartholin's cyst this time, go home get gear then straight to hospital - don't believe I was given a choice just get there NOW! I was beginning to think that just for once it would be good to at least have a medical problem I could understand or had heard of. Seems this gland had been damaged during childbirth and a cyst had formed. Gland is cut open, drained, under anesthesia thank goodness. New duct had to be cut and necessary repair work undertaken.

Fabian came to hospital with me, the following morning he was handed to me to be breast fed, I obviously no longer smelled like his mum, he struggled at first, seeming confused as to whether or not he should accept me. His little face was red and swollen from prolonged crying. Hunger overpowered any doubts and he settled in for the much need nourishment and comfort.

In the meantime my little daughter had started kindergarten, so twice a day it was push pram to school and back, (what I considered must have been a relatively minor operation - wasn't) there were times I would make it to the school but didn't have any idea how on earth I was going to get back home. All uphill and most of the journey a gravel footpath, try pushing a pram on that surface, think you are going ok then - sudden halt - huge piece of gravel stuck under wheel, oh that jarred on some occasions.

I felt weak, tired, sore, pain wherever the cut was; why someone didn't realize I wasn't in any condition to be making that journey twice a day I will never understand. Oh well, I suppose what doesn't kill us, makes us stronger - right? In retrospect, why didn't I ask for help, I am sure one of the other mothers in our street would have come to my assistance? But why didn't I ask? What had stopped me? Why did I feel like I had to do it alone? We had some wonderful compassionate people in the street so why didn't I avail myself of their assistance? Did it go back to my early vow to look after myself? Were my thoughts influencing my actions?

My father-in-law had remarried following his wife's death with cancer. His new wife did not have any children, one night whilst visiting she was in the bedroom with me while I was changing Fabian's nappy, she had tears in her eyes. She left to return to the lounge room. I continued changing him. A male voice (quite loud) said "Make the most of him you only have him for a short time" I spun around in an attempt to determine to whom this voice belonged - there was no one there. Shaken I continued dressing my baby son, too scared to tell anyone in case it came true. I had had so much trouble even getting to this point why would anyone want to take this precious bundle from me. If I didn't say anything maybe it wouldn't happen, I could forget those words. The voice was definitely male and quite loud - it sounded like it came from behind and above me, I certainly didn't imagine it. I knew to whom it must have belonged but for years anytime it came into my mind I dismissed it quickly, I could not bear for that statement to become fact.

At that moment in time, I didn't know whether I wanted to be an emu or ostrich, bury my head in the sand or run like the wind and hope that statement didn't catch me!

I wished with all my heart for that statement to lay dormant and never see the light of day.

CHAPTER SEVEN

This was just the beginning of things to come.

When I look back, I think to myself - obviously no one wanted to take up the position of my second child. Miscarriage followed by hydatidform mole, a position which was vacated twice due to lack of a suitable candidate.

It obviously had to be someone extremely special in order to undertake the difficult path which lay ahead for them, or did I have to learn what it was like to lose my children, was this a sign of things to come?

By now you will be wondering if I have totally lost my marbles. Believe me when I say there have been times even I started to think I had. Luckily I was blessed with an open mind, faith and a strong will. If I don't understand something I search for answers, weigh up the available data and then make an informed decision re best course of action. I listen to other people, read books but it doesn't mean I will take everything on board, I question most things, then use what my **intuition** tells me is valid and above all 'right for me'. I have found placing my trust and faith in my inner wisdom serves me well, I try not to second guess myself, usually the answer which comes to mind first it the correct one for me at that time.

I believe intuition is the greatest gift we are given on Earth; it serves us well if we choose to listen. I cannot stress enough how important intuition is. It is our guide, our conscience.

*I believe we are here on earth to continue our soul development, to learn, to undertake our role in the 'big plan', I believe we are given **signposts** along the way to aide us in choosing the right path at the right time. My only regret is that I didn't always recognize this at the time for what it was, it was only following recent events that everything has fallen into place and I can even begin to understand the enormity of why we are here on earth. I thank God I was given the blessing to see, the faith to listen and the enthusiasm to continue to learn.*

… The local GP voiced "This must be your first child", No I replied, but the first didn't have difficulty breathing or swallowing. Smug … I wasn't impressed as you can imagine. He was insinuating I was a new mother panicking for no reason. Fabian had problems right from birth, I would feed him, lie him down and I could hear him trying desperately to swallow but unable to. Needless to say that particular trip to the doctor achieved absolutely zilch and I was left with more questions than answers. Fabian was born congested (hence no sound of a crying baby until the medical staff had cleared his airways), the congestion problem worsened with each passing day.

I breastfed Fabian for eight and a half months, Fabian gained weight rapidly, me losing it equally as rapidly, I decided it was time for the bottle - umm bottle for Fabian, not me that is. Solid food was the beginning of even more problems for Fabian, although I didn't know or understand this at the time.

He had eczema over his little body and the swallowing problem of a night worsened.

He would vomit thick revolting mucous, no wonder the poor child couldn't swallow, nothing would have been able to penetrate this thick mesh like substance. Fabian was one child who should have been accompanied with a 'how to' manual. It would take him hours of dry retching before this mesh of mucous would be released and my baby would return to his happy self once again.

He was a bundle of fun and mischief, always ready with a huge grin.

We lived at Blackmans Bay; I discovered the local Salvation Army Corps and began to attend Church, officers of the Church change regularly. Fabian was only about nine months or so when I introduced myself to the new officer, advised if she needed anything to let me know. She did need something ....someone to teach Sunday school. Consequently each Sunday my little daughter, Fabian and I set off for Church and Sunday school, milk bottle and all.

Fabian used to stand on the chair and look out the window while his sister was at school, waiting for her to come home, I was worried that if he ever managed to escape, school would be the first place he would head - looking for his sister who meant so much to him.

He wasn't born brave, he had a toy caterpillar, a pull along toy - it was called a clatterpillar because it made a noise as it was pulled along - the noise scared him so much he would run all the faster crying as he went because the clatterpillar was chasing him. The thought of letting go, did not enter his little mind. That poor clatterpillar didn't get much exercise for quite some time.

When Fabian was about nine months old I wanted to learn to play squash. My memory has let me down once again and I can't remember how it all came about. Anyway, my husband laughed at me, said I wouldn't be able to play because I had absolutely no coordination skills whatsoever. So be that as it may, I wasn't deterred. To my amazement as much as anyone's I absolutely loved the challenge. I became quite good at the game. I loved the fact that it was as much about mental stimulation as it was about physical ability - quite an adrenalin rush the two combined - I became hooked. What a confidence boost.

Fabian came with me, the sports centre ran a crèche for us mums, Fabian turned into something of an escape artist, no matter what obstacle blocked the path he always managed to find a way over or under in search of his mum. Don't think his minder, will ever forget him in a hurry. Not long ago I ran into her and she spoke of minding him at the centre. He seemed to make an impact, must have been that cheeky grin or maybe the amount of time she spent chasing after him. Well after all is was a fitness centre, Fabian was probably only ensuring she remained trim, taut and terrific.

He would be outside in the garden with me, I would turn around and there he would be hose up to his mouth getting a drink from the hose where it had sprung a leak, guess when a person has to drink they have to drink. Water would be running down the front of him, but he wasn't deterred, summer or winter the outcome always the same. Don't know whether it was pure thirst or merely fun.

We had baby white rabbits on a few occasions, Fabian couldn't bear the feel of their fur, the look on his face was priceless when one came too close, he wasn't scared of them, just couldn't cope with their fur. I would love to have known what was going through his mind and why the fur was so abhorrent for him.

Fabian, his sister and I went to my sister's for a short holiday during the summer months one particular year. I went out to check on the children playing in the swimming pool, all seemed ok; I went back and sat down in the lounge room where it was definitely cooler. Then something made me get up (I didn't understand, I knew my two were quite ok) I had to go out once again only this time take a closer look. My sister's husband had one of his Maori friends and children visiting. The youngest (a baby girl about 18 months old) was floating face down in the water. No wonder I was guided back to the pool. I shouted and from memory my brother-in-law retrieved the limp body from the pool. We managed to get her breathing somehow - none of us were trained in resuscitation or first aid. We wrapped this little mite in a towel and phoned emergency to see what we should do. We were given instructions, she was ok - thank you to 'whoever' was watching from above - she definitely had her Guardian Angel watching over her that day. I had been brought up believing in God, but it was like he was in another dimension, never thinking he was actually 'hands on' so to speak. I knew I was guided (almost pushed) to go back to the pool with the words **'take another look'** imprinted in my brain. It definitely wasn't her time to go 'Home'.

Fabian would be playing outside with the other children, he would come inside, give me a hug and kiss then go on his way, without saying a word, maybe he needed reassurance I was still within range. My little boy was so very precious and lovable.

I used to tell the neighbour's children I would peg them up by their ears on the clothes line if they continued to leave our side gate open, mind you they were all way too young to understand the repercussions of an open gate. Sure as eggs, I'm cooking dinner this night, one of our neighbours walked past the kitchen window. I'm standing there thinking - gosh a baby like mine ... oh dear, penny dropped, he was mine. Fabian had escaped through that infernal open gate. How stupid did I feel, a normal mum would have instantaneously recognized her own child, maybe it had been a l-o-n-g day.

It was 1981, I finally put my foot down and demanded I reapply for my driver's licence and we buy a car for me, I told my husband I was feeling like a sack of potatoes, being picked up and deposited here. Picked up for somewhere else and deposited elsewhere. I was playing pennant squash and relied heavily on a good friend I had met through squash to collect me each and every game and then deposit me back home. I had had enough; it was time to take a stand for independence. In those days this lady was another of my angels, without her, the Salvation Officer and squash in my life I don't know what I would have done to remain sane.

I had obtained my drivers licence in the early 1970s. My husband wouldn't allow me to drive the car unless he was with me, I would panic under his scrutiny, so me driving just didn't happen, consequently I allowed my licence to lapse, didn't see the point in paying money for something I was unable to use.

So it was back to the driving school - I apologized about 100 times per lesson, the instructor finally said "For goodness sake stop apologizing - how do you expect to learn if you don't make mistakes, it is expected, so no more apologies please!"

I hadn't realized the impact my husband was having on me - I obviously apologized continuously and didn't even realize, I suppose that is what happens when everything you do is wrong (well wrong in the eyes of others). Didn't seem to matter what I did with him it was never right. The impact was played out during the driving lessons, if it hadn't been for those lessons maybe it would have taken a whole lot longer for me to figure out - who knows! Another lesson noted and filed.

Yes I got my licence, the first go no less and more importantly minus the continuous stream of apologies. Then it was, let's talk about a car. We found a lime green mini; I thought it was the bee's knees. My beloved husband wouldn't give me the money for insurance, so dad told me to drive down and collect the money, he would pay, then it would be 'our car', he informed me.

Driver's licence - car - now I needed work! We were fast running out of money, my back had been really bad - as in, couldn't even walk up a flight of stairs bad. The Salvation Army Officer had suggested a chiropractor - this proved to be one of the most useful suggestions of my entire life. A few treatments later I was running up the stairs, what a difference. Problem was we had had to purchase a new bed, of the hard mattress variety and money was a scarce commodity.

I have since undertaken regular visits to a chiropractor, my body has endured quite a lot over the years, I have asked it to endure tasks one should not expect of something so petite and it has taken its toll. Regular visits ensure everything is where it should be and allows me to function more efficiently; it takes quite a panel of experts to keep this little body running in peak condition.

I telephoned the Commonwealth Employment Service; spoke to one of the staff with whom I used to work. I had worked with her for years, we were good friends, both from the country, we had a lot in common. I explained I needed part time work as money was almost nonexistent. This wonderful friend told me about a vacancy which existed and the fact that they required a temporary receptionist.

I phoned and was consequently interviewed standing in the reception area, I was asked if I could commence then and there. I explained I had two children at home for whom I had to find suitable child care but would commence next day if required. Can't say I had ever been interviewed before standing in a foyer of an office building. Am so pleased the gentleman in question was the personnel officer at the time, I will always be thankful to him.

The rest of the day I was in full throttle trying to find a child care facility and after school care. Everything happened so fast and with ease, it was meant to be!

A new chapter of my life was about to begin and I was so excited.

CHAPTER EIGHT

Child care secured, I commenced my second round of employment in September 1981.

Yes my life was beginning to take shape, a new chapter was definitely beginning, I was no longer just someone's mum, I was Denise again, starting to gain control of my life.

After school some nights, the Salvation Army officer would collect both my children from the crèche. One hot afternoon she collected them, rounded a corner near the school, heard a thud, she thought Fabian had thrown his school bag out the window.

Unfortunately, it wasn't his bag, it was him. She brought him home to me (after stopping off at the local GP). The first thing she said was "Are you still my friend?" I didn't know what she meant. She explained Fabian had fallen out of her car - again I didn't fully understand, I thought she meant he had fallen in the drive way as he was trying to exit the car. She went on to explain that as she rounded a corner what she thought was his school bag bouncing on the road at least three times, turned out to be this little boy. He hadn't thrown his bag out the window he had in fact, fallen out of the car.

He had been checked and apart from bruising and loss of skin he appeared to still be in the land of the living with no permanent damage or broken bones. When I bathed him that evening he had three major lumps on his head one on each side and one in the middle (that accounted for the three thuds she heard), poor little boy he did look a sight.

I had only been at work for two months, knew having the next few days off work was probably impossible, I telephoned my parents to see if they would look after him for a short time. I drove all the way to Crabtree, explained to mum and dad and to Fabian that I would be back in a couple of days when he would be well enough to return to school (that is what he called the crèche). Fabian turned to me with pleading eyes and said "I stays with mummy", so yes he came back home with me. He did look a sore and sorry sight, after those words how could I leave him? I loved that little menace with all my heart, it was awful seeing him so bruised and battered.

1981 seemed to be Fabian's 'Year of the Accident' - March 1981, I was playing pennant squash - it was finals and night time - he was getting tired but still racing around - he fell straight into a glass support and split his forehead open - what a mess. I was actually on the squash court at the time. When we arrived at the hospital emergency they decided he may have been the victim of child abuse. To say he was accident prone was an understatement, probably no more so than most adventurous little boys. He once rode his bike over a step; why? It was there and he could, or at least thought he could.

Previous scars clearly visible, the nurse in emergency decided had it not been for the fact I was known to her, she would have been convinced to take the matter further. Luckily Hobart is a small city eh! We had attended high school together.

March the same year he fell at the crèche and this time split his cheek open (just for the record I wasn't there at the time - see I was innocent). November 1981 he fell out of the car - not a bad effort for one small child in one year.

If I had a day off work, to save money, I would keep Fabian home from the crèche. He would sit in the lounge chair and glare at me; he loved the structure of the crèche. He couldn't or wouldn't think for himself, playing solo didn't seem to be an option for Fabian. He was happy being told what to do and when, what to play with and what not. The scowl on his small face made me somewhat mad at times whilst suppressing a grin at what he was trying to achieve. One little arm on the lounge chair, face resting on his hand, big scowl, large old fashioned lounge chair, small child, it was quite a sight. He was so small he was almost lost in the huge arm chair but his scowl? Well that was hard to miss.

I discovered it was cheaper to enrol him into a private school than pay crèche fees, so in 1983 he was enrolled in Collegiate with his sister (a school for girls I might add). Boys were accepted in kindergarten. He looked absolutely adorable with his school uniform and blonde hair.

It wasn't until Fabian was four years old and in the private school, a hearing problem was suspected and it was suggested he undertake a hearing test. The school couldn't understand why he appeared so intelligent yet couldn't speak.

One night my husband had telephoned me at work to say Fabian was crying with an ear ache. I got home, Fabian was more than crying, he was in pain; I telephoned the doctor to request he stay at the surgery until I could get there. His dad all the time saying, he is alright he is just tired and wants attention. On the way to the surgery Fabian was in the back of my car saying "Take me to the docket Mum, quick, take me to the docket". Now from a child who wasn't overly impressed about trips to the doctor this meant heaps. Diagnosis: Fabian had an abscess in each ear, instructions: for goodness sake don't let him lie down flat tonight because the pain will be unbearable, prop him up continuously until the antibiotics take effect.

I am so pleased I made that trip to the 'docket' that night and didn't listen to my husband's speech about attention seeking. In my heart of hearts I knew Fabian wasn't acting. He had a high pain threshold so if he cried with pain I could place a bet that he was definitely in trouble and needed help.

The school asked me to be present at the examination. Fabian didn't hear much of that hearing test. So it was off to the ear, nose and throat specialist for an overhaul.

No, he decided, structurally everything was fine, so an allergy specialist was recommended. Fabian was allergic to seventeen out of the twenty one samples with which he was tested. The discussions inside obviously hit home, as we walked calmly away from that visit, his little hand in mine, he looked up at me and said "Mummy what will I be able to eat?" I replied I had absolutely no idea but we would work it out. He was still so small; it didn't seem fair that he should be subjected to this harsh reality of life. No child should look that worried at that age, it just didn't seem right.

At least I had an explanation now as to why there had been a continuous stream of ear aches and abscesses.

When he was about two years old we heard a car horn blowing, we looked out the window and there was Fabian oblivious to the fact that he was holding up traffic. The adjacent neighbour had their sprinkler on; Fabian was enjoying an afternoon shower (right in the middle of the street). I rapped on the window to get his attention, I thought he was deliberately ignoring me, little did I know, he just couldn't hear me.

Housework went out the window, I had to research various foods, to learn what on earth I could feed this child before he starved to death or choked, dependent upon my chosen course of action.

He was not to have the same food twice in four days, this had to be continued for at least two years if Fabian was to have some kind of normal hearing without being blocked by mucous caused by the allergies.

The specialist advised, because I didn't speak loudly Fabian had never heard the beginnings of my words, hence he couldn't speak properly. He used to point or look to his sister and she would speak for him, how she knew what he wanted to say is beyond me, but Fabian got off having to speak, merely point and the words came out his sister's mouth. Both of them appeared satisfied with this arrangement.

… When the going gets tough, the tough get going … what is that saying? My husband by this time was in Antarctica, three months at Casey with the Australian Antarctic Division. The station rebuilding program could only be undertaken during the summer months so I was home alone so to speak, working during the day, night time wrestling with ideas for food when there wasn't much food to work with. The lounge room floor continually littered with allergy cooking books, any visitor could have been excused for thinking we had a whole new decorating theme going on.

I agonized over the whole diet affair. How could a child so young understand what he could and could not eat on what days? I prayed for help that night in bed, I wasn't having much success in trying to work it out by myself.

Next morning my prayers were answered. Coloured dots. A calendar with coloured dots. A marker to move each day would show Fabian what colour food he was permitted for that day, he didn't have to read, he only had to know colours and correspond them with food items in the cupboard and fridge. I said a silent prayer of thanks for such a beautifully simple solution to a complex problem.

So there it was, almonds, cashews, pistachios, peanuts, yellow, red, green, blue. Juices all four of them, all sporting coloured dots lined up nicely in the fridge or cupboard. A coloured marker on the calendar would lead the way to food for the day.

Ice cream was made from cashew nuts and fresh fruit. Jelly and jam made with agar agar and fresh fruit. Fabian's milk was made from almonds. Cooking usually commenced around 5am or soon thereafter. I made flat rice bread fresh each morning for breakfast; they were best eaten whilst still hot. Buckwheat pikelets were also on the breakfast menu as an alternative. Lunch was more of a dilemma, dinner wasn't such a problem, just had to remember, fish, veal, lamb, chicken, fish, veal, lamb, chicken, poor Fabian even years later he couldn't look at fish, those two years on this strict diet certainly took its toll. Each day was long, can't say I had any problem sleeping when I finally made it to bed.

Where possible and in support of Fabian we ate the same food so he didn't feel he was alone. Some foods like almond milk for instance were way too expensive for all of us to consume. In those days almond milk was not available in cartons as is now the case. Fabian's almond milk was made by me blanching almonds, removing the outer dark layer and blending the naked almonds with water. Whilst is would have been most likely healthier for us all to consume almond milk our budget would not stretch that far, so for the rest of us it was situation normal.

A week or so into the diet Fabian walked into the kitchen one morning, said hello to his sister and hello Mummy. We looked at each other dumbfounded (our morning greeting usually consisted of; throw himself into the kitchen and yell) who was this little stranger saying good morning to us in such a civilized manner.

Who would have believed a change in diet could make such a behavioural transformation. My eyes were being opened little by little each day.

Knowledge, I needed knowledge, education, input, data, but from where was the problem. I discovered an allergy group called ARM - Allergy Recognition and Management, they were a God send. I don't know what I would have done without them. Even Fabian's GP Doctor R joined the group so he too could understand more of this phenomenon which had struck our house. That step earned this particular GP my eternal respect, few are sufficiently opened mined enough to admit they too, need to further their learning on what could be considered 'out there' alternative options. At this time there certainly was not much in the way of information/documentation on behavioural problems relating to dietary intake. Who would have believed the intake of certain foods could create so many medical problems.

In my quest for understanding I took part in this group and also acted as a representative on the state committee, I attended many lectures and open days re the subject of allergies. I needed to learn everything possible. I had to understand what was happening, what food was available that still eluded me on the Health Food shop shelves. Not only what food items, but what to do with it when I found it. Many recipies failed - when I say failed I should say, Fabian and I didn't take too kindly to them so it was trial after trial with maybe three/four in ten being successful. Draining - most definitely but rewarding at the same time.

Following the revelations highlighted by Fabian, I am proud to say our doctor not only acknowledged and accepted the relationship between allergies and food consumption but also went on to further his learning in this particular field. Fabian's health, hearing and behaviour continued to improve. Fabian was only small but he was teaching all of us, including his doctor about the dramatic affect a change of diet can have on many aspects of a person's health and behaviour. From agro to placid, from sick to healthy - I was suitably impressed.

If we were all to maintain a whole food diet, free of additives, preservatives and sugars, would our children be less likely to require medications to correct behavioural problems at such an early age? Would behavioural problems disappear? I would like to believe that this could be one of the answers for our children of the future.

One night Fabian came home from school with a pocket missing from his shirt, I asked how this happened. His reply "I lost it". Now how on earth can a person lose a pocket, they don't just fall off - well not unless your name is Fabian that is.

Mind you, we did have a few hiccups, it wasn't all smooth sailing. After school and work one day I had to go to the supermarket. Fabian was zooming all over the place like a demented flea, an over wound toy would have been easier to control. I could not understand why, he hadn't eaten anything he wasn't supposed to … Or had he?

Later that week his friend's mum phoned, so I asked if maybe her son had shared his lunch with Fabian. She replied oh yes, he said Fabian never has party pies so he gave him a party pie from his tuck shop lunch. One party pie! Who would have guessed that one little pie could cause so much damage?

In case I ever had doubts about the hardship the diet caused - it just went out the window, I now had proof - the diet was crucial to Fabian's health and crucial for **my** peace. I would never have believed one party pie could turn my baby boy into a hyperactive terror if I had not seen the affect with my own two eyes.

And for the record - I discovered the story re the missing pocket. The boys had been playing slash rough playing and his pocket had come off with the help of one of his playmates. Yep, you guessed it, it was lost somewhere. Fabian's statement had been an honest one; he had definitely 'lost' his pocket.

By this time Fabian was attending Hutchins school, a school for boys. I asked the teacher is she had a problem with Fabian attending school with asthma (and all the coughing that accompanies such a disease). The reply was always the same, if you can't do any more for him at home then we would prefer he was here with us, medication and all. Fabian was four years old at this point. The school was fantastic, I explained to the teacher and the students why it was so important Fabian adhere to his very strict diet, all appeared to comprehend. The school allowed me the privilege of addressing his class, for that I thank them. They understood and were more than willing to assist Fabian cope through this very taxing time.

Mind you, I don't think it stopped some of them from smuggling him small amounts of contraband from time to time. I am happy to say we did not have a repeat of such a significant behavioural change as that infamous party pie had caused.

So for two years this diet continued, it had benefits for all of us. For years I had been taking medication for arthritis - I found my aches and pains had started to subside. Return, subside, then it would be red meat night, following this, back came my muscular aches, I didn't have arthritis - red meat was causing these problems. It took me awhile to fully realize what was happening. So ok, take note I thought, the results were always the same. Well who would have thought, here was I, learning more and more. What I didn't understand was; what was in red meat which would cause my muscles and joints to ache?

Lesson: my body obviously didn't like red meat, except in small portions occasionally. I have to wonder how many people go through life with the same symptoms never knowing the difference. If it hadn't been for Fabian I may still be living in ignorance and most likely still taking medication for nonexistent arthritis.

My Dr R reminded me recently of one incident, Fabian had been attending yoga classes as a means of trying to settle him down and hopefully get the asthma under control. The instructor suggested I allow

Fabian to go to sleep watching a candle burn. This he believed would take his mind off any problem and allow him to drift off to sleep peacefully. Well the aim was most likely achieved but there was one major hiccup. The very next morning following the candle flame, Fabian woke with a raging temperature, severe headache and nausea. No school or work on this occasion that was painfully obvious. So it was off to the GP. He was at a complete loss to explain the sudden onset of these symptoms. In desperation he gave me a list of potential allergy causes and said "Sit in the waiting room and go through this list to see if anything looks like a probable cause". Didn't take long - there it was - burning candle. Oh - another one of those oh geez moments. Oh well, one can only try these suggestions, in this case we certainly bombed out big time. No more candles in the house unless the power went out!

Fabian was addicted to both a vegetable extract spread and chocolate - he would want savoury on his toast for breakfast pre the diet, I thought I was doing the right thing. I wasn't to know he would become addicted; nothing could have been further from my mind. Same with chocolate, he would cry in the supermarket for anything that had a chocolate component.

I once read many years ago, it is children like Fabian with severe multiple allergies who are susceptible to substance abuse in later years - this was one statistic and theory which was to prove correct. I now wonder how many other people with substance abuse had severe allergy problems as a child. A tendency for addictive behaviour can certainly become apparent from an early age if one is aware and paying attention.

Fabian's health improved thanks to the rotation diet, after the two years he was able to tolerate most food. He would drink milk for a few days or longer, then he wouldn't be able to drink it again for weeks - his body didn't want it. Same with most food, if we listen and learn from our own bodies or that of our children you will see how we rotate food naturally without consciously thinking about it. Quite an education should you choose to be open to it, and quite a valuable lesson. This was only the beginning of my learning; I was to learn so much more through Fabian.

There will be times when your body will demand certain food, take note but don't confuse it with addiction. Demanding and craving are too different things but each will make itself known in no uncertain terms.

The foods we crave are more than likely to be the very foods to which we have an allergy or intolerance. Food our body demands are likely to contain a particular vitamin or mineral content which our body requires at that point in time.

CHAPTER NINE

Fabian had asthma from a very early age; there would be nights he and I would be up at 2am with his severe asthma attacks. His dad wasn't much help on these occasions he would tend to get angry (guess fear does that to some people - don't get helpful, get angry) so it was best he stayed in bed and leave us to it. Anger on these occasions only exacerbated the situation. Fabian needed understanding, peace and calm if we were to make it back to bed before morning.

One night in particular, I had given him all the medication that was possible, he must have seen the look of fear on my face as we sat in front of the heater waiting for the symptoms to dissipate. He looked at me and said, I will be ok mummy, I will. I had had to phone our GP at whatever ungodly hour to ask for instructions as to what to do next when the medication had failed to alleviate the symptoms. Nothing had been lost on Fabian, he had obviously realized phoning the doctor in the early hours meant serious. I followed the next set of instructions and finally the asthma abated and we were able to go back to bed. The most precious memory re that moment was the look on his little face as he was assuring me all would be ok. Severe allergies will impede normal growth, consequently Fabian was small for his age, small but adorable and definitely lovable.

There would be nights when due to the eczema Fabian's bed looked as though it had been the scene of a massacre, blood everywhere. He would scratch the affected parts until they were red raw. What a start to life.

Life continued, cooking, go to work, come home, go to squash, go to bed. The one huge moment came when after working for the Australian

Antarctic Division I was allowed to go to Antarctica on what was then called a familiarization visit. The ship left Hobart at midnight on a Sunday night, December 1984, we arrived at Casey at midday the following Sunday. Christmas Day was spent at sea - I was feeling so sea sick for the most part of the day I sat so still the other passengers could have been excused for thinking maybe I was a statue.

The first morning at sea I woke, felt ok, got out of bed, put my head down to extract some clean clothes so I could shower, sea sickness hit big time. If they could have taken me off on a mercy helicopter flight that first day I would have found the oomph to run to the chopper. Yes it was that bad. The ship went up and down; the accommodation module went back and across from left to right. Up, down, back, across, up, down, repeat a million times. What had I got myself into I thought. At this rate weight loss was definitely assured.

My cabin mate was running around (now where is the justice in the world) she was even running up and down the stairs to extract turkey after frozen turkey in preparation for Christmas lunch. I struggled to make it to the deck for fresh air and she was fit enough to be the turkey courier!!!! Some kind person had thrown up in the stairwell; that sure didn't help my queasy stomach in the slightest. Once on deck it wasn't a whole lot better, I had managed to walk to an area where the smell of diesel really churned my stomach at a faster rate. Walking through the kitchen - oh no, it was torture whichever way I went.

The second night I think I went close to throwing my soup bowl at the kitchen hand - not intentionally, just had to get out fast before I threw more than the soup bowl at him!

The first three days out of Hobart were definitely the worst, after that the waters calmed and once I gained my sea legs and learned to go with the flow it wasn't quite as bad. Please note! I did say wasn't *quite* as bad. I still sat quietly most of the time.

Christmas Day didn't feel like Christmas in any way, shape or form. This unbelievable journey was like leaving the world and going to another world far, far away. Problems at home, bad relationships, problems of any kind evaporated, disappeared, nonexistent. I found I hadn't even been thinking about my husband or normal life at all. I did feel guilty when I came to this realization, but only for a few minutes. I did miss my children and did feel as though I had deserted them when they needed me, after all Christmas isn't a good time to be without your mum. Unfortunately I didn't have a choice; this was to be my only chance to visit Antarctica. This new world was heaven I have to admit.

One morning about 2am one of our staff phoned our cabin to say "Look out the window", look out the window! After being woken at that time I could have given him a few clues as where to go, never mind where to look. It was so difficult to get to sleep in the first place so can't say I was particularly happy about being woken.

Well we were awake so might as well take a peek - snow white everywhere we looked. Bumper to bumper sea ice, penguins, seals watching us with inquisitive eyes. Day light I should add, by this time we were getting very close to the Antarctic continent so it was twenty four hour daylight.

Next morning the scenery was still the same, the ship was laden with supplies for Casey for twelve months so we were sitting quite low in the water. The seals and penguins watched us, it was like being in another land, nothing could compare to this - nothing at all. On one occasion the ship was heading for a piece of ice, two penguins sat watching us approach, they were having a discussion - probably wondering what type of animal we were. As we got closer and closer they finally realized they were in a direct line, one went one way and one the other (after a final hasty discussion) it did look quite amusing.

Whales swam with us and criss-crossed in front of the ship - it was an amazing adventure.

We arrived at Casey, once ashore even the land moved (well that's what it felt like) it was difficult to re-establish land legs, seems you get used to putting your foot so far and obviously wait for the ship to get to that point, so on land it was hilarious watching some of us mere beginners try to negotiate our way through the Casey tunnel.

Visits to Antarctica are deemed a privilege and as such, staff has to work to earn their keep. We had a choice of working in the kitchen or on garbage clean up detail. I chose the kitchen. So for six days we had to catch the chicken ashore so we were in the kitchen on station at 7am ready to start work. The chicken took us back to the ship at 7pm at night. Lunch break was after we had fed the locals and the visiting officials - only catch was - it took almost 20 minutes to get dressed in all required gear, by that time it was almost lunch time over - so needless to say we didn't get very far at lunch time. I should qualify one detail; the ship was called the Icebird. The chicken was her baby.

On the last amazing day, my cabin mate and I did get to fly in a chopper to Peterson Island with a graphic artist and another artist - what an experience. Elephant seal colony, snow petrels, birds in their hundreds. Only that morning we had been sitting by the edge of the sea saying to each other, "Wouldn't it be great if we could fly to an Island and see wildlife - just so we knew we were really in Antarctica".

You see, we spent six days, almost twelve hours each day in the kitchen so we could be excused for thinking maybe someone had painted a snow scene on the kitchen window and we really weren't in Antarctica at all. No sooner had we walked back to the main area of the station when one of the politicians on our voyage called out and told us to get our butts over to the chopper as there were two vacant seats heading out with the artists. Don't have to tell you we didn't need to be told twice and by the way, the version I quoted was the polite/censored version.

Think we spent about three hours on the Island exploring, taking in everything, disbelieving we were so close to the wildlife - someone pinch us please! The smell of the elephant seals was a reality check of sorts I suppose. The snow petrels were so beautiful, it was quite a noisy experience overall being so close to the bird rookeries but so very beautiful and rewarding. Six days x twelve hours of hard labour had been worth it.

During the week we had also been fortunate enough to drive out to Wilkes (the old American station) we spent a few hours at the Wilkes Hilton (accommodation akin to a shack) awaiting further transport. I don't think I have ever laughed so much in all my life; it was one of those occasions I know I shall never forget.

Whilst waiting for transport at the Wilkes Hilton we were in need of water to boil for a much needed hot drink. One of our staff had found water a few times during our final walk to the accommodation (accidentally that is) so it was decided he was the perfect choice to send out to complete this mission. Not sure if he agreed with our decision but being a good sport he accomplished his challenge with good humour.

One night about 9pm we also had a tour of a closer island (Shirley Island) which was home to penguins, penguins and more penguins, only drawback was, after getting back to the ship I was so exhausted it was so very difficult climbing the ladder to get back up to the deck. Those rope steps seemed to go on forever and my body felt like I had lead weights tied around me.

It was extremely difficult falling asleep when surrounded by 24 hours of daylight - the body clock loses its usual rhythm and I found it impossible to sleep at all. Tired, oh yes, but unable to sleep to save myself.

Would you believe New Year's Eve - we had a BBQ - yes you read correctly, glasses not required after all. I was so tired I couldn't even be bothered getting dressed, I ventured outside in my normal gear (normal inside gear is still winter woollies and thermals I might add) - yes I got cold but I was almost too exhausted to care or notice. We had had the normal days work to undertake - potatoes, potatoes - peel and more peeling, onions - oh so many tears in one day. Washing up, washing up and more washing up - yes all this was pre the modern age so all undertaken manually. We were feeding approx 120+ super hungry people. I had blisters on my fingers, bruises up and down my legs from climbing on stools to put the large boilers on a shelf. After the normal feeding routine we then assisted the chef with the preparations for the nights feast so it was a much longer day than usual. Height would have been a distinct advantage for kitchen chores, height would definitely have saved me from a few bruises. There are some instances where being my height is a distinct disadvantage!

Heading back to the ship after midnight, the only method to determine it was midnight as opposed to midday was the pinky tinge which appeared - weird I can tell you, your mind tells you it is midnight but the light says otherwise.

The whole week was truly amazing, each experience so very different from the previous. I shall always treasure those memories and am extremely grateful to have had the opportunity to experience Antarctica. My thanks and gratitude to the Australian Antarctic Division.

We sailed out of Casey on a Sunday, as we left the sea was freezing behind us, quite an amazing sight. We hit sea ice so thick the ship had to keep going into reverse in order to have a second go at the ice in an attempt to break through. It was like being in a rodeo - thrown about with the motion of the ship. Never even entered my mind we could get stuck solid, luckily we didn't, other voyages are not always so lucky.

This time around my sea legs didn't take so long to set in motion, we had made friends with the variety of people with whom we shared the voyage - politians, artists, navy personnel, staff from the Maritime College, School of Hospitality - you name it we had it. First time the Antarctic Division had a ship with the capacity to take visitors as well as expeditioners, accommodation had been fully utilized and was packed to capacity. We had quite a mixture of personalities and career choices aboard.

Parties and parties ensued all the way back home, it was wonderful, a real social experience. I found during this time, I was a different person - so happy - no one criticizing me, only extremely friendly and fun loving people who shared the one passion: Antarctica and all it had to offer. Enjoying the company of all - board games, videos, sometimes just sharing experiences - a diverse population such as this, we had a lot to talk and laugh about when we got to know each other.

We arrived back in Melbourne the following Sunday - from there it was fly back to Hobart - back home - back to the real world again.

Don't think I was fully prepared for how I had changed on that 3 week voyage.

Whilst on our way back I received a telex to say I had been promoted - now that was something to celebrate.

I don't think I ever made up my mind as to what was worse, sea sickness or air sickness like flying over Macquarie Island on an air drop. Back in the 80's the Australian Antarctic Division in conjunction with the Forces used to fly three airdrops a year to Macquarie Island - dropping fresh food, mail, even eggs at one time and any other item which would survive the crash landing. Items that were required pre the next sea voyage.

These items were flung out the back of the Hercules in a 'dizzy lizzy'. The Herc went around and around air dropping only a small amount as the isthmus came in sight at just the precise moment. Think we dropped for approximately one to one and a half hours - around and around, up and down, ended up with bruises from getting thrown around. Not exactly a smooth exercise, given the turbulence over the island. My girlfriend told me I turned green 'maybe that's why Macquarie Island is called the Green Sponge'. One friend had been worried when she saw the colours I kept changing to and from. I would have gladly gone out the back attached to one of the dizzy lizzies if someone had offered. I have never felt so sick in all my life. No escape on this one either. Yes I threw up, as did the pilot (didn't feel so bad when I learned that). You know the one excellent thing about being sick on a Herc? One gets to keep the sea sick bag until landing is completed – guess that is a small price to pay for such an amazing adventure.

So yes, both were truly unbelievable, once in a lifetime opportunities but no thanks I do not wish to have a return trip to either destination. I treasured those experiences but nothing but nothing would entice me to undergo a re-run of either.

Travel sickness can sure take the fun out of some experiences.

CHAPTER TEN

I knew before I went to Antarctica all was not well with our marriage, we had had constant arguments; my husband believed I was having an affair with someone at work. The first time he came up with that I started to laugh, couldn't even think of anyone with whom I would want to have an affair with let alone do it. When I realized it wasn't a joke I got mad, I had given him no reason on which to base this assumption. Where did it come from? Either way it was another nail in the proverbial coffin.

One night I had been to a work party - I had taken one of the girls with me, so that meant I also had to take her home. During the evening a friendship developed between her and one of our guys; I believe one of the parties was married which made events a little more complicated, hence I was extra late getting home. My husband had obviously decided I must have been having affair - pot calling the kettle black wouldn't you say.

Next morning I was so very tired, he told me I was a lazy bitch and dragged me off the bed and down the hallway - I had carpet burns on my elbows, I'm pretty sure he ended up getting kicked where most men dread - my only defence. Not one of my more pleasant experiences or memories.

Now back to face reality ...

I arrived back home from Antarctica, the kids started to argue (as kids do) my husband started yelling at the pair of them. I took myself outside, sat on my front lawn, looked at the Derwent River and wished that ship would come back and take me away - only this time for good. I didn't want my life back.

I wanted the peace and happiness I had found on my three week discovery of myself. I wanted to be loved not criticized. Loved for who I was, not who I should be to suit someone else. I wanted the happy person back, the one I found on the ship. I didn't want to be told all meals should be set out the same on the plates, I didn't care if the carrots weren't all cut the same size, I didn't care if each vegetable didn't look quite the same or was in the same place on all plates. What does all that matter - honestly? The army didn't know what it started when it taught him to cook and how to present food. He obviously took those lessons extremely seriously, probably more seriously than they were ever intended.

It was at that point I decided I wanted out.

Funny, I started with infinite amounts of love, little by little hurtful things happened and the amount of love gradually eroded until one day I woke up and realized the barrel was empty. I remember how scared I felt, how alone, like I was the only person in the world to ever feel this way. I would lie in bed at night hoping he wouldn't make it home and that life could go on without all the pain I knew was to come.

I made it through this period with the help of a friend and work colleague, she had been through a divorce, I talked to her, told her how I felt, she told me what she felt as she was going through that period in her life. I didn't feel so bad when I realized I wasn't alone thinking those same horrible thoughts. It was good to learn other people have felt the same, thought the same thoughts, same emotions. I felt more at peace learning this. Thank God for other people's learning experiences and for sharing, I will always be grateful for her and to her, more than she will ever realize. Thank you, thank you so very much.

Falling out of love - divorce - I hadn't factored either into my life plan.

The last morning on the ship, one of the passengers told me he had fallen in love with me. I went back to my cabin in a major state of shock, how could someone fall in love with me. Someone who was useless, fat and revolting, couldn't do anything right (well according to my husband anyway). I had tears in my eyes when I entered the cabin. My cabin mate looked at me - she said "He told you he has fallen in love with you"? I nodded; words escaped me at that point. How could anyone love ME! I didn't dress to impress, I had had my hair cut shorter than normal to make it easier whilst on the ship, I wore old clothes, I was just me on that voyage, how could anyone fall in love with 'just me'?

I had no idea my husband had managed to undermine my confidence to that extent. It took some serious internal dialogue to answer that one. I used to think 'how could I be so bad, as bad as he says I am, yet I am getting promotion after promotion at work', if I was as useless as he says I wouldn't get promoted at work - would I? I had to really dig deep at that point. And for the record…no I have never been fat, never sat still long enough to get fat except for my pregnancies when I was somewhat bigger than usual.

When your confidence is being undermined little by little it goes unheeded until one day it is like one huge revelation exploding like a nuclear bomb. Then what? Where to from here? The unknown can be extremely daunting.

The Salvation Army Officer used to say to me, 'I don't think he has anything to complain about, the children are always clean, you always have the housework done, lawns mowed, meals prepared' I can't even remember how that discussion arose. But it did make me think.

Sundays I would be sitting in church, and I swear I had given her fodder for the lesson that week, time after time it seemed to fit right where my thoughts or my life was. Maybe she was more of an influence than I had first thought. Maybe she was teaching me more than just religion. Maybe I was teaching her.

When it was time for her to move forward in the Salvation Army, I couldn't even summon up the courage to attend her farewell. I had worked with her for about three years teaching Sunday school, my world was falling apart and yet another piece was coming unravelled. She had been my one true friend, driven me to places when the need arose, took care of my children on occasions when I first returned to work. What would I do without her, the glue holding me together was melting too fast, could I cope?

I don't think she ever understood (how could she, I never explained, I couldn't trust myself to speak to her before she left) I knew I would lose control totally, if I started to cry I may not be able to stop. Don't think she ever forgave me. Maybe one day she will understand and forgive. I pray my book will find its way to her for that very reason.

I had to try to preserve what little of me was left. I had to survive.

Like most wives who are down trodden and not allowed to spend money I used to hide any clothing I bought for myself and the children. Get them out much, much later in time and pretend like they had been there for absolutely ages …. Sound familiar?

One particular night I thought I am not in the mood for this game. I walked in the door, threw two cheap track suits on the table which I had bought for squash. Said "Look at them now and complain if you are going to because then I can put them away". Quite a brave move for me I thought after the event. My husband picked them up, looked at the quality and cost and said "Gosh they were a good buy". I was stunned; I had done the hiding thing for years when I could have just taken a stand instead. I was so annoyed with myself for letting him treat me in the manner he had. Oh well, we live and learn. Some of us just seem to learn at a slower pace I suppose.

If there was a moral in that story it is to always be your true self, regardless of the situation, speak your mind, by speaking out, resentment has nowhere to sit and seethe. Left to its own devices resentment can build up to volcano proportions and cause untold damage to the holder. Maybe it takes a few years under the proverbial belt before we begin to come into our true selves and have the confidence to make a stand.

One night before heading off to play pennant squash I had cooked chops for dinner; Fabian looked at the one remaining lonely chop and asked if he could have it later. Next morning whilst preparing our lunches there was the little chop looking back at me from the very spot I had left it.

Fabian came into the kitchen, I asked him why he didn't eat it last night - his reply ….I was too scared to ask daddy for it. I just stood there in shock. My only thought …what am I doing to these children. How much damage am I doing to them by trying to hold the marriage together - is it worth it? Too scared to ask for a chop! I don't know how long I stood in the kitchen, I do know shock set in and I felt rooted to the spot whilst my brain tried to make sense of those words.

Who would have thought one solitary chop could be the catalyst for a marriage breakup, sounds ridiculous doesn't it, until you know the circumstances….and for the record Fabian never knew how much impact that 'chop incident' had on our lives. I would have gone to my grave with that information; no way in this world would I have wanted him to think he was responsible for the breakdown of our marriage. That little chop was merely the red flag, a final warning to take note and act.

At that point it wasn't a case of wanting to get out of the marriage and house it was a case of MUST get out before any more damage was done.

So where to now, I knew I had to leave him, how would I survive financially, two small children? I talked it over with them - it had to be their decision too, if they didn't want to leave then I would have to re think. My beautiful daughter would have been about ten, Fabian six - I found a house to rent at Coningham - a beach side suburb south of Kingston. Both children wanted to get away from their father so the decision was made and set in motion. I explained if we left their dad they would both have to leave their respective private schools and go the local public school - to my surprise my daughter didn't have a problem. In retrospect Fabian leaving his school was a negative moment in his life, I believe that did have major consequences for him. Consequences which would remain unknown for many years.

1 July 1985 I made the move … anyone who has been through a separation has probably been through the same experience. People would say to me "Have you thought about what you are doing", thought about it …

they had to be joking, who packs up two kids and moves out not knowing how in hell they are going to survive and …not think about it…. I swear if one more person had said that to me they would have received a whole lot more than they had planned for and it wouldn't have been pleasant and it would not have been in keeping with Thumper's philosophy.

Life at Coningham was wonderful, the three of us used to bike ride from where we lived down into Coningham Beach when we got home from work/school. Going down was fine, coming back, hill most of the way, took a few weeks before we could master the uphill stage and stay on the bikes at the same time. We had our own beach close by the house, it was so easy to walk down to the rocks and de-stress. Walk down to the jetty and sit and watch the small fish swim by and listen to the water lapping at the wooden supports. The location was both peaceful and beautiful. Life's problems seemed miles away during those precious moments.

Housework didn't matter because there wasn't anyone to tell me I hadn't dusted in particular locations. Life took on new meaning. The three of us knew happiness and peace at long last. Criticism had been banished from our life.

Well meaning people (upon hearing news of my separation) would say "Oh, I'm sorry", my girlfriend laughed one day and still does when she recalls my words - another oh I'm sorry came forth - my reply, don't be, I'm not! Guess that well meaning person was a lot more careful with their words from that day forward.

If I thought life *with* my husband was bad it was about to get a whole lot worse *without* him. Neighbours, friends all showed their true colours; you see I was the one who left so I had to be the one in the wrong. I was the one who went back to work - tsk tsk we all know what happens when wives go back to work. Gee, and I thought I went back to work because we ran out of money, silly me.

Seriously, that comment made the rounds of the street apparently, the cause of the marriage break down was my return to work. Doesn't pay to heed gossip, no one knew what went on in our house, note I said house not home, but those of us who lived therein.

Years later one neighbour said these words to me: "I knew you were unhappy, I would see you through the window pacing around your house", funny, I never realized or thought about it, but yes, she was correct, I had paced but not thought anything of it.

My parents turned against me in a big way that really hurt. I was their daughter yet they chose to believe the lies my husband told them - it wasn't until 18 months later after dad had died that mum learned the real truth from him and said to me "Why didn't you explain" - I replied I didn't feel as though I needed to justify my actions to anyone. I

had a valid reason for leaving him, I was the only person I had to justify my actions to, it didn't have anything to do with anyone else.

I only justify myself to two people, one of whom is me, the other - the Man Upstairs. I am not responsible for other people's actions or thoughts nor can I control them, they will think what they want regardless. I can only be responsible for me.

My husband turned up on their door step night after night crying. He told them I had left him for another man - yes they believed everything he said. Dad had only just started talking to me again before he had a massive heart attack and died.

Due to family pressure I gave in and my estranged husband came to live with us at Coningham - my logic was - this was a second chance, at least I would have tried and known definitely if I had made the right decision in the first place.

It was one of the most miserable twelve months of my life (up to that point anyway). It didn't work; I have to wonder if it ever does. Friends find it hard to know where their allegiance should lay - family try to go on as if all were normal. We were all miserable.

At one stage we had to go to marriage guidance counselling, the counsellor asked how did I see it - my reply - like a book I have just finished and am ready to move on to the next one. Blunt, yes it probably was, but that is how I felt. Years of mental abuse will do that to a person I discovered.

My beloved had even told my mother he was putting money aside for himself just in case I ever left him again. No, in case you are wondering, it never occurred to her to impart that tiny bit of useful information. He wouldn't help pay the bills, finally I had had enough, I asked him this particular morning for money to pay one of the many bills - he threw some money at me in the car - sure helps to make your mind up when someone does that to you. Yes I wanted out - only permanently this time!

…and about him putting money aside…mum told me that years and years later. To say I never felt close to my mother is something of an understatement, even today I can't say I know my mother because I simply don't. Why? I don't know. I don't have an answer for that. I never actually felt part of the family, maybe that was a starting point if searching for an answer; I always felt different but had no idea as to why. I don't ever remember mum showing her emotions to any great extent, she seemed guarded where emotion was concerned. Maybe it was because we never discussed anything as a family; any problems were hushed and not spoken of. The 'children should be seen and not heard'; the 'speak when spoken to' theory all contributed I would think. (*To this very day I still deal with my problems alone, I don't discuss until I have had time to process myself*). There could be a myriad of reasons. I may not understand her, but do I love her? Yes I do and always have done.

We are all human and as such none of us are perfect, we all have faults embedded in our DNA somewhere. We have different beliefs; some are more judgmental than others, some have peculiar habits….life would be boring if we were all the same. I have learned to deal with the fact that I may never truly know my own family.

Ok, miserable was about to get even more miserable from this point on for awhile. My husband had been given my dad's gun and he stored it under the bed, he told me if I ever went to leave him again he would use it on me. Scared, worried, stressed - yes I sure was.

My husband was out mowing the lawn one afternoon and I could see he was talking to himself all the while. I watched from the window a little more than a tad worried. He came in for a shower; I could hear him talking to himself so I went closer to the bathroom door. He was saying "I'll tell her I am just staying for awhile then I won't leave (or something similar) then he laughed the most blood curdling laugh - it was so unnerving.

I had never heard anything remotely similar to that type of laugh before. Yes I have heard it since, after Fabian got schizophrenia, it isn't a normal laugh, it is one which goes right through the listener and leaves one with a cold eerie feeling. A sense of danger prevailed from that point on.

Once a week I was attending aerobics class, this particular night the instructor caught me yawning every time she looked at me. I hadn't slept for about three nights so yes I was tired. I was terribly scared that gun might see some use after all these years and it was getting closer to me moving out.

I found a small but beautiful house in Kingston, almost behind the Antarctic Division, it was everything we needed, and I could afford to buy it (with the help of the Bank I might add). So the Bank and I bought this warm, friendly house and I moved in, in December 1986. Pleased to be safe once again.

I discovered we were more like friends after the final decision was made to split permanently, we were even able to talk things through, think he wanted to separate as much as I did but like all things maybe the thought was worse than the action.

CHAPTER ELEVEN

Life seemed to be ok again. Didn't have any spare money, but the house was warm, we had the most beautiful view of Mount Wellington from the lounge room window - how many people in the world have an active canvass to view, one which changes within minutes. I loved that house.

Work I loved. I loved the work I was undertaking at the Antarctic Division regardless of which particular area I was involved. At one time I was joking with one of the ladies with whom I worked, she hit me hard on the head with a pile of files and scolded me for saying whatever it was. I think I had called the Man Upstairs 'Ralph', she thought this to be disrespectful hence my scolding. My reply was always the same "It's ok, I am on first name terms with the Man Upstairs, he wouldn't mind because he too has a sense of humour".

I can no longer remember how or why this came about but he has always been 'Ralph' to me as long as I can remember. I would say or do something and then apologize to Ralph if I thought it was disrespectful to whom my words, thoughts or actions had been directed. I would ask him for guidance, I often say "Sorry Ralph" out loud, especially when I am apologizing for my behaviour or thoughts. To me this was 'normal' and certainly not meant to be disrespectful.

That pile of files necessitated a trip to the chiropractor for a neck repair job. I told her about this and her reply was "I do that to my kids", I suggested she might like to cease that type of admonishment as it had the potential to have a lasting, damaging affect on her children. Our necks are not designed to take trauma of that type regardless of how innocent it may appear.

"I am on first name terms with Ralph, the Man Upstairs" many of my friends, family and work colleagues have heard that repeated over and over. I firmly believe it to be true, how I know that isn't clear, I just know and believe.

Another one of my favourite musings has always been. Ralph is somewhat bored, looks down and notices I am sailing along quite nicely and am stress free, so he says to himself, "Hmmm what can I give her now, she hasn't had any problems for awhile". I have always related my challenges to his boredom. He hasn't let me down; as soon as I hit the 'all clear' on any given challenge he comes up with the next one, usually bigger and better than the last.

For a short time my life was again happy.

One day I was driving over the Tasman Bridge, came up behind a slow truck, pressure applied to the brake, but no response forthcoming, my little mini just kept on keeping on. I took her to a mechanic; they repaired one set of brakes. Day or so later driving down another steep hill; braking capacity almost nonexistent again - so back to the mechanic.

See what I mean … was Ralph bored again?

On closer inspection they discovered one set of brakes had been cut (obviously for a while) the brake warning light also severed. I asked if they would give the report to me in writing - but like most brave males who like to cover their own butts the reply was in the negative. Guess they didn't want to end up in court as a witness.

My problem you see, there were only two people who operated on my precious baby car. The realization hit me and it wasn't pleasant, it scared and angered me. I always had people or children in my car, I used to give one of the women a ride to work and back each day, take it in turns driving to where ever squash was for that week - how could anyone take such action and risk all those lives? The drive to where we used to live at Coningham was full of corners; if the brakes had failed at that point I would have ended up in the water.

I knew I had to confront him when I could see his face, I would know from his reaction. He came to visit me, I told him about the brakes being severed - the look on his face said it all - I started to shake uncontrollably - it was him, he didn't have to say a word.

I went into shock; I can't remember how long it lasted. He stammered something about being unable to stop the brake fail warning light from being on permanently so they had cut the cable so the light would go off.

Yes, I probably should have taken it further, but I chose not to. What did I have to gain? I had my life, my sanity and above all, peace. I thought I was better off leaving it at that. He had to live with himself, he knew I knew the truth and he had to deal with that within himself, not something I would choose to do willingly. I couldn't live with that amount of guilt, how he could live with himself is beyond me.

Do Unto Others as you would have them Do Unto You - would have been useful if he had applied that rule prior to his actions. I believe in karma, it isn't up to me to 'punish' someone, at some point he will answer to a Higher Power.

My children came home one day after playing with children in our new street; they told me the children's surname. I'm thinking gosh I used to go to school with a guy with that surname, not a common name. Imagine my surprise when yes, it was a blast from the past. Our children became firm friends. Fabian in particular with their number two daughter, the two were inseparable.

Life in Willow Ave was really pleasant and quiet. I was so very happy with my little world and my little home.

During our time in Willow Ave Fabian was brought home in the arms of a neighbour - he had fallen off his bike going down the hill, he had a hole under his chin, his friend's dad had found him and carried him home. I had to take him to an afterhours doctor (first and last visit I can assure you). We walked into his surgery - the doctor stood there and said "Don't get blood on the floor will you!" - I honestly thought he was joking - he wasn't.

I had this child with a hole from heavens only knows what in his face and this guy was telling me not to get blood on his floor - please! Yes he mended, didn't appear to do any lasting damage, no foreign objects discovered, some part of the bike must have stabbed him as he crash landed. He was effectively stitched back together; he looked a mess, so much skin missing from his small face, his tears stinging as they hit the affected areas. The more he cried the more he tried not to because of the pain.

1987 sometime, I received a phone call from my estranged husband; Fabian had fallen off his bike at Coningham and severed the end of his finger. I was to meet them at our local doctor's surgery.

As you can see the accident saga continued.

The doctor was Indian - Fabian hadn't had much experience with dark skinned people, he kept shouting "He is trying to kill me, he is". The doctor chuckled as he repaired the severed finger whilst trying to assure Fabian all would be ok.

A few years earlier I had met a guy at a training course, he seemed to be really friendly, understanding and charismatic. We had become friends for a short time. I can't remember how we met up and came in contact again but we did.

The friendship grew and he moved in with us. The children were definitely not happy about this arrangement but accepted the inevitable. In hind sight maybe I should have taken more notice of their intuition. At that point I certainly wasn't listening to mine. I can honestly say it is one of the few times I failed to heed the advice of my intuition. My intuition has been belting me around since I was knee high. So why did I not listen in this instance? I don't know? Maybe I had lessons to learn from the experience I was about to encounter.

The day of my wedding, I went to my favourite hairdresser, I didn't want to go back home, a feeling of flight and fright had set in big time. I wanted to run and never look back. I thought about all the preparations that had been put in place, how his family had all driven down from Launceston. I turned coward and went back home with a heavy feeling.

We were married in December 1989. I suppose life for us began to deteriorate from that very day. I had heard the saying 'some people change from the day they married', well here it was for me in black and white - a definite change for the worse. Why? I don't know, just know it happened. It was as if he had spoken the 'correct' words at the right time, words I wanted to hear, now, when he was safe he didn't have to 'act' anymore and I was confronted with a different person.

On our wedding day, one of his brothers took me aside and said "If he ever hurts you let me know". I put those words of advice aside and didn't give them a second thought. It was some time later before I realized and remembered those words. They had meaning alright, if only I had read between the lines.

He would get angry with one or the other of the children and go for them continuously, then without warning, change to the other. Fabian copped it more so than his sister. Both would argue back which didn't help the situation in the slightest. If either child voiced their interest in a certain imminent television program, you could place a bet on the fact he would have a car racing video on at that very same moment, deliberately. Time after time this scenario repeated itself. Childish? Yes I believe it was; the reason for which I will never know nor understand.

I tried to keep peace between all three but the tension was mounting by the day.

It was akin to living in a war zone.

I was slow to realize I was pregnant this time around, it sure wasn't planned, I had gone off the pill with the hope of losing some puppy fat prior to the wedding. My new husband was over the moon at the prospect of becoming a father. Maybe this was my wedding present.

I remember thinking it would be unusual for me to become pregnant that easily given my age but reasoned if that is what happens then it was meant to be for a reason.

When friends and work colleagues discovered I was pregnant at - wait for it ....38 years of age - well that attracted more than the odd comment. I would reply "Well no one told me you could get pregnant in a second marriage" if you could have seen the expressions on their faces when I uttered those words. It was priceless. Some obviously thought I was serious. Have to admit the devil in me did enjoy watching their expressions change from ???? is she joking ???? is she serious? Sometimes I kept a straight face and walked off, other times I felt the need to put them out of their misery and explain - hey joke!

Fabian, thought it was wonderful, he used to come and sit with me whilst I had a bath so he could feel the baby moving around. His little face would light up each time he watched and touched the small hand or foot moving.

My daughter I wasn't so sure about; one of her friends from school was also pregnant so I suppose she found it a little strange and embarrassing that her mother could also be pregnant at the same time.

This pregnancy was definitely my worst. I was so sick for most of the time. The doctor started to lose his patience with me, not the same gynaecologist this time as with the other two, mores the pity.

In desperation I made an appointment with the local pharmacist who had been a member of the Allergy Recognition and Management group, he did a small blood test and examined it through a microscope. From this he deduced I had a pH imbalance in my blood. He suggested I eat certain food at certain times of the day. Eureka - it worked, normality returned to my body. Well as much as possible given the circumstances. As long as I ate in accordance with the diet he proposed, I remained healthy and nowhere near as exhausted. Alkaline foods are preferable for the body and this was sure true in my case during the pregnancy. Keeping the body alkaline, rather than acidic allows the body to let go of unnecessary fat cells, allows it to function in balance. From what I have read disease cannot function or flourish in an alkaline body. Food for thought! The Acid-Alkaline Diet for Optimum Health, Restore Your Health by Creating pH Balance in Your Diet by Christopher Vasey, N. D. explains this in some detail, in an easy to read and understand format.

Symptoms I experienced throughout my pregnancy until I visited the pharmacist were very similar to chronic fatigue syndrome, so extremely tired all the time. I was unable to sit for anything except short periods, felt like my skeleton was either unwilling or unable to support my body in position. I would go to work, by the time I walked from the car park to the reception area of our complex I would be totally exhausted and could have sat and cried. I would sit there for a while wondering how on earth I would make it down to my desk, let alone undertake a full day's work. My gynaecologist would not give me a medical certificate - he informed me I was merely pregnant not sick! I wish he could have tried to walk in my shoes even for a day, would have been an eye opener for him!

He just may have had a little more sympathy after that.

Previous pregnancies with hadn't been like this, I was used to being so healthy, fit and active *most* of the time. It was a long nine months.

My husband used to work on leather as a hobby. He made pictures, leather bags, belts. A week or so before Laura was born he had his leather spread across the lounge room floor, I had been so very sick during the pregnancy I had to eat soon after getting out of bed. There was no clear way of making it through to the kitchen without treading on the leather, so off I went and stepped as lightly as I could, given the circumstances.

He picked up the wooden hearth brush and hit my arm really hard, I got such a surprise. I was so fat I could hardly walk let alone get out of his way, I picked up the dust pan (plastic) and hit him - probably not a good move but I didn't even think, just reacted. He pushed me so hard I fell backwards towards my rocking chair. The baby had been stuck sideways for awhile now, the head protruding quite noticeably on one side, I knew if I landed the way I was headed, the head would hit on the wooden arm of the chair.

I managed to change direction a little to protect the unborn baby. To say I was in a state of shock was a mild statement, I felt dazed, confused, add a dash of mild panic and you come close to the emotions I was experiencing. I went over and over the whole scenario in my mind for days, trying to make sense of it. The large dark bruise on my arm a constant reminder that incident had, in fact, been real, it wasn't my imagination.

In retrospect I should have done something about it at the time, whether it was the pregnancy, shock or the fact I was hoping it was a one off, but I let it slide and failed to take assertive action. Mentally and physically it was certainly an inconvenient time for him to decide to start hitting me.

I had to have a caesarean birth this time. Laura was far too big for me to deliver normally. I opted to have an epidural. I wanted to see my husband's face when the baby entered the world. Whether I was too small in size, whether Laura was far too big I don't know but the epidural went horribly wrong. My arms now paralyzed, I was finding it difficult to breathe.

My husband was the only one who finally realized I was in trouble; I couldn't speak, so the only tell tale sign was the tears running down my cheeks. Finally the medical team took notice and on went the oxygen.

Pain now in my shoulder, so bad it was excruciating. No, I'm not normally a wimp but this pain was something else. The anaesthetist noticed I was in pain; he said to the gynaecologist "She has a blood clot go looking for it quick". No reaction, he continued on with his lesson in how to do what he was doing.

Blood clot! His voice was louder and more insistent this time. Blood clot located and on with the procedure. I felt sure the baby was going to be born without a head, he tugged and tugged at her feet with such gusto but she remained firmly stuck. Hush of amazement when Laura Erika finally entered the world and intact.

I heard one of the team say "How big do you think she is?" reply - "Oh about 9lb I would think". Meanwhile I'm thinking they must be talking about someone else. I couldn't possibly have a baby that size. Well I did - 8lb 15oz to be precise.

The staff asked if I would like to hold her - my arms wouldn't move, how on earth was I supposed to hold her. I was wishing they would get a grip and realize I was still having problems, they obviously still didn't get the fact that the epidural had gone up instead of down. She was so heavy I had to ask them to take her off my weary sore body. I looked at the huge baby which had been presented to me and couldn't believe she could be mine.

I learned during the operation they have ten layers to sew separately - hmmm I'm thinking, sewing machine would be a damn sight faster. Two layers to go they informed me ….oh by now pain was coming back into my body along with some feeling - not a good time for the epidural to stop working completely. I could feel my legs getting tingly, don't think that is supposed to happen at this stage. By the time those two layers were neatly stitched together, the pain was unbearable - I really did think I was going to die on that table.

Recovery now and I'm trying to explain that 'No, I cannot shut up and go to sleep' as I had been instructed by the very rude sister on duty, I am in so much pain - pain like you wouldn't believe. This sister obviously wanted a quiet time and I wasn't cooperating in the slightest. The anaesthetist was called; I was given another injection of omnipon or something. This didn't help much either. My body really can turn traitor on me at the most inopportune moments.

No rooms free so had to wait in recovery longer than normal. More calls to the ward, still no room free. That sister really did want me out of her sight. More calls, finally they took me anyway, the sister on duty had probably had enough of me. So I was given time out in another room while they waited for someone to go home from the maternity ward.

I had asked my friend if she would come to the hospital and stay with Fabian. I was worried about the fact he was a severe asthmatic. If he got too worried about the birth he might have an attack, I preferred he be closer to me and know what was happening, that way it might lessen his stress levels. My daughter at the time was visiting my sister in Melbourne, she was on a shopping mission for her Leaver's Dinner dress.

I had best explain; this particular friend and I met at work in 1982 when I had trained her in the use of the switchboard, she is eleven years younger and from that moment on we became firm friends, she was a major part of my life for quite some time and will appear frequently in my story. It was in fact she who used to keep saying to me "Who needs 'Days of our Lives' when I have you".

Laura was taken to the nursery quite soon after the birth as they were unable to keep her body temperature at the required level. Fabian was allowed to go with her to the nursery. I believe he remained with her for quite some time. He explained to the nurse he had in fact wanted a baby brother not a sister. She told me later she had said to him "Well, no one is looking shall I swap her", he said no!

There in that nursery began quite a big brother relationship which lasted for some years until schizophrenia became part of Fabian's life.

My throat was too dry to talk, dry from crying, from the oxygen and whatever the epidural going wrong caused. My friend fed me ice chips – my husband was less than useless. Think he felt his job was done so he was off the break the news of the birth to anyone who would listen. Hell! I could look after myself - well I had the whole damn hospital there didn't I?

So, now the room was ready. Off we went. One, two, three…they swung my body on to the new bed, no, damn they missed, I rammed into the side of the bed. I am willing to bet that whole floor of the hospital heard me scream; I can remember my friend loudly abusing the staff in question.

By now I was out of this world with the pain, yes you guessed it, only one thing for it. The now frustrated anaesthetist was called up to maternity. Another injection of something. It didn't appear to do anything.

It was dinner time, where had the day gone, pain plus all day, I was given sandwiches - for some reason all the injections which did nothing at the time, started to kick in, I went to sleep with a sandwich in my mouth. I remember thinking when I woke, they couldn't kill me on the operating table so now I'm trying to choke me to death instead, the sandwich still in my mouth. My Guardian Angel must have been watching over me at that particular period of time. Goes to show how much attention the nurses were obviously paying, what is the word - observation? Observation must have been missing that day - trust me to go to surgery on a day when compassion and observation were on flex leave.

I Make Mark

Three excruciating days later the nurse assigned to me informed me they thought I was a drug addict. When the injections didn't work for whatever reason, they deduced I was a drug addict and that is why I didn't get much in the way of help or sympathy. How dare they! What gave them the right to jump to that conclusion? Based on what evidence? Didn't they consider it may have been prudent to at least ask me? Years later I read that omnipon or whatever it was needed to be given in conjunction with another drug in order for it to have the desired effect; well at least I had a theory as to why it hadn't worked.

I had marks on my arm where I donated blood in the past, but what on earth possessed them to think I was on drugs. Even if I was, who were they to judge? My baby was 8lb 15oz, healthy and happy to sleep when not eating. I was obviously healthy. Her statement defied gravity and left me outraged and speechless trying to fathom the unfathomable. I was in a Catholic hospital for goodness sake - they obviously stored their Christian beliefs in the basement because they sure were not visible or apparent on the ward. I was totally disgusted with the attitude of staff within this hospital. I shall explain the repercussions of this in my next book.

My stay in this hospital did have its funny moments. Laura was far too big for the hospital baby suits. I soon learned which day and what time the fresh laundry arrived in the nursery. You guessed it; I would be standing in wait. One day I put a grow suit on her, as bad as I felt I had to laugh, she was so scrunched up, she looked so funny, it was the largest they had at the time - I couldn't do that to her. If I waited for the fresh laundry, I got to choose the largest night gowns - this meant she wasn't scrunched for at least a few days.

I was lying in bed one afternoon, one of the cleaners came in (*off duty I might add*) said do you mind if I show your baby to my friend. Thinking this was quite a strange request but I didn't mind, regardless of her motive. Next thing "See this is the baby and this is the mother - see I told you didn't I!?" Yes, another person who couldn't believe this tiny mother could have this huge baby. I was obviously a talking point for the staff and their friends. No I didn't take it personally I was still having trouble believing it myself. Plus the action of the cleaner had managed to bring a smile to my face; it was hard to believe someone would actually do what she had just done. Just as well I have a sense of humour; her actions may not have been appreciated by another patient.

Thanks to the caesarean and Laura's size I couldn't hold her to bathe her, she was far too heavy. I know that probably sounds ridiculous but my body wasn't capable of holding the weight given the circumstances. If I have a 'next' life I am going to request a larger body or at least a larger frame, trying to get though life with a body my size is hard work.

No one thought to warn me that when the nerve endings have been tampered with in a big way the body cannot necessarily tell when it needs to go to the toilet. This particular morning I had pains in my stomach, which wasn't unusual. I shuffled into the toilet and it was like one major bladder explosion, I really didn't think I was going to make it out of this hospital and live to tell the story. When I repeated this episode to the doctor he made it sound so matter of fact - well thanks for the warning ….after the event. So yes, seems this is usual and you need to go to the toilet and do the brain work for your body until it is capable of registering this minor detail for itself.

Left me wondering what other minor technicalities they may also have omitted. Where is the check list of 'can go wrongs' when you most need it?

One morning the doctor came and checked on me, all seemed sort of ok. Two hours later the nurse happened by to do her checks, she lifted my still swollen fat stomach to view the stitches; my scream could be heard all around the ward. I sure had one severe hot spot embedded somewhere below the surface. The nurse phoned my so considerate gynaecologist - his reply - "She was alright this morning so what is the problem?" end of story. He didn't bother to undertake any checks to ensure I didn't have a problem he may have overlooked.

Some people have so much charm you wonder how they cope!

The day finally came when I was supposed to leave. So here I was all set up ready to go. Doctor no show. Hours later and he was still awol. He was called in for another birth; yes! I thought I might now get action. Still nothing! Somehow, someone finally persuaded him to visit me so I could escape, ignorant prat - a little bedside manner wouldn't have gone astray. Get the feeling I really wasn't his favourite patient; I really hope and pray he didn't treat all his patients with the same degree of contempt and indifference. Days like that one I truly hoped karma is a reality and not merely a word!

When we finally got home I had to go lie down, I was totally exhausted from lack of rest during the day, sitting on my bed all day thinking I would go home any minute had taken its toll. When I woke and it was time to get off the bed, I couldn't. My stomach was far too sore, I couldn't turn over and get up that way, I was stuck folks, until help arrived. Help finally secured; my husband then went off somewhere, this was usual for him. I was left to cook the evening meal. This I did crying in pain as I went, how could he be so inconsiderate? Where in the world could I get justice, ten horrific, pain filled days and now this, I wanted to just give up and go die somewhere peacefully. Honestly, I felt that dejected.

I stated previously I research any challenges I am given, facing a caesarean I did just that, I read what I could re caesareans but nothing but nothing prepared me for what I experienced. None of the articles I read had any adverse comments re associated problems or likely problems. This truth thing still keeps raising its little head.

I can't have been the only person to experience adverse reactions, why these issues are not raised so someone having to make a decision re which method to choose can gauge the full implications of their decision? I would have liked to at least been partially prepared for what could go wrong. I wish I had been stronger at the time, or had more help on the home front. I would have put my discontent to print and outlined the different stages I went through. I realize that probably 99% of women are lucky enough not to experience what I did, but I am also sure that 1% need some form of literature which helps them feel not so alone during these 'oh geez' moments. I didn't have a choice about whether or not I chose natural childbirth or caesarean, Laura had been stuck solid for weeks pre her birth, hence my hot spot when the nurse examined me. Her feet would kick off from the same spot day after day until I was so sore I screamed each and every time she landed another goal. I was convinced she was a boy, I was so surprised when they told me it was a girl, I felt for sure those kicks came from a promising AFL player.

Fabian used to tuck Laura inside his jumper and let her go to sleep, then nurse her for hours in that position. She was a child who didn't know what it was like to sleep in a proper bed; it appeared there was always someone on hand for her to sleep on. She wasn't so much as spoiled as smothered with love on every level possible.

Her dad used to go into the bedroom and just sit and watch her. Then of course, pick her up. After he had been successful in waking her he would bring her out for me to take over. Thanks for nothing! She didn't have a sleeping pattern to speak of; no one gave her a chance to sleep.

I ended up buying a queen size bed just so I had some bed left for myself. I went back to work when Laura was about eleven months old, I needed my sleep.

Life didn't improve the way I had hoped it might. We got by is all I can say - with a lot of arguments.

CHAPTER TWELVE

My beautiful small house in Willow Avenue, was just that. Small! We started to look for a larger house, my eldest daughter was in high school, Fabian needed to have room to himself; they too needed sleep. Maybe things would improve in another house. Yes, I actually believed it might make a difference. I like to live in hope is all I can say in my own defence. I thought a house we had bought together might make a difference.

For anyone thinking a move, a marriage, another baby is the answer to your problems, stop right there and consider your options because any of the above only add more complications. Complications which you do not need to add to what may already be a complex situation.

The only house my husband would agree too was a rundown weather board house almost sitting on the main road at Blackmans Bay. The only up side was, it had four bedrooms plus another small store room. I figured it couldn't be all bad, well other people lived there after all.

> *... As I sit here writing, it is 11:45pm, unable to sleep, partly due to my medication which has been changed only recently, probably also due to the fact that work is so very busy at the moment and my brain is in full gear all day, yesterday I was at work for eleven hours. My body is physically tired yet my mind showing no signs of sleep.*
>
> *A girlfriend reminded me only this week. I was explaining how Sunday night I couldn't sleep so I got up to work on my book. She said remember you have to go to bed when the wave hits – like her*

I remember reading ... Sleep is like surfing you have to catch it on the wave, if you miss the wave it doesn't happen and you have to wait for the next one. Oh how true, how very true. In this case I think I missed the whole damn ocean, not just the wave!

I have to wonder if other people have this much in their lives to write about. It couldn't be only me who has action packed life stories to show and tell. Sometimes I wonder too, how one person can fit so much into one life time - I feel as though I must be making up for lost time. Maybe I slacked off in my last life and have to work doubly hard this time.

Why did I give myself so many challenges in this life?

I look back; sometimes it seems like yesterday, sometimes like light years away. I know I feel happier within myself these days, I have learned a great deal and am totally at home in my own space with my own thoughts. I was perfectly comfortable and happy turning 52 a few weeks ago, even proud of it. It was the happiest birthday I can remember having, ever. How many people can say that? I felt happy and free.

I have different friends, I take people as I find them, I accept we all have faults and we accept our friends, faults and all. Most of all I want peace, peace to sit and write; peace of mind. I believe I am so very fortunate and I am thankful for my little life and all that it holds.

I went back to work from maternity leave. My first day back - I was met with congratulations; you now have responsibility for security keys, telephones and furniture as well. So yes, things had obviously changed in my absence. It was good to be back.

My working life was my sanctuary of sorts.

One of our neighbours kindly took on Laura's day time care, this was a relief and the arrangement worked quite well for some time. Fabian went to her after school knowing his sister would be home if he needed to get into the house for food or anything else. Fabian loved his carer, he used to say "I love cuddling her; she is so soft and cuddly". Life was bearable once again.

One night my husband came home ropable - Laura's carer had told him Fabian had said something which I can no longer recall, anyway he couldn't wait to get to him. He found Fabian in his bedroom, he made him pull his pants down and he hit him hard. Later I asked Fabian what he had said, something he hadn't bothered to do. Fabian had said something quite different but it had been misheard - he had been innocent but found guilty and punished. When I listened to his explanation it was easy to see why the words had been misconstrued - his allergies had left him with many holes in his vocabulary.

He was at a loss to understand why he had been in trouble.

At night when I would get up to see to Laura I would sometimes see a shadow cross Fabian's room. At first I thought it was him, but after checking and finding him sound asleep knew that wasn't the case at all. I saw this 'shadow' quite a few times. One night after getting back in bed the same shadow appeared in my bedroom door way - I thought to myself 'yes I am alright thank you' the shadow departed. I knew it had come to check on me, I wasn't afraid; it wasn't there to hurt any of us, merely ensuring I was alright. How did I know this? I don't have an answer for you, I just knew.

The shadow wasn't like a real shadow but had shadow like qualities, the main exception -it would be where a 'person' would stand and how a person would stand, whereas a normal shadow would fall on the wall or floor. The best way for me to explain it to you is to call it a shadow so you have a vague idea of what I was seeing.

The shadow didn't belong to a tall person, I thought it was my father but I may never know if my assumption was correct. Well hopefully, not for a while anyway. I'll check when I get back Upstairs; either way I suspect it was my Guardian Angel. Once I had given my assurance I was ok, it never returned.

How did I know it was a soul from the spirit world? Why wasn't I afraid? How did I know what it was thinking and why it was with me? I was obviously correct as it left following my reassurance. Another of those life experiences filed for future reference.

The move to a different house didn't change a thing. Night times were full of arguments.

This house made me feel quite depressed; some rooms smelled of damp, furniture took on new angles where the floor had sunk slightly in patches, the house needed a major make over. I kept trying to tell myself we were better off; we had heaps more room to spread out. It didn't help! I planted new garden beds in the hope of improving the atmosphere. I wanted it to be friendly and inviting, the garden helped but only slightly. At night time the television had to be a few notches louder until the peak traffic time passed. It really wasn't a 'me' house at all.

One really good period during this time was a trip to Queensland. My girlfriend had managed to secure cheap flights so she, Laura and I set off for sun, surf and shopping.

First day in Queensland and we were waiting for the lift to go down from our hotel room, Laura had been leaning up against the wall, her feet slipped from under her, she hit the floor and looked up most indignant. Queensland dropped me she exclaimed, her little face was priceless. According to Laura she didn't have fish on her bathers, she had *shish* on them, she was happiest when she was walking around exploring, not being pushed in the pram. It was a most memorable break from the real world for all of us.

Whilst in Queensland we visited Movie World, Laura in her pusher, we encountered Bugs Bunny - he came up to talk to her. She put her tiny hand in the air and said "Gives me sive" Bugs Bunny kindly obliged and gave her a high five. She was absolutely delighted.

Queensland was a blessing, it was peaceful and fun, if only life could remain like that I would have been happy.

Christmas that year turned out to be not so Christmassy – my husband was yelling at Fabian this night, I walked into the kitchen with Laura on my hip, he was washing up. I said to him "Wouldn't it have been better if you had explained why, not just said no?" I didn't raise my voice, I was calm.

My husband had metal serving tongs in his hand. The look on his face was frightening. He lunged forward as if fencing and as the tongs hit my cheek he closed them, my face stung from the encounter, blood appeared where the tongs cut into my cheek. Later that night I asked Fabian to photograph my face, I thought I might need evidence. I had been carrying Laura; once again he didn't think about her safety, I might have dropped her when he made contact with my face - did that thought enter his mind do you suppose? I guess not!

Next day at work people asked me what happened to my face. I explained my husband had hit me. The reply was always the same as each person asked - "No, don't you mean you ran into a door". I would then repeat - "No, he pinched my face with metal serving tongs". Again … "Nah you ran into a door right"?

What is wrong with some humans, why can't people accept the truth? Experience has taught me that the majority of people would prefer a lie than deal with the truth. I was confused, I hadn't experienced anything even close to this type of reaction before and it was difficult to handle. I was telling the truth yet people kept insisting on putting other words in my mouth. Didn't they want their perfect little worlds soiled by even the thought of domestic violence?

So another learning experience ensued, filed away for future reference.

One male contractor with whom I was dealing through work, found it extremely difficult to believe that a husband could do that to his wife. He later said "You know, when I see a woman with bruises, I now wonder if she really got the bruises like she says or if her husband hit her. I look at it differently now". I was so pleased to hear his words; at least he was prepared to look deeper than the surface. Pity the world didn't have more people like him; at least he wasn't hiding from the truth.

I phoned one of my sister-in-laws, explaining what was happening and that I didn't know what to do anymore. She wasn't sympathetic toward him at all. I learned he had also hit his last wife and her children and that was why he had left Queensland. Nice if someone had thought to share that with me *prior* to the marriage.

At that time I was still so stressed that I forgot those very words I had been told on my wedding day....if he ever hurts you let me know....he tried to warn me but I didn't listen.

So now what?

I went to the police which was quite difficult in itself. Yes I did want to get out of this situation, no I didn't really want to press charges just have peace finally. That night I packed mine and the children's clothes and hid them in the wardrobes and drawers ready for a quick departure in the morning when he left for work.

A policeman took me to the Women's shelter. A counsellor met me and ushered me into an interview room. As she sat explaining the characteristics of a domestic violence perpetrator I couldn't believe my ears. It was as if she knew my husband more than he knew himself, she described his traits perfectly. I was amazed to put it mildly. So now I knew the reason behind his actions. That made it easier to comprehend. Some consolation!

Sometimes I think having to know the big picture is a curse. I am more at ease with the world when I can understand at least part of it. Far worse is not knowing, not knowing can cause untold damage. Face the truth head on, deal with it, understand the associated emotions, then move on, this is yet another of my survival tactics. Burying events or emotions can cause far too much damage in the longer term, always try to find the strength to face the problem, no matter how difficult it is, ask for help, the Man Upstairs is available 24/7. He is there for you. Have you heard of 'Footprints in the Sand"? It is most appropriate and so very true. Counsellors are available from various, specialized fields, available to you when required. Avail yourself of their services; they will respect you for your courage.

> *'LET GO AND LET GOD'* – *please take the time to locate and read this very meaningful verse, it will help you understand how*

we ask for help but often fail to let go and allow the Universe to carry out our wishes.

I was shown to a bedroom which would hold all four of us and the rules explained briefly. Stress levels were at a premium I am here to testify!

The current baby sitter (by this time another person was Laura's carer) didn't want to know when the proverbial … hit the proverbial fan so I frantically went in search of an alternative. I had to keep working, I didn't have a choice.

What did I say about what doesn't kill us makes us stronger? by now I must have the strength of the proverbial ox and the whole entire extended family!

We were housed in the shelter for a few days, Christmas was fast approaching.

The staff at the Women's Shelter had just purchased another house to use as a half way house. By now it was Christmas Eve; the staff went into overdrive to make the required purchases in order for me to move into it and not have to spend Christmas Eve and Day in the shelter itself.

The shelter was clean, efficiently run, counselling on tap, with one counsellor sleeping over one night each week to talk to us around the table at night after the children had been settled. It was nothing like I would have imagined a shelter to be. It was like a normal home only on a much larger scale and with more rules. The residents had a roster to cook and clean the communal areas, laundry provided onsite for all to use. Supplies of spare clothing for emergency purposes, plus a play room for the children.

The staff in question, have my undying respect and love, I cannot speak highly enough of them. The time and effort and speed with which they undertook this mission was extraordinary. They were truly amazing and dedicated.

I moved into the house late in the day on Christmas Eve, my girlfriend stayed the night to keep us company and give the three children some semblance of normality. Think we broke every rule in the book, in my own defence I didn't know they had these rules.

Rule 1 - no guests unless the shelter knew about it - well that is obvious to one who has all their brain cells operational ….me, well it didn't even occur to me at that moment in time.

Rule 2 - no alcohol - we usually share a glass of wine Christmas Eve - one of the few days a year I would have any form of alcohol.

Rule 3 - no men - well man, hmmm debatable – my ex-husband called to collect Fabian and his sister on Christmas Day.

Not bad, been there for less than twenty four hours and three rules go out the window. I am not usually this disrespectful where rules are concerned.

I got to share the house with another lady and her three children, she was from the country. I occasionally run into her at a shopping centre, it is good to meet up with her from time to time. Funny I can't even remember her name now, think a lot of my memory is still in storage - sometimes little bits come back but only with prompting.

I looked at this experience as a weight loss initiative; my puppy fat fell off me readily during this time. It is amazing how one learns to blend into a wall when one spots the husband in the local shopping centre during these times. I'm sure I turned into a chameleon at those moments. The bank wall and I became one on more than one occasion as I was hurriedly trying to extract funds without him seeing me. I am most grateful for my warped sense of humour; as usual it got me through once again.

My eldest daughter wasn't impressed with the whole exercise; guess it was an age thing. The house was a whole lot better than the one we owned at Blackmans Bay, two levels, really modern, like I said; I think it was an age thing. I had so much on my mind at that time my children were the one area which fell through the cracks. I tried to make things as normal as possible given the circumstances, I did the best I could, was it good enough? Possibly not, but I definitely gave it my best shot, of that I have no doubt. I did the best I could given the circumstances and I can't ask anymore of myself than that.

Fabian was fine with it most of the time, he made friends with some children in the street and so his life continued - cricket on the street after school, food on the table and he was mostly happy.

Laura was too young to know the difference, she was only two. My eldest daughter slept in the downstairs flat, but we all wanted to get back to the house we called home. It wasn't much, but it was our home.

The Women's Shelter had explained my social bracket was the hardest to get the message to. Some women would willingly go to the shelter when the need arose but the middle class were most likely to suffer alone. Shame, ignorance, guilt, pride all took their toll, they suffered in silence behind closed doors.

They tell me I was a wonderful ambassador for their cause. It allowed other residents in the street to see that domestic violence can happen to ordinary people as well. Their reasons for resistance were less founded, no husbands ranting and raving, no screaming coming from the house, just a normal person trying to live in peace.

Women now go to the shelter due to my promotion, if I recognize a female I think maybe a victim of domestic violence, I manage to bring into the conversation my positive experience in the shelter. Friendliness, hospitality and above all - safety. I don't ask them any questions merely explain my circumstances. If I only manage to help a few without them even knowing I suspect, then my experience was worth it.

The respect was twofold. If ever I had the chance to give something back to the Women's Shelter staff I would do so in a heartbeat.

The experience of living in this kind of situation made my life seem so less intimidating, I was the only resident who had a job and the means by which to support myself should the marriage fail completely.

Some women didn't even know how to shop; they had not been permitted to go out of the house. One old lady asked me if I had children, when I finished explaining, I asked her if she had any, her reply "No dear, I used to have, but children wouldn't do to their mother what mine did, so no, I don't have any". She had disclaimed her children, as I said it was Christmas, her children had taken all her pension money and left her with absolutely no money whatsoever at Christmas. The police had brought her into the shelter. She was dealt a devastating blow by her own family whom she trusted. She was definitely at a low ebb in her very long life. Other women would leave the shelter only to go home to yet another beating, to return days, weeks or months later … and so the cycle continued.

There is another world out there behind those dreaded closed doors of so called "happy families". A world full of pain, suffering, violence and horrific stories.

My husband promised to go to counselling if I came home. He had grown up with domestic violence, for him it was a part of life. A beating after church was a common occurrence, one family member or another would be the target. Life wasn't always a happy family affair whilst he was growing up. He did not appreciate it happening when he was a child yet he chose to follow the same path and refused to admit or acknowledge there was a problem. Or more importantly, that he was the problem.

It is impossible for a person to grow up in that type of environment and come out unscathed, it isn't something which should be buried and not talked about. It is this type of non-action which causes damage. He refused to speak to or about his father except to outline some of the abusive actions which occurred. He would not seek counseling or assistance with the level of hatred he kept bottled up. It was a recipe for disaster.

I believed I owed it to him to at least let him try to come to terms with his past and accept counselling as a lifeline for our marriage. I hadn't fallen out of love with him, I wanted this to work.

So he attended maybe two counselling sessions. The first time I walked in the door the counsellor said "… But you are so small" - not very polite I'm thinking to myself as I searched for a seat. "And he is so tall, you must have felt quite scared" - pleased he thought to qualify his initial statement.

I agreed that yes, this was the case. Not a pleasant experience one hopes to emulate.

End of counselling sessions for my husband - my fault it seems, but then isn't it always. I was so used to being the scapegoat; everything with husbands and children is always someone else's fault, never theirs, so suppose it comes with the territory.

Lesson for all parents: allow your children to take responsibility for their own actions. They too are here to learn particular lessons for their soul development, it you take away that responsibility the next lesson will be more difficult for them. You are doing them or anyone a disservice if you take responsibility for their actions. Help them by all means, with guidance, listening and understanding. Taking responsibility for them is *not* helping.

We moved back home, the kids were home but not happy, my husband was still there. Life improved slightly for a short period … but not for long.

I didn't get hit again just verbal abuse now - guess that was better at least. I didn't say acceptable …just better than physical abuse.

You see the thing about physical abuse - where he was concerned, there was never a warning first, the times he hit me came out of the blue, calm prevailed first, so I never knew when he would strike. Life was one of constantly walking on egg shells. He thrived on arguments. (I guess that bottled up anger sought any excuse as an outlet).

One particular evening I refused to argue any more, I must have been unpacking in the storage room, I was trapped, can't even remember what had started this debacle. Next thing I knew my head hit the wall as I was thrown against it, this happened at least twice before I realized I had to get out or possibly die, didn't think my head would take 'take three against the wall". He then held me fast against the wall, his arm under my neck. Somehow I managed to bite and draw blood; it was a risk, but a risk I had to take. He released his grip enough for me to break free, I made it out of that room at break neck speed (pardon the pun); don't ever want to be in that situation ever again, once is enough. Stress levels once more at an all time premium. Would the teeth marks instigate another blow? Would I live to see tomorrow? I honestly didn't know at that point.

I can no longer remember what happened for the remainder of that evening, don't imagine I went to sleep too easily, would have been praying for the next day to come quickly so I could escape for work and at least be safe for the next eight hours.

Fabian and his sister both had to have their dental check up, both required braces and dental work. My daughter burst into tears during the examination by the orthodontist, no way was she going to have braces. I didn't push the issue; it had to be her decision also.

Fabian was a different kettle of fish, he had too many teeth for his mouth, some of his front baby teeth were not coming out of their own volition and his two front second teeth were far to big and had to be filed down. Four of his baby teeth had to be extracted, the roots hadn't dissolved; I got such a shock when I saw the size of them. Poor kid no wonder they weren't falling out of their own accord they were stuck solid, it was like comparing it to an iceberg, two thirds below the surface. Those teeth are still with me in a small specimen bottle. Some things I just can't bring myself to part with. He had ulcers in his mouth for weeks after the braces were fitted. Eighteen months on, he had the most beautiful teeth but no way was he going back for further ongoing treatment; once the braces came off he had had enough. He endured a lot of pain to have his teeth corrected.

I hoped that somewhere in the future, life for Fabian would be less painful and less problematic.

Neighbours from our previous address used to visit every so often. One night we were all walking down from the back yard, my husband and I had been having an argument prior to their arrival. Without anyone even realizing, he kicked me quite hard on the back of my leg. Later on when our guests had departed I broached the subject. No he didn't do it and if he did it must have been an accident. Yeah right - like I believed that, the bruise was really deep and obvious. Accident huh?

As you can deduce life certainly didn't improve any. Somewhere, somehow it had to get better, at that stage I certainly didn't think it could get any worse!

CHAPTER THIRTEEN

One night Fabian and his sister were arguing about loud music, my daughter was holding Laura, my husband intervened and slapped her - I didn't see her again for maybe two years, she left the house that night, unsure if she exited through the window or the back door. At midnight I was driving around our suburb in my dressing gown and slippers trying in vain to find her. My world was unravelling once again. My beautiful, precious daughter, the one who walked everywhere with me when she was so young. I had let her down badly. I couldn't find her anywhere.

I didn't know it at the time but that night I lost the daughter I thought would always be my best friend. It is the biggest regret of my life.

College wouldn't help us, privacy issue! As a parent, you get to hate that seven letter word. My daughter, my child was assisted in remaining separated from either of her parents. She refused to go to counselling on the grounds she was too angry with us. When I say parents - she had two sets of parents – her dad had remarried as well, so even if the College and the associated counsellors wouldn't speak to me they could at least have spoken to her father.

We drew a blank at every turn, so had to face the inevitable - she was taking care of herself and putting herself through College at the same time. Brave move for a child of her age.

Fabian remained relatively happy (at least openly) he was always smiling, he had a beautiful smile. Laura was growing up from a baby to a toddler. Still, my eldest daughter left a big hole in our lives from the moment she went out the door. Life was never to be the same for me.

Part of my family was missing; it is something I never came to terms with. I can honestly say my life changed forever the evening she left.

My husband couldn't wait to take over her bedroom for a sitting/reading room for himself. That really upset me; he didn't seem to notice in the slightest.

The contractor (whom I mentioned previously as the one willing to see the bigger picture) and I had formed a close bond through all this; he was one beautiful piece of my disintegrating life. The few stolen moments we managed to secure was the only thing which kept me going at times. At night I would curl up in bed pretending to be asleep, hoping my husband would just let me be. I would be thinking of how my friend had kissed me that morning, with a kiss that was ever so gentle yet passionate.

Pretending to be asleep didn't work all the time, having my legs forced apart by a demanding husband brought with it all kinds of feelings. Pain, physical and mental. Hate, contempt. I would get out of bed and walk away for a while hoping he would fall asleep before I came back. Wishing he would die before I came back, it was that bad at times.

Rape within marriage is largely unreported but it is still rape and should not be tolerated. As with domestic violence, there is a way out, no one but no one should be anything less than safe, particularly in their own home. So should you find yourself in this situation take steps to move past it in the safest possible manner. Talk it over with a professional and work out the best course of action for you.

I promise you there is a way out of any situation, you just have to find it and have the courage to follow that route to safety.

I only have one word of caution - if you discuss with a religious professional be very wary as they may say "Keep it in the family" and this is not to be condoned, domestic violence should not be 'kept in the family', it should be handled with care.

Discuss with someone you know you can trust both for confidentially and practical purposes. How do I know this: because I knew a person in that very position, her parish priest told her to keep it in the family. She did this until one of the children sported a bruise and this was one bruise too many, she then took steps to remove herself and the children from the situation. She should be commended; it takes a strong person to be able to make that decision, particularly when they have strong religious faith.

Maybe for some people this may work (religious counselling for both parties) but as is the case with everything ….do what is best for you….only you can make that decision.

I am not saying that all religious advice should be disregarded, this is not the case. I am merely trying to alert you to the possibility that their counselling may not always be in your best interest. I do not believe in stay *in the marriage at all costs*, sometimes the cost is just too high a price to pay.

I would sit and think of my precious stolen moments and take myself into another happy world for awhile. Get back into bed, think gentle kisses, imagine his kind, loving eyes filled with pain and love, then drift off to sleep with those beautiful thoughts in mind. Those thoughts undoubtedly saved my sanity at that moment in time.

I remember one morning he said "You taste so good after having your coffee" I hadn't had coffee at that time - so that was a really nice compliment.

I would be able to smell his after shave on my clothing for hours, those moments were so precious. One day one of our staff was explaining to him what she needed, he was looking into my eyes at the time - next thing I hear is "Run that by me again", his concentration had been lost momentarily.

I was under a desk on another occasion passing him a piece of equipment - the occupant in the room with us, he had found my hand and he was holding it - my face becoming a dark shade of red, all the time wondering if the occupant realized what was going on.

I was devastated when the affair ended, how could this beautiful person leave my world? The one person I was able to say to "When you said that it hurt my feelings" I had never been so open with anyone before.

I Make Mark

Never been able to say what I really felt or thought without being afraid of the consequences.

I cried for days.

I now realize that some people come into our lives when we most need them and help us through difficult times. We had helped each other; he was going through a marriage break up at the time. I don't regret what transpired; I am truly grateful to him and always will be, he undoubtedly saved my sanity when I most needed it.

One other major lesson I learned through this relationship was one of psychic connection to someone. I would know when he was driving onto the complex, I would look up and sure enough he would be driving down the laneway toward the building where I worked. The phone would ring and I would know beforehand it was him. I had not had this type of connection with anyone before. Can't say I understood it fully but it was a learning experience. Soul mate probably best describes what this relationship felt like; I had never had that connection, I could only surmise that this is what people mean when they refer to that terminology for a relationship.

> *27 years on and we are still friends, we phone each other on occasions. Who knows what may have happened if things had turned out differently. I still wonder …*

My husband asked if I was having an affair - I replied yes! - he looked at me, started laughing and strode off down the hallway - that truth thing again, why ask the question if you don't want the answer. Would have been an interesting exercise to see what he would have said (or screamed) had I replied in the negative.

My philosophy has always been "If you don't want the answer, don't ask the question", I don't like to lie so the truth comes out - hopefully with love and grace on most occasions.

Humans really are an interesting species. I would dearly love to study psychology. Maybe one day I may get the chance, as I stated previously, I live in hope.

One morning just before I was ready to get out of bed I heard a loud knock on the front door. My husband hadn't left for work; I assumed it was one of his friends. Like most wives who have been through a bad time you lie in bed until the husband leaves for work - pretend like you are asleep and it saves an early morning debacle, one argument less for the day. Husband leaves, then you go at break neck speed to catch up with what you need to do before leaving for work yourself ... I often wondered what 'boring' would be like.

I could hear voices outside the bedroom, they were in the garage. I got out of bed, looked out the curtains, could hear one voice calling out an item (sleeping bag) and another repeating the same words, he had a clip board in his hand and was taking notes and making a list. (*No, unfortunately for me it wasn't near Christmas so I knew it wasn't Santa - making a list and checking it twice*) though that is exactly what came to mind when I heard the voices. Like I said, I have a warped sense of humour - I thank God for that quality.

I started to shake so hard I swear I almost jack hammered myself right through the floor boards. We were being raided, there was no other explanation.

My brain (bless its white and grey cells) was arguing with my eyes. My eyes seeing what was going on, my brain all the time saying "Nah we are not being raided, this doesn't happen to people like me, these things happen to other people, my eyes saying nah it's happening alright I can see it" I swear I am not lying I had an argument going on between my bodily parts. I was caught up somewhere in the middle it was as if I was merely the host in which the argument occurred. Talk about out of body experiences; that's what it felt like, it was as if it was all happening and I was looking down on it all without any form of participation.

When the debate finally subsided, I thought, "Gosh if they are searching the garage, the house is probably next, so I had better get the two kids up, bathed and dressed just in case".

Fabian, was so scared, he said "Mum will they search my room, and if they find anything will I get into trouble?" poor kid, he didn't deserve this, no one did. I explained as briefly as I could that no, he wasn't the one in trouble here, it would be ok.

As expected the four men in suits entered through the back door soon after I finished showering and dressing all three of us. I took one aside and explained that I wasn't naïve enough to ask what was happening I could see that, but why? That I did want to know! Remember I said I am a big picture person - well if that makes me inquisitive then so be it - but I wanted answers, I felt they owed me that much.

The gentleman in question took me outside, explained that they were from the Hobart Police and Defence Special Investigation Unit from Sydney, they had been watching the house for the last week or so, knew I wasn't involved. They believed my husband had a 'pack rat' mentality; he had squirrelled away so much gear, gear he could never hope to use in those quantities. Defence for some reason wanted their property back. Funny that! He also explained they had discovered two car loads of Defence property and he would most likely lose his job and be charged by the police as well.

I asked if I was allowed to go to work. He stated they would be completed soon and be out of my way, after that I was free to leave. They had absolutely no interest in me whatsoever - thank God for small mercies.

While I was trying not to go through the floor boards but still trying to peek out the window I thought I had best phone my girlfriend and explain what was going on. I told her I thought we were being raided, that I would probably be late for work and I would explain as soon as humanly possible. It was one of those 'don't worry - but' moments.

The police had come to a screaming halt in front of our house it seems, you know, like you see in the movies, I kid you not. The cars parked dangerously on the main road partially blocking traffic. At the time, practical me, thought, ok I can't control what is going on in here but I sure as hell am not prepared to see some poor innocent motorist come to grief on this corner by smashing into a police car.

I asked if they would relocate their precariously placed cars out of harms way. It amused me when I thought of it later, how can one manage to be so practical when their world is collapsing? Maybe my brain was still arguing with my eyes about whether it was or was not happening. Who knows, the body and brain do funny things when stressed.

When I got to work and explained to one of my close working colleagues he said "Oh it must have been so embarrassing, wondering what the neighbours must be thinking". You have to be joking; the thought hadn't even crossed my mind. Didn't really care what they thought to be honest, I was too busy wondering what I thought. Aren't some people strange? If the situation had been reversed I would have been worried about his mental and physical state not what the neighbours may or may not have been thinking. Sometimes I am grateful I am me.

Yes, definitely another learning experience in human emotions and reactions, filed away for future use and contemplation.

My main worry for that day was the state my husband would be in when he returned home at night after being bundled up and taken away by the police for the day. Would he be in a foul mood? Would I get hurt that night when he came home? If I could have stayed at work all night I would have done, I was a mini nervous wreck. Sure delayed going home that evening, any excuse to remain at work a little longer was taken willingly.

My girlfriend took the next day off work to make sure I was ok. I bought some green paint, and between us we painted everything in the backyard that didn't move. Sections of the garden had been contained with brown bricks - they in turn became green bricks. Quite a transformation did wonders for my stress levels. Other normal people might have had a nervous breakdown; I painted brick work. Well you have to admit, sure saves on medical bills.

Brave move on her behalf when I think about it, she too may have been in danger; there was no way of predicting what my husband's mood would be like. That's dedication on her part with a capital D.

It was squash night, I was still playing pennant squash, I had to go, we didn't have sufficient people for replacements, I didn't have a choice. I remember we played the team who were on top of the ladder; I hadn't beaten my opponent previously. This night I focused on that little black ball like never before. I didn't see the ball, I saw my husband's face, so each time it came my way I hit and hit hard. In the end my opponent (who for the life of me I am unable to recall,) don't even remember seeing her face that night, said "If you want the game that bad it's yours". I hadn't realized I was playing so hard, winning not even on my mind at that point. Only knew I had a lot of anger, frustration and disappointment to work out of my system.

I felt much better after playing that game, mind you I am willing to bet that ball needed retiring afterwards, I doubt it was in any condition to make it to another game. Exercise is a good way to help with stress levels, beats sitting at home worrying I suppose.

Being raided was the proverbial straw that broke the camel's back. My husband went home to Launceston one weekend soon after we were raided; my girlfriend and I got to work and relocated all his clothes from the main bedroom to one of the smaller bedrooms. Not a word was said in front of Laura. It was 1993; Laura was only two and a half.

He came home late on the Sunday evening; I was beside myself, stress levels over the proverbial moon, wondering what was going to happen the minute he noticed all his clothes relocated. He came into the room, I held my breath but felt for sure my pounding heart could be heard in the next street, I thought if he hits me this time, its going to be big.

Laura and I were in the lounge room next morning when she heard him entering the kitchen, she spun in mid air, went racing into the kitchen shouting as she went "It's alright daddy, it's alright, even your own pillow is in that room for you", I couldn't believe it, she was only a baby but she was trying desperately to pacify him so I wouldn't get hurt.

How did she know? She pre-empted violence and was trying to calm the situation, she obviously thought the pillow was the clincher. I thought I had seen a lot of things to date but this one took the cake. I was mesmerized. Totally blown away! Adults who believe children don't understand what is going on are fooling themselves; children obviously take in and process far more than we give them credit for. Laura was living proof.

At some stage following those stressful days, I asked him what he wanted out of the relationship because I had had enough. That was the final straw. I went as close to a break down on that one as I wanted to get, I wasn't prepared to hang around for more, I wanted out of the relationship. Funny, sure I remember those words from some other time in the past. Hmmmmmm.

I always said I didn't fall out of love I was kicked out and that can make a huge difference. We were married in December 1989 and it was now only 1993, what is it with me? I had had seventeen years with my first husband only four years with this one, I felt like a total failure.

My husband finally moved out into a flat in another part of Kingston, for that I was most thankful and grateful; he left willingly and without another major argument.

Some of my experiences instilled the following: each and every person I trusted to take care of me let me down to the point where I decided me and only me would have the responsibility for my well being from here on in.

Maybe one day I will learn to trust again and allow someone special to share my life, but for now I think this is one learned experience that will stay with me for some time.

It will take time for me to put the past totally behind me and move forward with love and grace.

CHAPTER FOURTEEN

I was talking on the telephone one evening after work, I turned around and there was my husband standing right behind me, he had let himself in and was standing there listening to my conversation. Another 'oh geez moment', I was getting too jumpy to let this keep happening, something had to be done.

I knew I would have to take assertive action to show him this was no longer his home, he wasn't welcome. Whilst I remained in that house he would always think he had a right to be there. It was my home!

I think I should qualify the 'my home' statement. All the money in the property was mine. He had not had any monetary input except for helping to pay the mortgage payments whilst we were together. The money required for us to have a joint property was again compliments of me so I felt I had the right to say 'my home'. I was not trying to do him out of anything that was rightfully his. I had even given him money when he needed to purchase a second hand vehicle. So yes, the property was mine.

I began to look for another house, one I could afford. In the meantime locks were changed for at least some form of security and solitude.

By now it was December 1993, a training course came up with work, one I desperately wanted to undertake, a three day course on 'Emergencies in Buildings', covering everything from bomb threats, physical security, fire training.

Day two and afternoon, theory and practical at the Fire Station, practical achieved and stored in my brain and it was on to the external part of the hands on training. The fires were lit with a petrol/diesel mix, we were behind buildings in an indent, I suppose the idea being it was sheltered from any breeze.

We were taught how to put out certain types of fires, oil pan on stove, how to aim fire extinguishers for maximum gain and speed to extinguish a fire with efficiency. I started to feel a little nauseous, thought maybe I'm scared about putting out the fires. After all the supposed oil pan on the stove was a tad high for me, so my theory was I'm just scared, I'll be alright when it is my turn. Wrong. I started to feel sicker and sicker and then the shaking started.

I walked out of the dip onto high ground; at least the smell wasn't as bad. One hitch though, I couldn't hear, so I had to proceed back down into the smoke filled area. This time I felt even sicker than previously. Finally it was over, all the participants began to leave the site and head back to their respective vehicles, another day over.

They found me in the car park leaning up against a car; I was shaking so badly I couldn't walk away. Some kind person took me into the office at the Fire Station, I was put on oxygen and proceeded to go into shock. Charming! This is all I needed!

The ambulance guys were called from next door. Lucky they didn't have to go far - that had to be some kind of consolation for them. For once in my life I wasn't guilty of totally inconveniencing people; at least I tried to minimize the inconvenience this time!

Seemed everyone agreed I was obviously sensitive to the fuel, extinguishers etc, obviously a petro chemical sensitivity of some type. The ambulance guys wanted to put me in hospital, I explained "I have two small children at home I have to go home sick or otherwise". Who else would look after my children? They would be scared.

Two of the course leaders wrapped me in a fire jacket and drove me home, against their better judgment, in hindsight maybe I should have gone to hospital, but at the time all I could think of was my two children who would want me at home. Mothers do that, don't we? We put everyone else first, seems to be part of the job description.

I Make Mark

I was sick all night. No way was I going to miss the last day of this amazing course though, I needed this course under my belt for work purposes, so off I went next morning feeling more than a little hung over and the worse for wear.

The course leaders had played mix and match with our name cards, I do hate it when they do that. I suppose it takes me out of my comfort zone to some extent, especially in unfamiliar surroundings. A lady walked over next to me, deposited her bag and jacket on the chair and headed off for a caffeine fix. The pulse in my wrist just about leaped out, it started to pulsate so hard. Perfume, it must be her perfume I thought. Yesterday's episode must have made me more sensitive than usual.

The lady returned and sat next to me, pulse rate accelerated once again, nausea set in, I started to shake, I left the room. The course leader came out, I explained what had transpired and suggested/requested he seat me next to someone not wearing perfume as I really wanted to finish this course. He sent out a plea and I was seated near a nice man not wearing after shave.

I made it through the day.

It was getting awfully close to Christmas and I hadn't made much progress to date as far as undertaking Christmas present shopping. My girlfriend and I went into the city to make a start. I said to her "I didn't know the city smelled this bad, I've never known it to be like this". The whole place smelled absolutely revolting. Why was I noticing it today - yet had never noticed previously?

We entered a large store - my pulse rate accelerated dramatically and I started to shake. I suppose it confirmed my suspicions that the Fire Station incident had made me sensitive to all toxins.

Monday morning and it was back to work, I explained day two's incident to my supervisor. I had to complete an incident report. This achieved I went off to make a photocopy. I didn't feel really well whilst at the copier but didn't take too much notice. The photocopier was of an older variety whereby fine particles of toner were dispensed upon operation.

I returned to my desk, my boss took one look at me and asked if I was alright, I explained that I thought the photocopier had made me a sick, he was turning white - imagine what I must have looked like! It was as if someone had blown up my lungs then tied them like a balloon, I could not breathe - my lungs were out for the count. Then all of a sudden the air was released in a single whoosh … My pale faced boss telling me to put my head down as he went racing off to seek medical assistance.

Right at that very moment my life was about to take yet another turn for the very worse. At least that is how I looked at it at the time, I now know differently. This was meant to happen for a reason, another of life's little challenges, another learning experience.

Fortunately for me we had medical officers on staff. One came to my aid with oxygen , I was taken to the surgery, took about two hours before I was sufficiently stabilized and allowed to go home. Driven home that is, driving certainly wasn't on the agenda that day.

From there I became progressively more and more ill. Small amounts of any type of chemical made me so sick to the point where I was bed ridden for most of the time.

My girlfriend would come and cook the two children dinner, if she cooked chops I would have to leave the house and go sit as far away as I could possibly get in the back yard. Even the fumes from grilled chops were way too much. Not a life I recommend!

I wasn't able to drive in a motor vehicle unless absolutely necessary; again my pulse rate would go sky high. It was a year or so before I could even drive my car into a service station to be refuelled - again girlfriend to the rescue. I couldn't go to the supermarket or shopping unescorted. At work I would continue to have severe allergic reactions to minute amounts of chemicals.

My local doctor wasn't what I would have called helpful. He had obviously decided all of this was in my head and really didn't have a solution. I was supermarket shopping one day - solo I might add - one of the freezers obviously had a minor gas leak, between that and all the people and their assorted perfumes, hair spray, conditioner, after shave, I got so sick I couldn't remember where I was or which supermarket I was in.

I forgot to mention, mental confusion or brain fog is a major by-product of this disease, I struggle to find words, names, where I am at times, *'chemical cross up'* is my version.

Trying desperately not to panic I'm standing in the aisle thinking to myself, just try to remember which way you were going, Coles the check out is this way, Purity it is the other, slow down and work it out. I did try unsuccessfully; nothing looked familiar, I had to ask another customer which direction I had been travelling - yep she definitely thought my marbles had gone astray.

For someone who believes and considers myself in control to have this disease thrust upon me was so totally confusing, scary, horrific - my world was out of my control and I had no way of knowing what on earth was happening to me.

I got through the check out somehow, found my car, threw the groceries into the back and went storming into the doctor's office to say "This is what happens when I go shopping". Take a look at me - does this appear normal to you!!! I was livid, I wanted action, confirmation it was physical and above all, I wanted treatment.

My fingernails all turned inward and cut into my fingers, this happened directly after the intake of chemicals. I had to cut them so short. I did leave one intact so I could do a show and tell with my doctor. His reaction - you are probably not eating sufficient meat. Oh no - I couldn't believe my ears. I was in his too hard basket and he wouldn't even listen to these horrible symptoms, symptoms which were scaring me to bits. What was happening to my body - I needed some answers before I went completely nuts.

I had been his patient for years yet this little man couldn't think to himself "Gosh for years she had been quite healthy and stable but now something has gone drastically wrong, maybe I should find out". Seemed those thoughts didn't so much as enter his head. He was too busy thinking this was all in my head. Where was my previous doctor when I most needed him?

Maybe I am being a little harsh, but consider how I felt, my life had suddenly turned upside down, from healthy to extremely ill, the symptoms were debilitating to say the least. I was no longer independent I was dependent upon my girlfriend or any other kind person who would assist me.

I felt let down, frustrated, betrayed, scared and very much alone.

Symptoms I was experienced scared people; it is another case of the 'afraid of the unknown'. If they could have only put themselves in my shoes instead of concentrating on how they felt and try imagine how I was feeling, maybe things would have been different. When I would stop breathing or experience difficulty, most around me hit the 'panic' button in lieu of the 'help her' button. For those who assisted me I thank them most sincerely.

For months I had wrestled with the THEM v ME issue. Is this illness in my head or isn't it? When you are constantly being told it is or at least it is insinuated then it becomes extremely difficult not to believe them - after all - many of them. Only one of me!

I would think to myself - but I didn't know going into that building was going to make me sick, I didn't know that person passing would cause that reaction. I was not having a panic attack - I was reacting to something in my surroundings - wasn't I?

My finger nails would distort upon entering a building with sub-standard air conditioning or upon eating food with chemicals or preservatives, I could watch it happen in front of my eyes. No wonder I was looking way older than my age, I couldn't be imagining these symptoms! My imagination never excelled in the past, so why start now.

All those years where I had to be independent were now paying off, I had to believe in myself like never before, I had been independent since I was a child, maybe this was the very reason, maybe my life up to now was my training ground.

My daughter whom I hadn't seen for quite some time heard about my illness and the fact it was debilitating and quite serious. She came to visit me. She was so incensed re the treatment (or lack of) I had received from my doctor she phoned him outraged at his lack of action re my condition. I believe she pointed out in no uncertain terms how sick I actually was from her perspective and that I needed assistance and needed it now!

I would cook a baked meal for all of us and I could guarantee I would sleep for two hours following the meal - something in the meal actually acted as a sedative; my body was way out of control.

I often wonder how different things may have been if my previous GP Doctor R had remained in the area. When I ponder that statement the one thing that comes to mind is: I believe one of the main lessons from this little known disease was for me to believe in myself. To trust my own intuition. I knew I wasn't having panic attacks, I knew I wasn't imagining any of the symptoms. My task was to convince the medical profession and others that there was a valid reason for everything that was happening to me.

The local GP volunteered to come and visit me at home that evening. My daughter must have made quite an impact.

Workers compensation had accepted my claim thanks to a visiting allergy specialist. Even this thought appeared to scare my local GP. I was sent to an allergy specialist who visited the state each month. He listened; he understood and finally gave it a name - Reactive Airways Dysfunction Syndrome - meaning: one intake of chemicals shuts down the whole detoxification system. Multiple Chemical Sensitivity or 20th Century Disease is the short version. Hard way to live I can assure you!

I was and am akin to the 'boy in the bubble' just didn't make it quite to his stage thank God. I can have times when I go out and am ok, the next I have to head back home early with tears in my eyes and give myself permission to feel sorry for me and wonder what 'normal' would be like for even a short time.

I do not recommend this disease for the faint-hearted. I had to have lots of internal dialogue with myself as to where to place my trust and faith. I had to believe in myself like never before. That isn't so easy to do when one has been put down for years.

Where did the inner strength come from? Did I have sufficient to see me through? Would I ever be rid of this obscure, little known disease? I really shouldn't say it like that. Yes it was unplanned, unfortunate, untimely, but I learned a great deal from this disease - I was given this challenge for a reason or reasons.

My sensitivity to my whole world increased - I could smell things most of the human race is incapable of - I became my workplace's very own Canary. I was far better than any VESDA (Very Early Warning Smoke Detection Apparatus) unit.

I can have minor to severe allergic reactions to minute amount of chemicals both natural and synthetic, someone walking past with a potent perfume, some types of paint, cigarette smoke, a painter with turpentine on his overalls, diesel fumes on mechanic's overalls, standing next to someone who has recently had their suit dry cleaned, all take their toll on my body. I can go into a shop with good intentions but have to leave due to any of the above, makes getting served really difficult. I have to admit, sometimes I get so very frustrated I have tears streaming down my cheeks as I depart without whatever I had intended purchasing.

It isn't easy being me sometimes. Kermit I understand completely!

I had one teller in the local bank, she would come and serve me in the car park, pharmacy assistants would hear me tapping on their window and come and serve me on the footpath, what some people do for attention eh? I had to face facts, there were some places my body just couldn't cope with, there are some very compassionate and kind people in the world one discovers on these occasions. I don't know what I would have done without them; I still have moments where it is necessary for them to serve me on the footpath outside their workplaces. My thanks and love to those very understanding people.

Pharmacies which have perfume stands placed right in the pathway near their front entrances please re-think the location. It was because of this I could not enter one particular pharmacy, women would 'test' the perfumes and because of the location I would not be able to walk thru the pharmacy to have any prescriptions filled or to purchase my much needed vitamins and probiotics. Acidophilus is a must for my body. I understand the logic as to why the placement is as it is but for sensitive people like me it is deadly. I needed to undertake other shopping in order to live and any exposure would and could stop my shopping for that particular day. Please help us to be as 'normal' as possible.

Please put the lives of others first and profit second on your priority list, put yourself in our position and think how frustrating and dangerous it is for us. Thanking you in advance for your consideration.

Driving was also difficult, my journey still consists of 'keep windows and vents closed when driving in peak traffic' if I don't not only do car fumes make me so very sick but also passing service stations and garages where bodyworks and spray painting are being undertaken.

Water, my body became unable to tolerate water from the tap, too many chemicals. I couldn't even put the glass close to my face. I could tell when the council had re-dosed the water. Even cleaning my teeth with tap water became a challenge. I love to have a bath to relax and de-stress. If the water had been freshly dosed - a bath was out! I was unable to sit in the bath water because of the smell of the chemicals, I would feel so sick. So needless to say I have had to have filtered water ever since, it is the only way I can cope and still drink water my body requires.

I would have huge big red angry lumps on the corners of my mouth which no one could identify or treat. They would come and go at will, didn't matter what I did no action on my part could encouraged them to disappear. I never discovered what they were or what caused them except to say that I now sport scar tissue in those two areas. My list of unknowns just kept getting bigger and better!

Seriously, it is not something I recommend you try, but it makes me wonder what untold damage chemicals are doing to our bodies. I am merely YOUR early warning system, think about what you are using in your home, what chemicals you are putting on your body, think long and hard and help to reduce your risk of becoming sensitive to the world.

Think about your make up and all the chemicals contained therein, think about whether or not you really need that hair dye, think about whether or not you require perfume. I get sick from *you* wearing it so imagine what it is doing to you.

I do not understand why people who have experienced and beaten cancer continue to dye their hair, drink copious quantities of alcohol and continue life as before. The disease was given as a warning that something in their lives needed to change, so why continue to scoff at the Universe and not heed the warning? We are given a warning for a reason; the next warning may not leave willingly if we fail to listen.

I believe in this philosophy: the spiritual message of cancer is to remind you to treat your body as a pure temple and to live your life in joy, happiness and love. Cancer sometimes sets in following an emotional ordeal of major proportion.

Maintaining a pure body is a body free of toxins, stress, anger, guilt, resentment, limit these factors as much as you are able, given the age we live in.

I don't allow the chemical sensitivity to control my life, however a good dose of commonsense has to prevail when one has to continue working and living. It does not stop me from doing what I want or going where I want, I just have to be conscious of the fact that I may get to a specific destination and have to leave at any given point depending on my body and its tolerance to the surroundings.

My body is akin to a walking environmental barometer - I have levels by which I can cope with small amount of some chemicals, should this level elevate because of increased exposure the next exposure will blow the limit and I have to retreat to somewhere safe. Somewhere safe can also be limited, my home, the beach providing gas heating from nearby homes isn't heading my way, or somewhere where the air is totally fresh with absolutely no vehicle exhaust fumes. It is the same with wood heaters, I have to be extremely careful in winter where I choose to walk; smoke and gas are extremely toxic for me.

New electrical equipment can be quite toxic along with new furniture and fittings - it's akin to walking through a mine field. I never know when an explosion may occur. It is for this reason I had to believe in myself like never before, I would not and still don't enter a different building or unknown territory believing the worse may happen, I go in there as a normal person then retreat if and when the need arises. More often than not I am ok, occasionally though I may need assistance to exit quickly. At times my body freezes and I am unable to walk away from the toxic substance, other times my eyes shut tight and I am unable to open them until I am further away from the offending substance. It is moments like these I have to rely on some kind person to assist - that is if I am capable of talking at the time - life can be fun.

What did I do for entertainment pre this disease I hear you ask?

I learned our bodies have various ways to detoxify - different pathways, if one pathway is blocked it searches for another, as such my collections of symptoms following exposure varied from time to time. Just when I thought I knew the symptoms and the carefully prepared route they would take, it would change. I couldn't even get complacent about this particular part of my life!

Still searching for boring and normal!!!!

Food is another unknown quantity for the un-initiated, packaged foods can be a nightmare; freshly prepared foods without preservatives and additives are a much safer option. Some foods actually make me feel sick just smelling them, it is my body's way of saying "Don't go there, or go there but beware there will be consequences", if I don't heed this warning I pay a high price.

I felt like a washing machine - I have cycles just like a washing machine I just don't click to signify the end of a particular cycle. Sequence goes like this - have allergic reaction, shake (at worst stop breathing or eyes shut and won't open), nausea, dry retching (*I call this fur balling - yes I sound and feel like a cat with a fur ball, my airways fill with mucous*), go on cold cycle, unable to keep warm, get extremely sleepy, lethargic, lose my balance, stutter, slur my words. The more reactions close together the worse the symptoms and the longer it takes to recover.

During this period where I was bed ridden most of the time my favourite Uncle came to me one night whilst I was asleep. He was in hospital seriously ill with cancer, he told me he knew I couldn't come to him so he came to me to say goodbye. He leaned over to kiss my cheek, he was freezing and I woke with a jolt from my sleep. He was so cold I knew he had already left his body. I was shivering with the cold memory of his touch. Uncle departed this world soon after. I loved him and had always wished I had a father like him, one who played games with his children and loved them to bits. Obviously we had quite a connection for him to take the time to come and say goodbye to me. I knew he had cancer even before it was diagnosed (another of those 'I know things without knowing how I know'). He was diagnosed with cancer soon afterwards. He had always looked so fit and healthy and on this particular day I looked at him, he looked thin and gaunt and I knew! I love him for coming to say goodbye, it meant so much to me.

Did I tell anyone? No, not many as most people choose not to believe - unfortunate but true and a great loss for them personally. If only they were open to such love they would gain so much.

This experience was one of the most beautiful I shall remember from my time in my Roslyn Avenue house. Heaven knows most of the other memories from that period are certainly in the 'I would like to forget category'.

CHAPTER FIFTEEN

Still in search of a new home, this disease made investigating prospective new homes almost impossible, challenging? It certainly was.

I was home one day, bed ridden as usual (getting to be a normal state following the continual stream of allergic reactions) - the current real estate representative called on me, he wanted to sell it to a lady who was interested, but only interested if I took a major reduction in asking price. I had to get out of bed to answer the door. He literally stood over me in the doorway, me less than 5 feet him 6 feet tall and demanded I accept.

Needless to say, a less than friendly partnership was terminated at that point. I was not going to be intimidated by a real estate thug, he could take a hike.

I phoned another agent, the guy they sent was like a God send. He knew what I was thinking before I knew or at least at the same time. He was excellent; he would make sure his car was non-toxic prior to collecting me to look at a prospective new home.

He was just what I needed under the circumstances. Thanks for being you and for caring.

Some houses I would stand at the door, unable to enter because they smelled too bad (*please note - not that anyone else would have noticed - just too strong for the canary*).

No, I am not now studying birds, nor have I turned yellow, canary as in 'canary sent down the mines to detect toxic gasses'.

Damp was out. If the previous occupants smoked - that automatically excluded a house because I was unable to tolerate even the faint hint of smoke. Brand new was out - still far too toxic for my body. Carpet deodorant houses were also off limits along with any home recently painted to impress buyers. Frustrating? You had better believe it!

I needed a real estate agent with the patience of a saint!

I learned it takes eight years for sufficient off-gassing to occur to make a new home habitable for me.

Then one day - in a quieter part of Kingston - there it was. It had a lot going for it except personality - the vibes inside the house didn't feel good, almost as if it was a shell without any love. Not a single picture on any wall. It was a house not a home.

I agonized over this house, I liked it, it would look different, more importantly feel different if it belonged to me - I would make it a home. Now one much larger problem loomed - I couldn't afford the asking price.

The lady who wanted my home wouldn't budge as far as cost went so I was literally in no man's land. The owner of the house I wanted to purchase came to see me one day - then soon after advised they were prepared to take a lesser price if that would help me.

Help me - it sure did - I have now been in this beautiful, warm, friendly home for ten years and loved every minute of it.

Came the day to vacate the revolting house in Blackmans Bay - one minute problem - the doors being opened wide during peak traffic made me so sick I had to be vacated to my new home - getting sicker today wouldn't help anyone.

So off I went to the new house and awaited the arrival of all my bits and pieces, leaving my daughter and my friend to take control of the vacating process. I felt so guilty, like a rat deserting a sinking ship. The fact I didn't have any choice didn't ease the guilt in the slightest.

Next problem, formaldehyde from the boxes piled everywhere the eye could see, suppose you can guess. The formaldehyde was making me so sick; this meant the boxes had to be unpacked with record speed which isn't easy when the body is more than a tad sick. Why does everything have to off-gas, life would certainly be easier if this didn't occur. Would sure like to get hold of the person who invented off-gassing, he has a lot to answer for!

Well at least my new home didn't make me sick. It turned out this house had been built in 1986, so the carpets, paint, everything had settled down. Built in the year when I had moved into Willow Avenue and at approximately the same time - was that an omen? It was built for me. Welcome to my new home!

Laura wasn't very old when I went to Margate with my girlfriend to purchase fresh fruit and vegetables, some of which were locally grown. Laura had never liked baby food; there was no quick fix for her where meals were concerned. This particular day, food secured, all strapped in and we set off back to our respective homes. From the back of the car all we could hear was rattle, rattle, crunch, crunch - Laura was within reach of the vegetables, she was ripping into the raw vegetables like she had never been fed before in her life. I kid you not. It was hard to believe, raw silverbeet, lettuce whatever was within her small grasp went into her mouth and was demolished within seconds. No wonder she didn't like baby food, smooshy food, she wanted raw. Another lesson for me, another child giving me lessons in 'watch, listen, learn' and above all 'take note'.

It was a waste of time buying vegetables and fruit without Laura being present unless they were definitely organic. She could sense chemicals on food and would not have a bar of them as a result. How she could tell still remains a mystery as she was far too young to allow us access to her thought process. I would hold her near the desired purchase and if she put her hand out to take one I knew it was chemical free. Same with meat products, no point in purchasing a normal sausage from the supermarket; had to be preservative and chemical free from selected butchers.

Breakfast would consist of a punnet of strawberries, stewed fruit (stewed fresh without sugar and frozen for consumption throughout the year - the freezer was full), processed cereals were mostly off the shopping list. I had to cook vegetables for the family; Laura's would always remain raw. It was years before she would eat any vegetable cooked.

Her baby teeth were worn through - not from decay but from eating raw vegetables, they certainly got more than their fair share of work during their working years. I froze kentish cherries in handful packs; these Laura would have for dessert. Not a cheap way to live but healthy, definitely!

A lesson beautifully displayed and taught by a toddler. I hope one day I shall learn how she could tell whether or not the vegetables were organic and safe for eating. She couldn't talk other than the normal baby words, so how did she know?

Somewhere around this time I bought a kitten for Laura, only problem was Fabian was so allergic to this tiny animal it was a case of 'get rid of Fabian or the kitten', one of them had to go, hmmm deliberation time. No, only kidding, Fabian had asthma so bad it was a case of the poor little kitty had to go to another home. Alternatively we could have tried having a permanent bed ready at the nearest hospital as Fabian would have definitely been a regular visitor - had he survived that is, yes it was that serious. Fabian's asthma was in the extreme category. Girlfriend came to our aide and took the kitten in so at least Laura could have visiting rights and know she was in a safe home and was loved dearly. Pretty sure Laura wasn't real impressed with my choice as to which one had to leave home!

Laura was now a little over three years old, we planted trees and shrubs which would encourage native birds to visit our garden. Now the fairies needed somewhere to live - so in went the rose bushes and azaleas. The azaleas in the fern garden made a fairy paradise if ever there was one.

Mum would recite this verse to my daughter my eldest daughter when she was small:

I wonder, I wonder, if anyone knows
What lives in the heart of a velvety rose,
Is it a Goblin or is it an Elf
Or is it the Queen of the Fairies herself.

Laura has now heard that verse over and over as we sat quietly awaiting the arrival of the fairies in their new home.

Ok, there are some things that never cease to amaze me, I should no longer be surprised but I am – I decided I had best finish at the last full stop and make a phone call to my girlfriend to see if she had heard from Laura. My girlfriend agreed to collect Laura today from her last night's sleep over. Full stop initiated, I arose from my chair, took two steps and the phone started ringing. Yes it was her, no doubt in my mind it wouldn't be. Laura had just sent her a message to say she was ready to be collected.

Timing eh? So now I have approximately three quarters of an hour left to continue before my baby daughter returns home full of news from the weekend and my peace and thoughts come to an end.

Fabian would have been fifteen when we arrived at this house, he would only have one particular bedroom - I didn't understand. I actually needed the largest bedroom to accommodate Laura and her toys, but Fabian was insistent he could only sleep in this one bedroom.

I think I probably got a little annoyed with him but I wasn't to know. I now wonder if he was already showing signs of schizophrenia and was too frightened to sleep in the back bedroom which was closest to the highway. Although we lived in a quiet, out of the way suburb, we had the Southern Outlet directly behind our back fence. This Outlet was the main thoroughfare for the residents of Huonville to access Hobart along with everyone on the way and residents further south. Log trucks frequent this highway along with trucks delivering all those essential commodities – so yes it accommodated considerable traffic.

Fabian had had problems aplenty at primary school. Where the private school would take him asthma included, the state school didn't want to know about it. If he had a cough he had to stay home. His asthma was quite often caused by flowers in the classroom. I would, time after time, explain that daffodils and other potent flowers would exacerbate his condition, all to no avail. Then I would have to keep him home until the asthma abated. I found this situation rather frustrating as it occurred on many occasions.

His reward! .... at the end of one particular year, his male teacher named him as the child having the most absences from school for that period - Fabian was so embarrassed and hurt. How dare a school willingly humiliate a child to that extent - some instances defy gravity. Where was this man's brain at? I hope this teacher has found a new vocation far away from children.

Fabian must have felt so small and insignificant and such a failure. His absences were out of his control. It was the school which had failed, it certainly wasn't Fabian. Although I imagine the experience helped to set the scene for what was about to come!

His father had been dominating. As much as Fabian had loved him, he was scared of him. Changing to the state school, meant a change in teachers, Fabian was presented with a male teacher for the first time in his school life. Fabian had been too scared to ask him questions ……so he didn't.

Between the male teachers and the attendance problem, his school work deteriorated - I explained he had been in the top percentage of his class at his previous school. The teacher almost laughed in my face.

At a parent/teacher interview for my eldest daughter at this same school. The teacher said "Well, what do you want?" I explained as it was a new school for her I was anxious to know how she had settled in. Her sarcastic reply "Well, it's obvious, she attended a private school". End of story. Interview terminated soon after. What is their problem? This school had a definite problem. What had I done to my children?

My daughter had not attended a private school for very long, her grammar was impeccable, she was quiet and polite, she was merely being her true self not a private school upbringing coming to the fore.

Somewhere, sometime life has to get easier I kept telling myself, if it hadn't I may not be here writing my story, I had to **believe** my life would improve.

CHAPTER SIXTEEN

I was a single parent, working full time, with three children. I obviously let a lot of things go through to the keeper without meaning to. When I look back, some of these things were glaringly obvious, but at the time I didn't see what was happening under my own nose, I was too busy just trying to stay afloat and keep on keeping on.

Would the outcome have been different if I had taken more notice and followed up more? Or was life meant to occur this way as part of the grand plan, will I ever learn the truth?

> *Even now, years later, one of the hardest things I find in life is to devote the required time to everything, it is impossible. I work full time, sometimes exceedingly long hours (not because I want to, but because I have to, to stay on top of my work load). I had to work the last two Saturdays which left me one day per week to undertake all the housework, washing, ironing, relaxation time, visit my mother, supermarket shopping, mowing lawns, spend time with friends – you know how it goes. On top of this my sleeping patterns are well out of kilter and I am averaging far less sleep than my weary body requires.*
>
> *I get home from work, exhausted some nights, then have to find the physical resource to still cook dinner, a load of washing, take Laura to netball, get those few items from the supermarket I forgot. This would all sound only too familiar to quite a few readers.*
>
> *It is easy to feel guilty. I survive by doing what I can, anything over and above that has to wait until the following weekend. Sun-*

day, I was totally and utterly exhausted; I did the ironing so we had clothes for the week. Undertook a small pile of mending and had to acknowledge that that was it. Housework had to wait for another week. There was only so much I could do without making myself sicker than I already am.

Today, following eleven and a half hours sleep (YES!) I have managed to undertake all the housework, ironing, a little stretch of relaxation (that means doing absolutely nothing except watching TV) and above all, time at my precious computer. I have come to the conclusion that each weekend should have an additional hour attached to the Sunday - especially for us working mums. Last night day light saving ended, what a bonus - a whole hour extra. One whole hour to spend as required. It was a most welcome reward for two long hard weeks at work.

A work colleague asked me how I fared without a partner in my life, live-in partner that is. I explained I had been on my own for ten years now, and at the moment I physically didn't have the time, inclination or required energy. Yes, I sometimes wish that were the case, but I ended an 'on and off' again four year distant relationship. We had grown further apart, our differences highlighted once too often, and I couldn't fit another something into my life, I just didn't have enough me to go around and I felt like I was going nuts. Felt if I didn't get time to myself I would self combust - I needed time out from the world. Unfortunately, my relationship was the 'fallout factor'.

I need more time to myself. More time to write - I feel like I have been taken over and have a destiny to fulfill - I gain so much from writing our story it is hard to get off the keyboard at times. I don't realize how cold I am getting because the fire has gone out, sometimes I forget to look at the time and I realize I only have four hours sleep before it is time to get up and start another day.

Lonely? No, can't say I am - at work I have approximately 300 staff to keep me company and action their respective requests, telephones ring constantly, at home I have Laura, at home I have my own peace and space.

I am perfectly at peace and happy with myself - now that is quite an accomplishment. It has taken a lot of hard work to get to this point and I am still learning.

Fabian's sister would try in vain, repeatedly, in earlier years to help Fabian understand his school work, it always ended badly, with one or the other storming away from the kitchen table, steam coming out their ears.

Whilst she found school easy for Fabian it was hard going.

I would imagine by the time Fabian reached high school he was way behind the other children - why wasn't I told, why didn't someone say something? I don't have an answer to that; just know it didn't happen, if the school tried Fabian certainly didn't pass on the messages of concern.

I don't know the age at which Fabian started smoking marijuana - did the smoking come first or the schizophrenia? I will never know the answer to this one either, I suspect.

Our garden started to grow, Laura and I were delighted, to help her adjust to her new home I started a fairy book - with photos of fairies in the flowers on the rose bushes, sitting on the fronds of the ferns in the fern garden, on the Christmas tree. She was delighted and we gradually added to her book. I told her the fairies were so shy they wouldn't normally allow their photo to be taken. They allowed me to take photos especially for her, but only when all was quiet. I explained she should feel quite special. What little girl wouldn't have been taken aback by the sheer joy of it? She had love written all over her little face. Why couldn't it remain like that…… forever?

The fairies were paper, I cut the silhouettes out from fairy gift wrapping paper, the idea worked perfectly, I carefully placed them in various flowers and shrubs, Christmas tree for their respective photo shoots.

When I was young mum used to do a similar thing at Christmas time, put a paper cut out of a fairy princess on my bedroom window, I was supposed to be in bed pre the arrival of the fairy or Santa wouldn't be happy. Occasionally the fairy made it to the window before I made it to bed. Mum would affix her to the window with water, when the water dried the fairy peeled off and fell into the garden below. I remember my dismay if I looked at the window and there she was before I made it to bed, suppose it did make me that must faster the next night though. I didn't want to get Santa off side at that time of year. It was many years later before I learned my fairy princess wasn't real.

The native birds discovered the native shrubs - it was all starting to happen - it was beautiful, our hard work was now rewarding us twofold. Some days we have up to seven different types of birds in our garden. Hakeas in the backyard are a major draw card for Black Cockatoo - the noise - the destruction - the absolute awe of it all. We feel so honoured by their presence. The native shrubs in the front and side gardens are a source of food and water for the honeyeaters, small wrens, wattle birds and others, we watch in silence, it is amazing and so beautiful.

They have water, food; we have the sheer pleasure of watching them in action - a perfect partnership. Following rain the small wrens enjoy a shower under the droplets of water on the leaves. Some of the most precious moments are when the babies leave their respective nests and they too are brought here to experience all the garden holds. We are able to watch the babies being fed, disciplined, yes disciplined - I wasn't even aware that birds would discipline their offspring, but I now know they do. Sometimes I just sit and watch never quite knowing what will happen next. I love every moment and I say a silent 'thank you' for allowing me to be part of their lives.

1994/95 wasn't altogether a fun time or years I would willingly choose to repeat. Life seemed to go from bad to worse; I forgot the meaning of peace completely.

Laura's dad would take her for his normal visits, on many occasions Laura would only go by force, crying "Help me mummy" as she went.

I was stalked, no other word for it. In October 1994 I had an insurance sales rep kind enough to visit me at home considering I worked full time. Laura's dad drove up the street three times during that two hour period. Fabian had been in the street playing with his friends and had seen him and taken note.

Laura would repeatedly say "I don't want daddy to steal me again", that's what she called it when he took her for visits and then refused to bring her home. On one occasion I asked my girlfriend to collect Laura from the crèche and take her to my mother's house as I had to work later than normal. Laura requested my girlfriend stay at mum's until my arrival, when asked why she once again stated "I don't want daddy to steal me again". She obviously thought (all of four years old) there was safety in numbers.

Arguments over clothing, school fees, visitation, you name it, it caused an argument. He didn't require any excuse he revelled in arguments so the slightest word from me and he was off in a never ending cycle of verbal abuse.

I lost count of the number of times I went to bed scared, his constant driving past my house was sending me slowly but surely around the proverbial twist. It was constantly on my mind, it became akin to an obsession with me. I wanted to be free but didn't know how to achieve this state.

February on a Saturday night, I had a friend visit, car in my driveway, Fabian watched him drive up and down my street approximately eight times during that period, he obviously wanted to know who it was and why - what did he hope to gain?

Would my life ever be mine again? Would I ever know the elusive state of peace?

February 25, could only happen to me. Laura had a boogie board; girlfriend and I had taken her to the beach. Laura had decided it was my turn for her to tow me on the board, I was lying on the board when all of a sudden a huge wave hit (ok yes it was more like a small ripple but that would spoil a good story and make me look even more stupid). I put my hand down to steady myself, just as I made contact and thought I was on an even keel another one of those huge waves struck. My hand had gone into the sand at right angles (I was in at least 25cm of water - now stop laughing), the next wave had pushed the board and my hand rolled as a result.

The pain was something else in my left hand. The weight of water on the affected part way too heavy, can't say I had ever experienced anything like this before.

I was on 24 hour call out with work at the time, wouldn't you know it, the pager sounded and I had to attend - alarm in one of our demountable buildings. Twenty six separate alarms had been set off in the one building.

My girlfriend drove me to work; luckily we had gone to the beach in her car.

I walked into the demountable, a spider had set up camp in front of the movement detector, each time he walked across he registered on the trip meter, the security company phoned me to ensure I was ok and hadn't come to any harm.

The guys were terrific, if I was on call and they sent me in to check on an alarm regardless of the time of day or night they would give me approximately 15 minutes then phone to ensure I was ok.

I assured security monitoring I was fine, that I had found the intruder and killed him. I explained it was a spider causing all the problems and he had met his demise. I couldn't drive so I had absolutely no plans for an immediate return should this spider decide he really liked that position and repeat or better his last twenty six alarms performance.

It took the doctor a few days (with me in pain every so often as the broken bone moved), to register that I had in fact broken a bone. Upon viewing the x-ray initially he had been so astounded at the state of my bones (apparently akin to that of a 60 year old) that he had forgotten to look to see why I was in so much pain. He obviously took a second look days later and realized I had a more pressing problem other than poor bone density. Like I need another problem or two, wasn't like I had enough already!

I was plastered on my birthday, March 2. Yes, maybe my problems would have seemed less if it were that kind of plastered but it was of the broken hand type plastered just incase you were thinking otherwise.

My girlfriend, Laura and I went to Scamander for the long weekend. It was nice to be somewhere where I didn't have an estranged husband driving around looking for me.

She used to say as we got further from Hobart she could see me relaxing, upon our return, the closer we got to Hobart the more tense I became. I would find my fists tightly clenched, I didn't even realize I was doing it, I had to make a conscious effort to check, then try to relax, only to find next time I took note, those little fists were back to their original tense state.

Arguments continued, the stalking continued all hours of the day and night. I didn't know what it was like to have a normal stress free life.

During March Laura told my girlfriend her dad referred to her as the good year blimp - what kind of message does that send to a four year old. How childish. Why couldn't we just agree to disagree and live peaceful lives?

I have to wonder at the damage all this did to Laura at such an early age, if this child turns out to be even close to normal, I for one, will be more astonished than anyone.

Rather than use the lounge room and be in full view should he decide to visit (on one of his at least four occasions per day) we relocated to the family room. Here I could shut the doors into the area and could not be seen by any one approaching the front door.

He would knock loudly on the door, I would ignore. He would then bash on the window until I thought it would break from the sheer force and anger. I would still ignore, he would then put his hand over the fence and bash on the family room window (couldn't see, only bash).

I would be shaking with both fear and anger, anger because I felt I had the right to feel safe in my own home, I should be able to live in peace at least here, in what I thought and hoped would be my sanctuary from the world.

I was talking to a male colleague from work on the phone late one evening; my phone was situated near the kitchen window. Whilst I was talking I saw a hand come through the gate and unlock the latch … geez …I knew it was him without even seeing his face. My blind was shut but there was sufficient space to see the hand on the latch. What did he hope to achieve? Did he wish to listen to my conversation? Was he checking whether or not I had someone in my home? Who knows, one cannot apply logic to stalking!

At times like these I knew if I didn't get a restraining order I would be in court for murder!

I would be sitting having coffee at the beach with my girlfriend, de-stress time, time to solve the problems of the world because I sure as hell couldn't solve mine. A bet could be placed as to how long and how often my ex husband would patrol that stretch of road during that time, I felt like I was continuously under a microscope. I felt as though I must have some type of detector attached to me, he managed to find me anywhere and everywhere anytime.

By the end of March the situation turned quite ugly, Laura wouldn't talk to me or look at me, goodness only knows what he had been telling her. At one stage Laura had told me "Daddy makes me hate you", I didn't ask how.

He would land on the doorstep and for the next three quarters of an hour shouting would emanate from my property. Not once did any neighbour seek help on my behalf, yet they would have known at times I was in trouble and needed assistance.

I would shake life a leaf just seeing him, tension, stress at an all time high on these occasions. After twelve years of knowing him I still could not predict how he would react to any given situation.

April 4, he flatly refused to return Laura; I went to his flat, he informed me she was asleep. I stated I was going to the police for help in retrieving my daughter. Police station closed, of course, isn't that just my luck.

Phone box handy, just then police car came into view. They informed me there wasn't a thing they could do to help me, my best course of action was to leave her there for the night with him (if I thought she wasn't in any immediate danger) and to go lawyer shopping the next day.

Next day I phoned the Law Courts to find out what I needed to do to apply for a restraining order and legal custody of Laura.

I found a local lawyer, explained he either represent me for a restraining order and sole custody or he would be representing me for murder because I was at the end of my tether. I couldn't take anymore; My ex had pushed me way too far. If I had seen him strolling down my driveway one more time with that smirk plastered all over his face I would have totally lost it. I was scared for me, scared of what I might be capable of doing given the wrong/right circumstances. I was just about begging for assertive action to be taken on my behalf. I needed someone to go to bat for me. I can honestly understand how a person can kill another without any hesitation, without wanting or meaning to, something snaps at that moment when you know you can't take any more taunting or abuse. Please don't think I condone this behaviour; I certainly do not but I came close enough to have an understanding how it can occur unwittingly. It gave me a greater understanding of why and how some people end up in prison.

Restraining order set in motion. Magistrate turned down the application - respondent had right of reply prior to the order being given. Back to square one.

One highlight of the day - plaster removed - poor little arm quite skinny compared to the other one. At least it was now free. Well I had one part of me free, suppose that was a start! If only I could work out how to free the rest of me.......I would have been happy.

The magistrate refused the restraining order - I hadn't been hit for two years so what was my problem. I kid you not, those were his words, my jaw hit the ground when this statement was relayed to me by my lawyer. Obviously stalking and intimidation in the eyes of this particular magistrate; was acceptable. Where did he get his law degree from? Yes,

I too, believed it must have been found inside a cereal box, how could someone seemingly so intelligent be so stupid and ignorant. This attitude was certainly unacceptable from a professional who should know better.

My lawyer may have been blind but was certainly not deterred; he submitted an application to the Supreme Court in the hope the original decision might be overturned. I think he did an amazing job, he obviously did not see his inability to see as a handicap to helping and assisting others. Thank you so very much for the time you vested in my case, I certainly appreciated your efforts.

Restraining Order finally issued by the Supreme Court, temporary measure only, but at least that was better than nothing.

May 9 had to attend compulsory counselling at the Family Law Court - the counsellor left a lot to be desired - he was extremely intimidating and should not have been allowed to counsel any female who had experienced domestic violence. Even his body language was intimidating. Must be something to do with the name. I pray this man has found a new vocation.

Yes, I did impart my feelings when he phoned me at work one day. I requested a different counsellor if this mission was to prove even slightly successful, I refused to be intimidated by someone who was trying to 'streamline their paper work' by trying to force me to make a decision I didn't wish to make. Don't imagine he thought much of me either but that was his problem. Me? I had bigger problems than men with their own agenda.

The restraining order was issued for a period of two years; by June 26, my ex had breached the order on three separate occasions. I knew I had to take a stand or the breaches would continue and it would be a waste of - wait for it - $7,000.

Courage in hand I forced myself to go to the police station to report the said breaches, I felt so sick. Statement recorded. Even the police didn't like dealing with him, he argued in circles, it was impossible to find a beginning and an end. Hours could pass without any resolution to the original problem; I knew only too well what they had to contend with and why they found it unpalatable.

When we were together he would leave for work so happy some mornings because he knew he was going to have an argument with one of his many work colleagues. He certainly 'got off' on arguments; he thrived on them to put it mildly.

He was charged with two of the breaches, at least that may have discouraged more of the same, I could only hope. The police officer apologized and said he just couldn't go another round with my ex and had settled for guilty on two breaches.

I was later informed that the police had picked him up near my house one night prior to any of this; someone had reported a man acting suspiciously, the policeman who imparted this statement apologized to me for not realizing sooner why he had been in this area and for not being more proactive at the time. His excuse at the time was obviously sufficient for them to take it at face value, they weren't to know.

Back to the $7,000 price tag, that amount gained me a restraining order for two years, legal custody of Laura and so he would finally get the message the marriage was over, divorce (mind you the magistrate who disallowed the restraining order should have had an invoice from me for his part in prolonging the proceedings and for his flippant comment and approach to a very serious subject).

My lawyer discussed my financial problem with my bank, they agreed to re-finance my home loan to accommodate this amount.

My ex was constantly on my mind, I was allowing him to take over my life, my every thought, every waking moment. I hated him for what he had done to me and my family. I knew I had to get past this hatred or end up seriously ill. I prayed night after night for guidance as to how to forgive and let go. I had to get my life back, hatred is a wasted emotion it only hurts the owner, the person who is the object of the hate is oblivious. I was only hurting me. My prayers were finally answered; I was able to stop thinking of him and the pain he caused. I will never accept what he did, but I no longer hate because of it, I treat it with indifference and try not to dwell on any part of the past.

I forgot to mention earlier that at some point after I relocated he purchased a unit within 'viewing' distance of my home. He moved in just across the street, from his letter box he could see my home, whether or not I was in/out, whether or not I had visitors. How is that for dedication? Maybe I had some magnetic appeal? Once the two year restraining order had expired he could come across anytime he so chose.

Wonderful! I felt like I was living in a goldfish bowl, my every movement monitored.

CHAPTER SEVENTEEN

It has been at least 7 weeks or longer since I have been able to sit here and work on our story, I have been so very sick, sicker than ever before. I knew I was reaching the exhaustion stage, but thought it was due to a combination of too much work and insufficient sleep. Not so. Seems my body took exception to my recent change in medication for Crohn's disease, being overworked probably didn't help the situation in the slightest. (It is now May 2004)

Coincidence once again, April 1995 which is about where we are at in "Days of My Life". I was diagnosed with Crohn's disease, other people collect stamps, bears, perfume bottles – seems I collect diseases. Funny this very serious adverse reaction could coincide at this very stage of our life's story, right when I am about to detail my first encounter with this very disease.

Firstly I will mention that shortly after my encounter with the environmental disease I began to notice I seemed to have a problem with Candida albicans, as soon as I ate some items which were extremely sweet I could tell straight away it wasn't a good idea. I hadn't had problems previously except for the odd bout of thrush but certainly not enough to even rate a mention.

I mentioned this on at least two occasions to my visiting allergy specialist to whom I was going for treatment for my RADS. He finally took me seriously and decided to undertake an allergy test. My body took exception to the additional Candida invasion, that laid me out in his surgery for some time afterwards, how lucky could

I get I was allergic to something that inhabited my body, something which obviously had no intention of leaving. My medical record just kept on getting better and better.

The Candida had flourished due to my depressed immune system, this may not have been a problem if I was even slightly normal, but I had to be allergic to it.

He told me if he could cure me of this he would write it up in the medical journals as he had never heard of it before. Oh how unusual for me to be the obscure example for him! I will never know the outcome as he stopped his practice in Tasmania. I couldn't see compensation paying for me to go to Melbourne for consultations. These days I get by with a daily hit of acidophilus - of the heavy duty variety. It helps to keep the Candida in check along with a diet as yeast free as I can manage.

My biggest problem is that when I have an allergic reaction to something it sends a rather loud and clear message to my Crohn's disease and my bowel starts playing havoc at the same time. Great company the two are - they love to play and act up together. Pleased I can provide them with a really fun playground. Honestly, would you want to be me? I haven't met anyone yet who would willingly take over my body.

... At this time, in 1995, I was working extremely long hours, it would be about midnight and I would still be on the floor of the lounge room preparing documents for the next day's meetings. This particular night I realized I couldn't sit down properly on the carpet. It was as if someone had inserted a pencil under my skin across the cheek of my bottom. Weird eh? Painful, oh yes! But sudden also, that pencil wasn't under my skin during the day. Like always I didn't have that much time to dwell on it, this work had to be ready for tomorrow's meeting, I merely adjusted my sitting position so that particular portion of my anatomy was off the hard surface.

The head of our section was, at the time, on his way to Antarctica as voyage leader on a ship. The person acting in my position was quarantined at home with suspected hepatitis, an officer undertaking an accommodation review was also absent on Defence leave. This left me and a temporary employee. We had a huge responsibility and very few resources; I don't know how I would have coped without my work colleague during that period.

I could give her minimum instructions re a particular task and she was able to deduce the rest and carry out the mission to completion. Thank you, thank you so very much.

My rear end became progressively more and more inflamed and painful.

My local GP forwarded me onto a surgeon, he was definitely out of his depth and I was playing pass the parcel once again, with me as the parcel. Wouldn't you love to be me for awhile, think of all the adventures, all the challenges, all the pain?

Although this surgeon was wonderful he was at a loss to explain or name whatever was happening to me - he could only deduce it looked as though I had had an allergic reaction to something. I wasn't given any form of treatment or antidote for this supposed allergic reaction, hence the condition continued to worsen.

I would go to the toilet in the morning, the neighbours must have heard me screaming, yes it was *that* bad, I would shake from the pain for at least 30 minutes following this early morning ritual. It was horrendous, I would be walking at work, minding my own business, then out of nowhere it was like someone was piercing my bowel with a knife - a rather large knife, again I would cry out loud and come to a screaming halt.

I was certainly a regular patient for this particular surgeon. He told me he had no idea what was wrong and couldn't cure me - I walked up the street with tears streaming down my face, I almost walked into the path of a car (yes it was accidental - I couldn't see, my eyes needed wind screen wipers). It is devastating to have a condition that painful and be told - sorry but I can't do anything.

I had felt alone before but nothing could have prepared me for the 'alone' that I was now experiencing.

I was way up there on the scale of 'alone' without any form of map or compass to gain any direction to locate a way back to normal.

I began to get small blisters all over the cheeks of my bottom, even in my mouth, diarrhoea so bad I was almost crawling out of the toilet at times - I decided if the experts couldn't cure me I had to.

I searched pharmacies in the hope of finding some form of pain relief for my now, "had been examined too many times bottom", it was made worse with each probing examination, I was at screaming point. Truly I am not adverse to a little pain but this pain was totally off the scale.

Finally I found a lady who played squash for the same club I had once played for, she sold Chinese herbs, she gave me sample products, three products and suggested I trial them and see what happened. Within three days I was again running around the complex at work, blisters receding by the day. Herb stock depleted, blisters and symptoms began to return.

> *Needless to say I remained on these three products for quite a number of years, yes I also required other medication but they certainly helped me to regain my health (well as much as I could under the circumstances). The Chinese herbs alleviated the requirement for more toxic medication; I could at least get by without toxic for now.*

After five months of this excruciating pain I finally took myself off to the surgeon and demanded he handball me onto someone who could give me a diagnosis and better still a cure. I couldn't take the pain any more. Successful this time and it was off to a colorectal surgeon for examination.

By this time I was more than ready to put a bandaid over my bottom with a "No Entry" sign written in very large red letters. I honestly didn't think it was capable of another unfriendly invasion.

It had to get worse before it got better - enema required prior to examination by the surgeon, by this time I seemed to have screaming down to a fine art. The enema was like the straw that broke the camel's back, burn - reminded me of that song …'I fell in to a burning ring of fire, I went down, down, down and the flames went higher'. Ok, so it wasn't a time to get trivial but unbelievable pain will do that to me.

Whilst the five months seemed to drag I had to maintain my sense of humour (or drive off a cliff) - so it went something like this - "They can't get to the bottom of it" - "It's a real pain in the butt"- "No end in sight". I had still maintained my warped sense of humour. I thank God for small mercies, without looking at or for a 'funny' side I seriously believe I would have found that cliff. The pain was indescribable, nothing but nothing eased the severity, I could not continue to live with this level of pain on a daily basis. I fully understand why voluntary euthanasia should be legal, this experience taught me one important lesson, we should have a right to end life if the pain threshold or quality of life becomes unbearable. It should be the right of an individual to choose Not a decision which should be in the hands of politicians who have their own religious agenda or beliefs they wish to uphold and inflict on the community as a whole.

In hospital again! Forgot to mention I had been there, done that, on more than a few occasions with the previous surgeon, all to no avail. Still didn't help surgeon number one come to a conclusion, only made my poor butt more painful to use. I lost count of the number of invasions my poor butt suffered all in the hope of finding a cause or cure. I am still uncertain as to why I had this problem but if a clue could have been left behind it would have been mighty useful at that point.

This time success - pain worth it - well it was if it meant we had an answer:

Crohn's disease and a bonus - you know the ad, not only do you get this but wait for it - you get this as well – me? I had two abscesses in my bowel as well as the disease. No wonder I had sharp stabbing pains, who would have guessed one person could be so fortunate and have all this to themselves.

> Crohn's Disease is inflammation of the full thickness of the intestine. The disease may affect any part of the gastrointestinal tract from the mouth to the anus, there may be many different clinical features. Common symptoms include, abdominal pain, diarrhoea, fever, malaise, nausea and vomiting, loss of appetite and weight loss.
>
> These symptoms are a result of inflammation and thickening and narrowing of the bowel wall. The early symptoms are often subtle and this can delay diagnosis. The disease tends to relapse or go into remission, but some people need continuous medical therapy to control the symptoms.
>
> Crohn's disease and ulcerative colitis can produce small ulcers on the tongue or on the lining of the mouth.
>
> Areas around the anus are more commonly involved in Crohn's disease. Skin tags, fissures or ulcers, abscesses or fistulae with a discharge may be present.
>
> Crohn's disease - cause unknown, the body attacks and destroys itself, immune suppressant drugs are used to try to control the disease.

Cortisone and flagyl prescribed to try to gain control of a disease with cause unknown, no known cure. Well at least on the positive side; I had a name for it now.

I returned to work, walked in the door and burst into tears, explained about the disease and the fact that thanks to the medication I would look like a budgie toy before I was finished. The thought of swelling up and becoming round didn't appeal to me in the slightest. I am so small in stature any additional weight goes 'out' as there is insufficient 'up' for it to go.

I gave myself two weeks to come to terms with this news and to stop feeling sorry for myself - I then had to request an extension. Well why not, it isn't everyday one gains yet another disease with no known cure,

I seem to have a real talent in that department. The least I could do was agree to an extension of time for adjustment purposes.

After two visits to hospital and numerous examinations I sure wasn't running anywhere in the short term, so slow and steady as she goes, body and face swelling from the cortisone - I felt like a balloon, my swollen legs and feet ached continuously.

My allergy specialist agreed an allergic reaction may have caused the onset of the Crohn's disease symptoms - even a small fissure in my bowel would have allowed entry for the Candida thus causing an allergic reaction, hence the "appeared to be only an allergic reaction" during initial examinations. I will never know the truth but intuition tells me I am pretty much spot on in this instance.

So somewhere between the Candida problem and the stress on the home front, no wonder my poor body had tossed a wobbly, it had probably had enough stress to last a few life times.

Whilst my hand was in plaster - from finger tips to almost elbow - it was fast food, frozen food from supermarket freezer department and whatever one could manage to warm one handed. My body wasn't used to junk food on any type of scale - bit like pinning the tail on the donkey - it could have been a combination of all three factors, either way I paid the price and have done so ever since. Moral of story - only have take away occasionally it you wish to preserve your body in reasonable working condition. Limit stress where possible and try to have sufficient rest at night.

Back to that 'balance' word. I imagine you are now realizing the value of that word!

Eat whole foods where possible, organic fruit and vegetables, limit meat and dairy intake, exercise regularly, keep preservatives and chemicals to a minimum and it should give you the basic recipe for healthy living.

Suppose the bonus is : I get to use fun toys like prednisolone suppositories, enemas, both of which dispense the medication right to the source - doesn't pay to be bashful with this disease! Oh well, one day at a time rule applies once again, along with a warped sense of humour.

> *...and you know what else you get with this disease? A can't wait card! To be presented when one needs to use the bathroom facilities in rather a hurry whilst out in public. Seriously, the Crohn's and Colitis Association issue us with this valuable item. My warped sense of humour likes this card. After all we are an exclusive club, not everyone has access to this card! I thank this Association from the bottom of my heart, they are a wonderful bunch of humans doing their best for those of us with this disease.*

CHAPTER EIGHTEEN

Back to May 2004

B I worked on two consecutive Saturdays at work, I was getting to exhaustion stage this particular Saturday at the end of March, I thought I was tired from work overload. Monday not much better so thought I had best go to my GP. Not a popular move, my supervisor was none too impressed, he had delayed one particular meeting and was angry he had to postpone once again. I wasn't looking to win a place in the popularity stakes, I knew I was sick and needed help. A bad tempered supervisor didn't even come close to a priority at that point. I left the surgery and decided I badly needed a haircut.

I was walking back to my car, the walk up the street seemed endless, my joints were beginning to ache. I made it to my car, drove to the chemist to get a prescription filled, by the time I reached home my head was beginning to throb.

I had the most excruciating, burning, throbbing pain in my lower stomach (thought it was a second part of my Crohn's disease yelling at me) then I got so cold I was shaking uncontrollably. I had taken a mild pain relief when the ache in my joints had moved into full swing, decided the best course of action was to go to bed, turn my electric blanket on high in order to get warmth back into my freezing body. I made it to bed, by this time I was in considerable pain, from the daddy of all headaches as well as the pain in my joints and lower stomach. My intuition was telling me to call for an ambulance but I managed to ignore that instruction – a move I was probably to regret.

I woke about an hour or so later; don't remember much about that night at all.

For the next nine days I drifted in and out of existence, I alternated between waking absolutely soaked, pillow saturated, bed clothes soaked, hair dripping wet to feel a little better must be on the mend. I would drag me out of bed to eat on the 'feel a little better' occasions, remember to take medication, only to go down again in a screaming heap a couple of hours later.

The headache continued through all of this time, my temperature so high I seriously thought my brain and eyes would melt (or fry). The constant heat was unbearable.

When the pain started, at first I thought I had maybe pulled a muscle in my back from lying down so much. I couldn't get off the lounge. I stayed horizontal until Laura arrived home from school. I explained I was stuck, that I couldn't move due to severe pain – "Show me" she said, Laura tried in vain to help me reach sitting position, I screamed so much we had to stop. Laura brought the telephone into me, I phoned the chiropractor to see if they had a solution – apply ice and phone back in 20 minutes. Yes the frozen carrots helped – well at least until I tried to move then oooooooooooh no go anywhere. Chiropractor suggested I phone the doctor after I screamed involuntary in her ear a few times due to the continuing pain.

I phoned the doctor – he suggested – still probably a virus, take panadol every 3 hours and rest.

My girlfriend had been coming in before work, lunch times and after work, she tried to get me up on occasions only to have her ears pierced with the screaming which by now was only too familiar.

Vomiting and diarrhoea set in just for added effect. Try vomiting when pain across the back is at an all time premium and the toilet bowl appears to have receded into the floor about one metre. I never realized before how low this much 'taken for granted' item is.

I really thought I was either having a baby which was determined to come out through my lungs (felt like contractions at times). Spasm, contraction – either way it was high octane pain. The other option was a thumping great footballer with sharp spikes on his boots kicking me full bore in both lungs at the same time, one boot for each side. Yes the pain was that bad, it sure superseded any previous ideas of pain that was stored in my memory bank.

Laura wanted to go to school on the Friday but was worried about how I would cope, I explained that my biggest problem was getting to the toilet, *rolling might be my best option, I wasn't going too well on the walking scale. I said hey maybe I could use Syd's kitty litter, that's it - do me a kitty litter tray and I'll be ok, with that she went off to school laughing and my girlfriend stayed home to look after me.*

Saturday night (day six) doctor called, me in bed, couldn't do anything, headache still so bad, body either super hot or super cold. Could be pancreatitis he said, not likely, but possible, blood tests taken as a precaution.

Wednesday (day ten) by 3pm I knew I was in trouble - I had vomited until there was absolutely no food left in my body to dispose of, whatever was coming up after that wasn't pleasant, diarrhoea wouldn't let up - I was still screaming with the pain in my back, accompanied by the pain which the diarrhoea caused. It felt like I had a dozen bulldozers in my intestines all scraping away with spikes on their wheels - I have never known pain like this and I don't want to again. My temperature had risen to 40 and was on the up and up.

My eyelids were blood red and to top it off my knees/legs wouldn't work, when I bent my knees it was so painful to try to straighten them.

I phoned my doctor to say I was really in trouble - he told me he would call in after work.

Yes he called in, at 10pm at night, by this time I was beside myself, my fried brain just wanting some form of relief, I couldn't and wouldn't take any more panadol type medication as I kept vomiting those up also, if he had suggested one more panadol he might have been told where to put it and it wouldn't have been pleasant.

I was so grateful my very dedicated GP made home visits; there was no way during those ten days I would have been able to make it to him. Thank you so very much.

Earlier in the night the wall in my bedroom had been getting further and further away - I was leaving my body - walls were no boundary I discovered as I rose higher. Then commonsense - hang on "I have a daughter and two books to write, I can't leave yet", then I had second thoughts. "Do you have a pain free thresh-hold up there" I asked, with that I was gently slid back into my body (I was only asking). The idea of a pain free environment did appeal to me at that point. Seems negotiation isn't one of the pre- requisites for entry

- I was back. This was the second time I had to say I wasn't ready to leave but the first time I had started to leave my body behind.

At one stage I saw mum coming toward me, I tried to sit up slightly to see if she had dad with her but I couldn't see properly, mum is still alive, why would she be sent to collect me - was dad there? I wish I had had a clearer view.

I still wonder what I had to learn from this experience, I guess it certainly confirmed to me that we go 'somewhere' after death. I discovered walls are definitely no barrier to the after-life otherwise my head ache would have been way, way worse than it was already. I learned that we are met by our relatives or people we know. But why did I need to learn this information? That was the question uppermost on my mind.

My girlfriend later explained that half the time she had no idea what I was saying to her - if the above is anything to go by maybe it was just as well.

I felt guilty for the times I said to her, just let me die I have had enough. I asked her to pack me a bag for hospital as I had had enough, I couldn't take any more and I couldn't look after me. She had taken days off work to look after me, on the odd occasions I could eat she would buy grilled fish or whatever I felt I could eat at the time. What would we do without friends?

She sat by the bed and put small pieces of ice in my mouth when I couldn't move my arms because of the severity of my head-ache or from the pain in my back, provide cold lemonade when the uncontrollable shaking occurred (true, I craved iced lemonade). Changed my soaked bed linen if she was on hand at the right time otherwise I crawled back into a wet bed if home alone. I really believe I would have died if it had not been for her - my throat would dry within seconds of the ice melting. No wonder I wanted out - who could blame me.

I had had bruises coming out on my legs since the previous Friday, by now they were on my arms as well; it was beginning to look like I had been bashed. My face was swelling - I should have had a before and after photo. It wasn't pretty.

Syd (our family cat/person) was beside himself by now, crying loudly and scratching at my bed, he had been meowing loudly while I was in pain earlier in the week but somehow even he too knew I was getting worse.

Examined once again, I asked if I could be put into hospital, I explained that I couldn't take any more pain. My GP phoned the Emergency Hospitals - rejected by the first I then headed for the second hoping and praying the bed would still be available when I arrived.

I was questioned, examined and blood tested. Drip inserted and put on fast mode, pain killers administered and off I went into pixie land. I have never had a more welcome present as the intravenous drip which was painfully attached to my right hand. From that moment on I knew I was in good hands and hopefully on the slow road to recovery. The doctor in emergency phoned and left a message for my physician to alert him to the fact he had one of his patients in emergency. I sure have this lifelong habit of inconveniencing any normal doctor assigned to me, unintentional of course.

The ward sister (or whoever) wasn't overly impressed about having an uninvited guest turn up at midnight, can't say I blame her but hey I wasn't going anywhere, no one was going to get rid of me, I would have hung on to that hospital bed for all I was worth, it took me ten horrific days of pain to make it to this particular bed and I sure wasn't leaving. It would have taken an extremely brave person to evict me.

Next day I felt like I had been hit by the proverbial truck. I even got to drink 500mls of liquid chalk - 250ml now in one sitting - 250mls in two other sittings at half hour intervals - seems I had a CT scan coming up - all I wanted to do was sleep.

CT scan was a laugh a minute - they really weren't having a good day in that department. Firstly I nearly choked when I was placed on the table for the scan (I had been given a child's size hospital gown so when they told me to lie down I almost choked it was so tight). That problem solved, pictures taken, then my sheet got stuck in the bed so I wasn't going anywhere until that technical hitch was sorted, same cheeky sheet then got jammed in the wheel of the wheel chair - one of the nurses dropped something with an almighty metal clang - laughter then erupted from all - could anything else go wrong? It was all treated with fun and in a light hearted manner. I was supposed to have some type of dye inserted for another scan but due to my environmental illness they decided to cancel and err on the side of caution.

This was the first hospital I had ever been in which took my environmental illness seriously - if I go back to hospital I vote for that one - the staff were totally fantastic, caring, all staff on the ward were fully briefed re patient problems, I was quite impressed.

Late that night I had to be changed from my child's gown into an evening gown (well at least that's what I called it) I woke soaked again, clean pillow case and I was ready for a nap from the exhaustion of it all. Next morning when the nurse came to help me shower she remarked that I now had a long gown on - I replied of course, this is my evening gown! The hospital gowns were useful when one is attached to a machine, all the better to extract you my dear! Reminds me of Little Red Riding Hood.

The verdict, it really was good news week, first it was - no it isn't pancreatitis, then a blood test confirmed it definitely was, CT scan confirmed presence of gall stones, oh yes, and my liver wasn't functioning properly, potassium levels also way too low. Crohn's disease also out of control, my poor doctor probably didn't know where to start first. Looking into his face, I felt so sorry for him, who needed a patient like me. He looked so concerned. Thanks for being the wonderful person you are.

He was wonderful, first couple of days visiting me twice a day to ensure I was making at least some progress. More blood tests, wasn't allowed to eat for the first 18 or so hours, mind you I didn't feel much like having a banquet, the soup at dinner time tasted terrific I must add.

So there it was, definitely no meat allowed, light meals only and lots of pain free sleep. It seems the likely culprit was my recently changed medication; I had been taking different medication for my Crohn's disease for two weeks prior to the onset of the symptoms. I must have been able to rate a tick in every box on the 'if you experience any of these symptoms consult your doctor immediately' column. Could only happen to me eh?

Didn't even occur to me at the time that my new medication could be the cause, though given how fast I react to 'anything' I may have suspected had I not been so ill. Pain seems to take away rational and was replaced with survive at all costs second by second.

I Make Mark

On the Friday my physician decided to give me a day of rest (no more tests until Saturday) - well it was Good Friday - then the nurse arrived with a little green basin - hmmm now what could that be for? Stool test required – see, it just kept getting better and better?

Meanwhile I would have a shower then fall exhausted back into bed, exercise over for the day, back to being like a little vegetable who was too tired to open my eyes or move a muscle. The nursing staff told me they love patients like me, no trouble whatsoever. I was way too sick to cause them any grief, even slight movement would leave me so exhausted, I slept most of the time.

I managed to collect an abusive next door neighbour - well abusive to his poor wife anyway. I could clearly overhear two phone calls, poor woman then visited him at dinner time. Dinner tray hit the floor or wall with a metal thud and echo. My heart rate now at an all time high wondering what was coming next and fearing for her safety.

Nursing staff too scared to enter his room but also knowing they had to - security called and waiting outside for good measure. He seemed to calm down. He went out for a time once his wife left the scene, he went past my door in such a rush I had a mild allergic reaction – "Hmm" I thought "No prizes for guessing what he had just been up to and I bet it wasn't tobacco he had been smoking". Thump as his fist or foot hit the wall, ok now this wasn't how I expected or needed hospital to be.

By 10pm my fists were clenched tight and I had been taken on a journey back through time - Fabian in his bedroom punching or kicking the bedroom walls when the voices would take over. (He would be happy enough, then it would be time for bed, he would be in his bedroom for minutes when I would hear "fuck off" and he would punch or kick the walls in frustration. On occasions he came thundering out of his bedroom at lightning speed as if his butt was on fire….I would look at him and ask if he was ok, course I am was the usual reply, he would then fall asleep in front of the television. I would find him in this position in the wee hours of the morning, give the bean bag a kick and send him to bed. What I didn't know was how much worse the voices became when all was quiet.

Holes in the bedroom wall, from his fist, his foot, the door handle and even a set of weights. I concluded it doesn't pay to try a weight lifting exercise in a drug induced state; it does create a rather large hole when a weight travels across the room solo.

The dent in my hospital wall now larger than life – it was as if it were years ago, I felt like I had been sucked back to the past as I lie there waiting for the next thud. I knew the risks with Fabian and schizophrenia; I knew it was those closest to them that were often the target of their aggression. Night after night I would lie in bed with clenched fists, wondering if the voices would be able to talk him into losing total control. No, this was too much, I needed sleep, I didn't want to be reliving the past, crying I went to the nurse's station to request a sleeping tablet and explained through sobs why I was so upset. Less than an hour later I fell asleep. By morning the world seemed peaceful once again.

Hospital had its ups as well as downs, apart from being 'good news week'. I would be out for my twice daily constitutional doing laps of the ward, I almost always encountered one elderly gentleman to whom I would say hi and an elderly lady both using walking frames.

I had to stick close by the hand rails as I kept losing my balance, I had to give way to these two in their walking frames, now that did amuse my warped mind, me thirty years younger and having to give way because they were faster and more competent with their walking skills.

At night time once the visitors had cleared and the coast was clear, my little man was out walking, when he first started off he would have to hold the hand rail as well as the walking frame, a bit later he would be motoring in his frame, this night I was lying on my bed reading and he was off at a pace with a walking stick, tapping his way down the full length. Next thing I hear is "Howim I doin?" to a nurse at the other end of the hallway. Reply echoed "Oh you are a machine", I was in hysterics by this time; I laughed so much my stomach hurt.

My mate was eighty two he told me earlier in the week; he had called in that morning to say Happy Easter and God Bless. That night as he went past he saw my now swollen, burning, tingling feet uncovered and suggested I cover them so I didn't get cold, he was worried about me. Bless his heart. He had been in hospital for 90 days and had another thirty to go he explained on one occasion, I hope he too is now recovering - I told him I wanted and expected an invitation to his 90th birthday.

So I guess the moral of the story - make the most of life regardless of where or how you are, even in his state of health he was caring, loving and retained his sense of humour and did not dwell on his illness nor complain about how many days he had to remain in hospital. He was certainly living proof that it is not the getting from A to B that counts but the journey itself. He was content with what life had dished out to him, unfair as it seemed and he was making the best of a bad situation. He was an inspiration to all of us.

He would tell anyone who would listen that I was a lovely lady, one night the nurse replied - and how would you know you are only supposed to be walking past - he replied "I know".

I have learnt one thing, it sure doesn't pay to cross your pancreas, treat it with care and respect because when it gets angry, it gets real mean.

Remember I stated earlier if we listen to our bodies they will tell us what we need to eat. Whilst I was seriously ill at home I would be shown a picture of a huge bunch of fresh parsley (in my mind), like someone was waving the parsley in front of my eyes. As sick as I was I would have to get out of bed and cook and omelet with heaps of fresh parsley, it wasn't an option, it was mandatory. Intuition was telling me what my body required.

When I came out of hospital I craved liquorice and brazil nuts, not normally a fan of brazil nuts, can usually only eat liquorice in small quantities. Here I was having my quota of both each day – it was a must. Not just any liquorice I might add, it had to be the real stuff or as close to it as I could get.

At one stage with Crohn's disease in full flight I sighted cashew nuts in a store, don't normally like cashew nuts they make me feel nauseous, but this day I had to have them. I looked at the cost and decided no, $6 was a little too much and I kept walking. Wrong decision obviously, before I knew it I was back at that same spot collecting a packet. My body wanted them whether I could afford them or not, I have long since realized it is no use fighting, I may as well give up and go with the flow, my body knows what it needs and doesn't let up until I succumb and eat. When I no longer need the nutrients/vitamins from that product, I no longer crave that item; it is as simple as that.

There are times when my Crohn's disease is so far out of control it isn't funny, times like this I crave two boiled eggs on toast, have to be boiled, cooked any other way will not suffice. Obviously cooking in different ways must change whatever it is my body requires from the egg. And yes, it has to be two. Potatoes - boiled, bananas and white bread are mandatory when my CD is screaming at me. Like I said, I have learned not to argue, it is a lost cause, my body doesn't give up until it gets what it wants. Bossy little structure it is.

Recently I bought a 'Vitamin Bible' book, this allows me to look up the particular item and deduce what I must be lacking and why - interesting book I might add.

Intuition - I cannot stress enough how very important it is to listen to the guidance offered by our Higher Selves, our gut instinct has a knack of keeping us safe, keeping us on the right path, keeping us healthy - but and it is a big but - it will only work if we listen to it.

I have now been off work for seven weeks; I have to gain some strength before going back into hospital to have my gall bladder and offending gall stones removed. My counsellor tells me I have to learn to slow down, these stones should be a reminder, you see I don't seem to have 'go slow' in my vocabulary or my life. I knew I was getting exhausted, I knew I badly needed to rest but there didn't seem to be anyway to achieve that - my body found a way!

I now read the newspaper more slowly, read more detail in magazines, spend time admiring my recently painted lounge room, always did appreciate the native birds in my garden but even more so now. The birds had been missing for quite some time, they returned only this week, I love watching the rain on the leaves and the leaves blowing in the breeze.

At night Laura and I light two small candles (that's about all my body can cope with) we have a small lamp in one corner under two plants (the effect is beautiful). One candle light reflects the water from the small water fountain. The whole atmosphere is one of peace and tranquility. Two words which have been missing from our lives for quite a long time.

I had to go into the city last week, everyone was complaining about how cold it was; me? I loved every minute of it - the rain on my face, the cool yet revitalizing breeze or maybe that was full on wind, either way I loved it. One salesperson remarked about how bad it was - my reply "If you had been too sick to be out of bed for four weeks you too would appreciate how good that rain and wind can feel on your face. I don't mind at all it just feels so good to be out of bed, out of the house".

A visit to my specialist - "you are still real sick aren't you?" my reply "yep 'fraid so". Seems like it will be awhile before I see my desk at work. He was reluctant to put me through an operation at this stage; he didn't think my body could take it. He said "I don't think you realize just how sick you were!" My reply "I got as close to dying as I want to for awhile", he said "well you weren't quite that bad, but with a smile on his face said - but I bet it sure felt like it!" … I didn't think it prudent to tell him about my little trip out of my body… thought it best to let that one lie.

I had to drink plenty of sweet drinks, my body unable to cope without something sweet at least twice a day (no, I'm not certain as to why), need small meals often, lots of rest, no meat, eat starches, carbohydrates, seems pancreatitis is about as bad as it can get. If I don't eat every couple of hours I get the shakes so bad I go out of control, can't walk straight, drop things. Seems this pancreas cross up has caused quite some damage.

So if you are thinking alcohol will solve your problems, think again because from what I am told most pancreatitis is caused by alcohol abuse. My physician kept asking me if I was sure I didn't drink, I laughed. I could count the number of glasses of alcohol I drink in a year on one hand, so yes I was sure. I was unlucky with the change in medication contributing to my state. Others who drink heavily may not be so lucky, pancreatitis can be fatal.

I badly needed a visit with my counsellor – I needed to get through this bout then mentally prepare for the gall bladder removal. He explained how pancreatitis is way up there (in the top five illnesses as far as pain is concerned) on the 'about as bad as it gets' scale. Seems I reached the equivalent of the speed barrier with pain - it doesn't get much worse than that - phew at least I know that anything from now on will be downgraded to 'discomfort' as opposed to pain.

I needed an explanation as to why I was going through this, he explained it is the journey which is important not the getting from A to B. *"Be true to yourself and live in that moment"* - have to learn to slow down, can I achieve that after my health improves - hmmm now let me see, that could be a challenge. Three gallstones, one for each child is how it usually goes he tells me.

The worst thing is feeling so useless and totally helpless; I was too weak after coming out of hospital to even go to the supermarket, having to rely on someone for everything. That feeling is exceptionally hard when one is usually independent and in control.

So it is one day at a time, I can do small amounts of physical work but only for a short time then I have to rest. I am learning to slow down, last week I did some gardening, any other time I would have done both the front and the back all in the same day even if it almost killed me - not last week. One day I did some work in the front yard, next day the back, then had to do absolutely nothing for the next two days, I was exhausted. See, I am learning to pace myself. There is hope after all.

You wouldn't think it could be so hard to just sit and write - would you? Well it seems for me it is. Since I last wrote I have managed to get slowly physically stronger, painted my bedroom and our spare bedroom, fell from the top of a step stool, been to hospital and now back home again. If you say it quick it doesn't sound like a lot.

Where have the three months gone? Once it was March and I was at work, it is now June and I sit here wondering where on earth the time went.

April passed with a mere turn of a page on my calendar, I didn't see April at all to speak of.

My bedroom was a breeze compared to all the other rooms I had painted, so by the Saturday morning a final quick coat before taking Laura to hockey and it was finished bar the shouting.

A couple of days later I started on the back bedroom, now that was a mess, tackling that room wasn't something one did voluntarily or for fun, Laura, much to my disgust had plastered the walls years previously with posters of all shapes and size. I had tried to take some of the posters down unfortunately the plaster followed as well.

Because it was a huge task I decided not to think ahead and to take one section of wall at a time and concentrate on that and that only. In a way it was fitting, little sections is how I handle the life challenges given to me, if the whole picture appears too daunting, break it down and tackle it in small portions, or take it minute by minute, not focusing on the bigger picture until mentally it is achievable.

I have found it best to live in the moment, don't dwell on the past and don't delve into the future, if you are having a difficult time concentrate on the here and now, if you can achieve that, the future will take care of itself.

I had outdone myself this time; quite a significant difference. I finished the painting and furniture layout then decided to cover the old brown wardrobes with a white sheet with purple stars. The desired result would be a 'mystic feel', just what our 'chill' room needed.

Step stool at hand and up I went; I had managed to slide the wardrobes too close together so I was having a spot of bother trying to get the sheet between the two. Then it happened……

I had over balanced the step stool and unfortunately for me I was standing right on the very top - the stool landed first - then me. Because of my size I landed right in between the stool legs - I slotted in - my left arm didn't, so it hit the leg with a thud - my right ankle looked as if it was broken (sure felt like it). I hurt in so many places; all I could do was just sit until the pain subsided a little. I reversed my pain racked body from the stool; I felt like a bruised banana.

I managed to struggle to the kitchen and make a coffee, I needed a break. I almost spilled coffee over me as my now swollen right hand gave way under the weight of the mug; caught and saved from that one. I finished my coffee and thought if I sit here much longer I am not going to move when I try to get up and I still have Laura's room to finish before my body gives in altogether.

So on I went, Laura was swapping beds, her bedroom was a disaster to say the least, junk everywhere from where she had run out of time the night before. Getting back up the ladder to wash the windows was probably the most painful experience for that afternoon.

At lunch time my girlfriend helped me get the bed back together and by the time she left I only had to remake the bed and finish off the room. I made it to the bath just before Laura arrived home from school, by the time she and a friend walked in the door I was sitting having a coffee feeling more than a tad wrecked.

To them I could have been sitting down resting all day for all they knew.

But the final look was something else for those two rooms - they were like new, I even had a clean-out of the linen cupboard - the house had never known organization and neat to this extent - well not since I had owned it anyway.

Monday I was getting so stressed about going into hospital, my Crohn's disease had gone into full swing, my butt so sore it hurt when I walked, hurt when I sat - no winning on this one. It is times like this I resemble a rhesus monkey - yeah I know the mental image which just flashed through your mind, funny yes, but true and oh so painful. Something I hope you will never experience.

I also need to undertake a weigh in for my hospital admission form. 50.7 Kg and 149cm - BMI 22 and have the printout to prove it. Oops looks like I could stand to lose a little weight, the printout tells me my optimum BMI should be 21. Oh well put it down to cortisone eh? Well that can be my excuse this time!

Wednesday arrived. No food after 7.30am - didn't matter because hungry wasn't on my radar at all - scared definitely was.

My girlfriend took me to the hospital, we waited, we waited and we waited, just before 5pm I said - I'm turning the TV on - suppose they will come for me now. Just as predicted they did.

I am pleased to say 'my driver' had a sense of humour - boy did I need that at that point - his offsider/bed pusher also a terrific guy - they even asked me if I had a stack hat as they weren't very good drivers. "I can see that" I joke. "The paint is off the door where you have hit it before". The second guy informed me he would do the bad jokes if that was ok by me.

My surgeon came out briefly to say hi and to see if I had any questions. A last look at the clock it was 5:15pm and I was off to the operating theatre.

By the time I struggled to read the clock next it was 6:50pm - voices - obviously my surgeon issuing instructions about medication - wish I could just wake up and listen properly - listening through a fog isn't conducive to asking questions and to see what happened and how the operation went. Cortisone at midnight - why would I need that and why such a large amount? Morphine - ooh must mean I can expect a fair amount of pain then. If only I could wake up. Oh back to sleep, not because I wanted to, didn't have any say in it.

I fought with my body to wake up but it wasn't much help, fighting a losing battle, the fog persisted.

My next memory was one of being told I had to get out of bed and walk around - now that amused me - I couldn't even fully wake up let alone be let loose on my feet. Anyway what can I say - miracles do happen - I walked as well and as much as one can whilst attached to a drip machine which was attached to my bed. One small step for man but a large step for mankind - or something. Anyway I achieved what they required.

My bladder obviously wanted to be emptied, I imparted this little piece of information to the night nurse whilst she was undertaking my half hourly obs - she wasn't' impressed. What can I say? "You aren't going to throw up on me if I take you to the toilet are you" - course not I replied - well not intentionally anyway. I thought she was joking - she wasn't.

She informed me that if I had a drip pole I could take myself to the toilet - I replied well yes I could, but I haven't, so I can't, I don't know how many times I apologized - not my fault I didn't have a drip pole. Sounds like something you would see in a comedy, except I wasn't laughing, this one was for real.

My bladder although screaming to be emptied, shut up shop and didn't want to know.

She wasn't in a mood for me to be making that extra trip to the, wait for it, other side of the bed so I could wash my hands - impatience now showing. But I stuck to my guns and washed my hands as best I could.

Hard to believe I was a private patient in a private hospital. She didn't have a clue what 'service with a smile' meant, come to think of it, the words service/helpful seemed to have eluded her completely.

I managed to fall asleep on three short occasions, each time I woke I scanned the window for signs of daylight, searched under my door for signs of light, if the hall lights were back on I knew it was morning. Oh no, I needed to go to the toilet again – where is a shift change when you need one? Yes she took me to the toilet – suitably unimpressed as usual.

Breakfast arrived, I felt so stiff when I tried to move. My surgeon came in; he told me I could go home when I was ready. Both he and I both thinking it would be late afternoon by the time I made a shuffled exit. I didn't ask any intelligent questions – wasn't feeling very intelligent at that point after having surgery, not a lot of sleep and a bladder intent on causing complications. Cortisone 50mg at midnight hadn't done a lot for me either, I couldn't work out why my face felt funny, when I finally looked in the mirror it was no wonder – my poor face was so swollen. I had the dreaded blowfish effect happening.

Enter next nurse – if I thought the night nurse was bad I hadn't seen anything yet!

She said the surgeon said you can go home – yes I replied but I can go home this afternoon can't I? No, you have to be out by 10am. Shock now set in. No way could I get this body out of bed, showered, dressed, packed and out all within an hour – I only came out of surgery 14 hours ago, did sympathy, empathy exist on this floor? Even a small quantity would suffice. I would have settled for any amount however small.

If I wanted to stay beyond 10am I would have to sit in the sitting area until my girlfriend could collect me in the afternoon, she went on to inform me. Yeah like I felt like I could sit up for hours in a chair, I was having enough trouble lying down in bed. Getting teary now.

She removed my drip, informed me it would bleed a lot so I should probably raise my hand above my heart should that happen – great I'm thinking and how in hell am I supposed to do that while I shower, dress and pack? I can only manage so much with one hand.

After she exited my room, I tried desperately to remove my leggings, now try bending over your swollen stomach 14 hours after having four holes stitched up and you will see why I was feeling rather dejected and teary. I managed to get my left leg free of this tight legging but I just couldn't get through the pain barrier to reach my right foot. It took my bed pusher quite some time to manoeuvre the legging under my name tags; to get them out in reverse in my condition was impossible.

With a firm grasp on the back of my hospital gown I shuffled down to the nurse's station to ask some kind person to cut my name tags so I could get free of this damn legging. Nurse from hell the only person around, this time she not only cut off the name tags but also offered to remove my legging – oh how kind! That was the least she could do. By now I was crying, I am in the process of trying to make it back to my room when my guardian angel emerged from another room – I had met her prior to my operation. One look at my teary face and she said "They are making you leave aren't they? – get back to your bed and stay there, you are not going anywhere, I'll phone the doctor".

My guardian angel, I was so grateful for her and to her. I was in no condition to be forced to leave the hospital at that time and she could see that, she was the only one who cared enough to fight for me. She phoned my surgeon, he agreed I should remain where I was, he would call in later in the day.

Friday morning my physician arrived pre breakfast to check on me. Now he was a welcome sight. He walked in the room, took one look at me and said "Oh look at your face it's so swollen" – at least he noticed, no one else seemed to realize or care.

I explained I was still throwing up when I tipped up – the bemused look on his face was precious. He did explain and issued a prescription saying I would need to remain on this medication until my swelling from the cortisone subsided. So maybe now when I tip up I will no longer throw up – the technical term is reflux by the way – my backflow prevention not working – how surprising for something in my body to be not working correctly. A plumbing overhaul may have proved useful, replace a few worn pipes; if only!

I didn't feel too great about having to lodge an official complaint re my treatment but believed it was justified and it may just save some other poor soul from the same experience. Or not! I can only hope.

I know hospitals have to operate on profit and loss like any business, but surely compassion and treatment in accordance with a patient's best interest should remain a high priority. Let us not lose sight of what is important in life. I ask you to treat people as you would like them to treat you, then and only then some things might improve.

I am now safely in my own home, Laura is staying over at a friend's house for the night. It is Monday – I felt so much better when I woke this morning, no pain killers today – how about that. I have been for two walks today. Or maybe I should say waddles, either way I waddled and that was good. My knees are swollen from the cortisone; they get even larger when I walk around. In hospital my legs reminded me of little elephant legs – yes they were that size and shape. Today they have been downgraded in size – no longer qualify for elephant size. After walking/waddling for too long they sting and hurt so it is back to my rocking chair and feet up.

Right now it is almost 11pm and time I was in bed.

CHAPTER NINETEEN

Now back to your own personal guided tour of my trip down memory lane - 1995 sure was an eventful year.

December 1995 just prior to Christmas - Fabian came home with a friend and he was clutching a Bible - now there was something different but also pleasing. Well first impressions can be deceiving and this one sure was, he was about to drop a bomb shell, one I sure wasn't ready for.

Remember I said earlier, knowing what I know now I should have sat my life out in a bomb shelter, at least that way the shelter may have protected me from anything heading my way. Well the following is one of the incidents I would have loved to deflect.

He informed me through tears he was now hearing voices and he thought he had schizophrenia. Oh man!

He asked if he could phone his sister. During this call I could obviously hear only one side of the conversation, enough to put me into shock and wish I had a major hearing problem, praying I could be beamed up to another planet. I didn't like what I was hearing - it went something like this …

"…I'm hearing voices

…smoked dope for the last 12 months

…oh about 3 times a day"

I can only imagine what the questions were from his sister but the answers made it pretty clear.

I swore at him at that point, I was so disappointed, scared, frantic. Later I tried to assure him he may not have schizophrenia maybe just a reaction to the marijuana he was smoking, if he stopped maybe the voices would stop also.

What a welcome to Christmas, if I thought Christmas hadn't been the same since my daughter left, that Christmas was certainly one for the record book, hopeful? Yes; Happy? Definitely not!

He began to attend the Church meetings with is friend. It didn't last.

He wanted the local doctor to give him sleeping tablets, which the doctor was reluctant to do, he did refer Fabian to a psychiatrist for further assessment.

The poem or statement of feelings Fabian wrote is inserted on the following page; his Father discovered it in his room much later after the actual writing.

Fabian was already in prison when it was unearthed amidst the mess in his room, I thought it prudent to insert at this stage so you can understand what he was dealing with. Understand how troubled he was, understand how worried I was.

When his father and I first read this poem we thought the words I MAKE MARK may have meant something sinister, like he was determined to do something 'big' in order for the world to remember him.

It was discussed with the prison hospital staff so they too were aware of its existence, aware of the I MAKE MARK, in the hope it could be headed off at the pass in case he was determined to do something bad.

Sometimes I would wish it may have been better if it had not been unearthed, I would have had less to worry about.

Ignorance is bliss; I could have lived with that thought at the time.

The psychiatrist was reluctant to diagnose Fabian with schizophrenia, he didn't want to give him a label because labels stick, I guess he wanted to be certain prior to confirming a diagnosis.

Fabian knew what he had, he had been correct. It was the rest of us who tried to hang on to any other theory other than the inevitable. Fabian had a friend whose mum had schizophrenia so he knew the symptoms only too well; he was fully conversant with the disease.

I Make Mark

Life is like a living hell, you fight one day at a time but with no success you think your on top of things but sudenly your below, you takes Suide but you take them in the hope that they work, you seek someone out there can here but are they gutless or a coward to tell the world is low. Society sux your life is nothing, looking forward to something but you dont what holding up 2 you you want the perfect body but dont have the looks or the Surety, you will be conquered but know one knows.

LIFE IS LIKE HELL
Society burns
you draw blood
but your life is nothing
Society is nothing
your the one to show the way
take control of everyone is they hear, Let them not sleep but can no one here is it in your head why cant anyone pick it up. all I want is mild sleeping tablets and I won't rest till I get.
I MAKE MARK.

Floyd

In this situation the wheels of motion turn ever so slowly, the gap between assessment, diagnosis and hence treatment were huge to say the least, during this time Fabian turned to heavier drugs and alcohol in order to cope with the voices. Unfortunately this method only exacerbates the symptoms when sober; so additional heavier drugs and more alcohol are used and required to mask the persistent voices.

I found it difficult to comprehend how a child; and that is what Fabian was, could adequately relate to this psychiatrist, a middle aged man dressed in what appeared to be a very expensive suit wearing gold jewellery. How could a child hooked on drugs relate to this image? He couldn't and didn't. Fabian became agitated at the slow progression, had he received the required treatment/medication at this early stage his life may have been different, but he didn't and it wasn't. Some things are not meant to be.

Please do not take this as criticism, the psychiatrist was exceptional in every way, he tried in vain to undertake the required course. I had trouble imagining how Fabian saw the image which to me was contradictory to everything **he** was going through. This man appeared happy, organized, family orientated, photos proof of this very ideal. Whereas Fabian's life was in total chaos in every way possible, his thoughts too disjointed to make sense of anything, all he could see was he needed sleeping tables to escape the world and to help him sleep.

I do strongly believe an assessment centre should be created, a centre where these kids are housed during the assessment, diagnosis stage and kept in residence until any required medication has been issued and monitored. Their condition stabilized prior to release. This method and this only would help so many people, people unable to help themselves; it may prevent the fast track onto the harder drugs and alcohol scenario.

I am not advocating a lock up prison type system, but a calm, friendly, caring centre with lawns, gardens, one which promotes the belief that life will improve, the fact voices can be controlled under certain circumstances. One where counselling goes hand in hand with medication, counselling which explains in full detail what is happening to them allowing them to see they are not alone, where they are with peers also suffering the same frightening voices or paranoia. A holistic centre where truth and education were paramount. A centre where HOPE was the key, displayed prominently for all to see and to strive toward. A centre where meditation, massages, kinesiology were as normal as a psychiatrist/psychologist or counsellor. My vision for the future!

Imagine how different their initial experience of schizophrenia would be if this ideal could be manifested. If only I had sufficient funds I would ensure this dream of mine could grow, if only 1 out of 10 survived the experience it would be worth it. I wouldn't feel so helpless. They say money can't buy happiness, but this is one amount of happiness I would sure like and would appreciate. Money in this case would certainly buy my happiness.

Selfish? Perhaps it is, I couldn't save my own son but maybe I could assist in saving a son or daughter belonging to another parent. I would feel as if I had made a contribution and make up for what I saw as my own failings. I would indeed feel more at peace. In this case, selfish would be good; it would be my indulgence to the world.

The reluctance by the mental health field (even today) to give 'labels' names to a particular type of mental condition is not helpful to the person concerned. I know the theory is one of being defined by who they are not be defined by an illness however there are two sides to this theory. Having been in a position where I had no idea what was wrong with me and hence no medication to assist was excruciatingly scary and frustrating. Like Fabian, whilst being given a diagnosis was admittedly scary it also came with a glimmer of hope and a major sigh of relief that it has a name….and therefore hopefully treatment. Different types of mental illness have different type of symptoms and people in general would be far better placed if they were given the benefit of knowledge. With knowledge comes understanding….it has the potential to benefit many and open up discussion on what has always been a taboo subject. Explain the characteristics and allow others the gift of understanding and hopefully acceptance will follow.

I know only too well how alone I felt when I was diagnosed with Hydatidform mole, miscarriages, Bartholins cyst, reactive airways dysfunction syndrome and Crohn's disease, I didn't know anyone with anything even close - same with the domestic violence situation. I didn't know where to turn for help and guidance when Fabian first indicated he was hearing voices.

Feeling alone can be the most frightening and daunting experience, there is alone and there is alone! That feeling can have dire consequences for some.

A centre would take away the 'alone', other people would be in a similar situation with similar experiences - alone wouldn't even have to exist. How wonderful would that be! I believe we would be half way to solving a lot of the accompanying problems.

I would have loved to visit a centre which explained any or all of the above; to me it would have been like being given a small piece of heaven. I would have been so grateful. I am not naïve enough to believe this would be an ideal scenario for everyone but I do believe it would be worthwhile.

> *Today (21 June 2004) I received news my first attempt at trying to secure funds in order to further a centre for treatment, education for people with a myriad of medical problems has failed. I entered a short story in the Women's Weekly Short Story competition. About 8,000 entries received, unfortunately my story was unsuccessful. So I now have to try another course. The successful author would be given a chance at having a book assessed for publication. This was the book I desperately wanted published in order to further my dream.*
>
> *My Dr Counsellor started a charity long ago - his dream was to have a relaxed complex where a group of practitioners with similar ideals about the value of holistic treatment and the benefits thereof*

practice together. A holistic centre where a patient would be treated as a 'whole person' not simply treated for one symptom. A centre where positive vibes prevail and those who want to receive and benefit shall. A complex where rich and poor are treated equally.

A centre where people can grown emotionally and spiritually.

What a wondrous gift to the world a centre like this would be.

Those of us in the otherwise 'reject bin' of life would certainly benefit from a complex for the complex.

A Centre which counsels families/partners as well as the patients, as many problems can be termed family diseases as they are not borne alone by one person, the behaviour of one can cause major disruptions to even the best of families.

I didn't have a plan tucked away in case this one failed so where to now I have absolutely no idea.

For a time life was getting me down, I wasn't improving as fast as I would have liked, Laura came home from school with a virus which I also managed to give a home to for a short time. My nose was continually inflamed where I had had radiation treatment for skin cancer – work wasn't going too great, I was really tired.

I knew I needed to get out of this depressed state or I would go further down hill, I had dug me into a hole and I needed to climb back out.

October 2004 five of us from work had thought about taking ballroom dancing classes, but it hadn't eventuated because work was so busy I just didn't get time to make the required phone calls.

I now decided it was time to act, so Wednesday 21 July five of us set off to the beginner's class and the social after lessons. I couldn't sleep when I got home, I was far too excited. I had forgotten how much I loved dancing. I had gone to lessons when I was 16-17 soon after leaving school. Returned to lessons about 1987 (for a short time) and had not danced since.

This particular night I learned progressive dances I hadn't previously heard of. Following the classes I then danced and to my surprise managed to execute the Palma Waltz, Quick Step, Slow Fox Trot, Cha Cha - I was overwhelmed, excited, ecstatic. Sick - who was sick, can't be me. Depressed, nah must be someone else I was on a natural high, happy to be alive.

Sleep was definitely out of the question. Twelve o'clock, one o'clock - oh how was I going to get up for work next day. Didn't matter I managed it somehow, I could have achieved anything the next day, I was on top of the world, nothing, but nothing could have spoiled that Thursday. What a buzz, depression now gone, self pity a thing of the past at the moment. I had had a wonderful time and couldn't wait for the next lesson.

I knew I had to do something to help myself before I got worse; I had even lost interest in writing my book - that wasn't like me at all. The dancing classes achieved the desired result, we have now been to two Wednesday night classes and socials and last night we attended the Latin classes - first night to learn the Jive - Yes! The Jive was the one dance we all wanted to learn but trying to learn it on a Wednesday night would have been mission impossible. Quite accidentally we had gone on exactly the right night - coincidence? Possibly not, it was meant to happen.

Since I last wrote, Sally, our dog resembling a cattle dog somehow was taken or escaped whilst I was in hospital for the second time. Two Saturday's later we heard a dog had been found dead near the highway, the description matched Sally. I guess Sally found life with me far too stressful or had she taught us all she needed to and left to go help another family?

Syd our person/cat went out one night and never came home. Why? We don't know. No reports of a cat being found, was he taken or has he gone to give someone else love they so badly required.

The pets in our home do not seem to remain with us for long, yet they teach us so much and never seem to act like animals – this will become clearer in my next book 'Beyond Description'.

Each time one pet leaves/dies another happens our way, it is as if they leave, having fulfilled their duty/lesson and make room for another. What/who will come our way next is anyone's guess; some of these people/animals find us not the other way around.

I seem to have digressed enough to last us for quite some time, so I shall revert to my initial intention.

CHAPTER TWENTY

In 1996 Fabian alternated between Bible and church and a burning desire to live on the streets. Many arguments ensued, what started off as marijuana abuse began to escalate into alcohol abuse as well.

In the very early stages of schizophrenia he firmly believed people were calling him a hunchback as he walked down the streets.

I sat with him for hours going through books and any magazine I could lay my hands on to draw the distinction between what he was like and what a hunchback looked like. I was making absolutely no progress so as a last ditch measure I took him to our local chiropractor. Chiropractor to the rescue.

Mission accomplished the hunchback theory was banished from our lives forever.

Fabian's posture was excellent, he had a straight back and carried himself well, it was the first signs of paranoia.

The following is one of the first signs of what appeared like compulsive, obsessive behavior; he would become transfixed on one idea and it was as if he just couldn't let it go regardless of what it was. He exhibited many other incidents of a similar nature; the only thing which differed is the idea or trait at that point in time.

I remember two officers from the Kingston police attending our home one evening - one very young the other more mature and much more experienced in dealing with obstreperous teenagers. The younger began to get angry with Fabian whilst the older started talking to him calmly, no raised voices. He patiently explained if he wanted to leave home and live on the streets it was his choice. He explained to him it was extremely unfair on me to place me in a position where I was forced to make him leave home.

If he wanted to leave, then leave of his own volition.

Full marks and my respect to that particular gentleman for a job well executed.

Fabian left home to live his dream on the street. The worst thing was that it was after even more arguments, I suppose that was his catalyst. I have this vague, somewhat sad recollection of him heading off one night in the pouring rain.

I alternated between a little relief from the pressure cooker situation to sadness and grief, wondering if I would ever see him again.

It would be ages and I wouldn't hear of any news or sighting of Fabian. I would pray for news so I at least knew he was alive.

Without fail in some way I would hear from 'someone' next day. Fabian had been sighted and he appeared to be in one piece. Thank you, the news was most welcome and I was always appreciative, thankful and relieved. I give love and thanks to all of those who helped in that manner. Thanks also to 'who ever' was listening from above in the Spirit World and helping me to retain my sanity. I loved my son and I needed to know he was at least alive and as safe as he could be given the circumstances.

At night I would feel guilty when I ate dinner, knowing it was possible Fabian was 'somewhere' hungry. I would feel guilty getting into a warm bed knowing he was probably cold. Life was on the miserable side to say the least.

I realize Fabian had made a choice. It was his choice. He had a right to live his life as he so chose but it was still so very difficult for me, as a parent, to accept. Guilt is a destructive emotion; I just couldn't shake it no matter how hard I tried.

As a parent I firmly believed I led the 'failed parent parade' I was way out there in front. At the time I didn't know we have our own 'Soul Purpose' and that it would not have mattered what I had done, the outcome would have been the same. Fabian was merely fulfilling his Life Path, his Soul Purpose, playing out his role in the Divine Plan.

I wish I had of known this at the time; it would have made the whole process at least bearable. I deal with things so much better if I understand the bigger picture.

It was during this time on the streets Fabian began his love affair with harder, more harmful substances. His drug and alcohol abuse accelerated.

I suppose it served the desired purpose until the effects wore off. The voices would be quiet for that period of euphoria or deep, deep sleep.

Unfortunately substance abuse exacerbates the symptoms of schizophrenia thus more and more alcohol and drugs are required to achieve the same result. Catch 22 situation at its very worst.

Survival on the streets is dependent upon handouts from charity organizations, accommodation shelters for the homeless and worst of all stealing.

During this period Fabian's mental state deteriorated rapidly, he began to get in more and more trouble with the police.

Most of the offences consisted of stealing (mostly minor items), disturbing the peace (I suspect drunk and/or fighting). Injury to property and unlawful possession.

Certainly not a long list (longer than I would have liked), but not a career you wish your son to excel in.

I often refused to answer phone calls, Laura's father was akin to a one man plague, arguments always guaranteed. This particular night Fabian had tried to phone and failed due to my non compliance re phone etiquette.

Mum phoned me; Fabian had telephoned her and asked her to tell me he loved me. To say her stress levels were at a premium certainly falls into the understatement category. Mum firmly believed Fabian was about to commit suicide. Not that he had said as much just the way he spoke and the message for me. He asked her to tell me he loved me.

I phoned his father, asked if he would come to the city with me to look for him. Well that was a waste of time, his reply - "What is the use, probably won't find him anyway", there was more but I am unable to recall the exact words only the fact that he wasn't interested.

I telephoned my girlfriend, asked if she would look after Laura for me whilst I went in search of Fabian. As is typical of her, no way was she allowing me to undertake this mission at night, in the city alone. She would come too.

So off we set; all three of us.

I got out of the car at the Mall in the Hobart CBD, my girlfriend and Laura would drive around the block either in the hope of locating Fabian or waiting to collect me. I set off determined to locate him and woe betide anyone who stood in my way, I was on a *Mum Mission*. Any mum on a mission will understand how I was feeling at that particular moment.

I saw Fabian; he saw me and started to run. My first reaction was one of - well if he doesn't want to speak to me, let him go, then determination set in, no blow him, he can listen whether he wants to or not. I wasn't prepared to let him die if I had a say in it, he meant too much for me to stand back and not at least try. I wasn't his father, I was his mother. I remembered that New Years Eve following his birth when he and I were in hospital together, I remembered my promise to him. I wasn't ready to give up.

I waited for him to reach the corner, then I took off at break neck speed, I needed to round the corner before he had time to escape completely. If I could keep him in my sights I had a fighting chance. Working hard has its advantages; I was still fit and agile.

He had crossed over the street, I could see him heading towards three boys of similar age, I thought one of them was about to fight him, now in full flight I ran across the street, narrowly missed being hit by a car (that was two of my lives used up, best not try for a third). No one was going to bash MY son, what I thought I was going to do was beyond me, didn't even think that far. Just knew it wasn't going to happen.

I caught up with all four, one of the boys said "Are you Fabian's mother? Fabian is this your mother? Did you think I was going to bash him? Did you come to save him?" I replied yes, yes and yes. God love you he said. He couldn't believe I was willing to try to protect him when I thought he was going to get hurt. In this kid's eyes I was something else.

Fabian was beside himself, he desperately wanted drugs, he couldn't stop pacing, I don't remember our conversation, he wanted money, I wouldn't give him money for drugs, I never did knowingly and I never would. He took off again and crossed the street.

Once again out of nowhere came these three young guys. One of the boys asked if I came to get Fabian off the street. I replied yes, he asked me to wait for him where I was standing and he would talk to Fabian.

So, with me standing in the Mall, Fabian around the corner whilst this beautiful soul alternated between the two of us, acting as an arbitrator on our behalf.

He informed me some kids are meant to be on the street, some are not, Fabian in his opinion, was in the 'some are not category' and he should be home with me.

He brought the two of us together, said Fabian hug your mum, be nice to her, she came to look for you, my mum never came looking for me. Your mum is alright you be nice to her.

He said "Fabian is due in court tomorrow, I'll take him home with me tonight, he will go to court then come back home to you tomorrow night - is that ok?". I replied "Yes that would be terrific", he asked if I had a car to drive them home to his flat.

Seems Fabian had gone to the Derwent bridge to jump off, when he got there he came back, don't think he even knew why.

Fabian's friend was the same age as my daughter (about twenty two), had been on the street since the age of twelve, bashed by his step father he sought refuge on the streets. He said "What chance did I have without an education; I either use drugs or sell them"?

On the way to his flat, he informed Fabian that if he mucked up with me he wouldn't have to worry about fucking killing himself he would do it for him. He said your mum is alright, she came looking for you, my mum never came looking for me, if she came looking for me tomorrow I would go home.

My heart went out to him that very night, he sounded so sad, if it wasn't for him goodness only knows what would have happened to Fabian that night.

He kept swearing, every time he did, he apologized to Laura saying "Sorry little lady". When we got to his flat, he wanted me to come inside and have a look. He proudly showed me his stereo system - he said "I bought this myself, ok I sold drugs but I bought it, it wasn't stolen" He informed me he didn't sell hard drugs. Hmm…….one can only wonder on that one.

Whilst he was ushering me inside the flat he was so obviously proud of, he was busy hiding his bongs at the same time. He kept telling me "God love you", he gave me a hug with tears in his eyes. He said to Fabian "if you ever tell anyone I was crying I will fucking kill you alright, now give your mother a hug and tell her you love her. If you muck up with her you will answer to me".

I informed him if he ever wanted a mother I would be it, he would be welcome anytime. He had my respect and love for life.

How could anyone so young, so mistreated, be loving, kind, generous and so very willing to help another kid get off the streets? Especially when it was obvious he so desperately wanted his mum to come looking for him.

He wasn't resentful toward Fabian as some may have been; he wanted the best for Fabian. He wanted for Fabian what he couldn't have for himself. I have never seen anything or anyone quite like him before or since. I hope he has now found love and peace.

He kept looking at me with tears in his eyes and saying over and over God love you. He may not have attended church but he was certainly spiritual. The only thing that worried him that night was the thought that if Fabian told the 'others' he was crying he would look weak. He obviously liked his 'tough' image, though from where I stood he looked so small, so young and so very vulnerable. His inner strength, his spiritual strength was what made him huge and strong in my eyes.

I doubt if his mum ever knew how much pain this kid carried around inside him. If she did, would he have been still on the streets? I would like to think not.

It did make me wonder though, how many other kids did he help on the streets; maybe he was there for a purpose. So mature and wise for his young age.

True to his word, he sent Fabian home the next night; mind you he was more than a little worse for wear when he arrived.

Fabian headed straight for the shower, I don't know what he had taken but standing and balance wasn't something to take for granted, the shower door cracked when he thudded against it. Shower over; he was ready to collapse into bed.

November 1996 he was in court for stealing, from memory he stole a pair of jeans, no he didn't need them, I have no idea why he took those jeans. Maybe he was testing his expertise in this field, the test obviously failed.

He would say to me "The neighbours can hear me thinking, go and tell them", this caused him much angst. What on earth he thought I was going to tell them was beyond me but come rain or shine he wanted me to go speak to them and stop them listening.

There were occasions he became so angry because of the perceived listening, I feared for their safety should he decide to take matters into his own hands.

He told me about this kid, he had met, how he could break into cars in about three minutes, he was so impressed with this ability. He was his 'car breaking into' hero. His smile was something to behold on these occasions, his eyes would light up and his face covered with love, his friends meant a great deal to him, he was so proud of their achievements.

The fact their achievements were in the 'definitely illegal' category meant absolutely nothing to Fabian, they were achievements!

I would come home from work, if Fabian and his mates had been on marijuana there would be food spread everywhere, one day they had tried to cook mince and definitely followed up with orange juice. Juice was sprayed everywhere including ceilings, walls and spread over two rooms. The mince? Well, that was definitely inedible to everyone except those off their proverbial faces. In their state it may have appeared banquet standard. Personally it made me feel sick just looking at it.

I stood in the kitchen and burst into tears, this was getting all too much. I had been at work all day, was tired, had to cook dinner sometime during the night, mess everywhere that had to be cleaned up before I could even think of cooking the evening meal. There wasn't any spare space to cook even if I had wanted to, so the mess had to come first.

I never knew what I would come home to at night; I didn't know what peace meant. I didn't know if I would have a house or if I would find a pile of smouldering ashes.

Another time I followed a trail of soil into his bedroom, there beside his bed, a tiny marijuana plant, unfortunately for the plant it landed in the rubbish bin, never to be seen again. Judging by the trail of soil Fabian wasn't in a great state when he planted it.

He began to take small ornaments Laura had given me, she had bought them from the school stall fund raiser for only twenty cents, Fabian would hide them under his pillow or wherever he thought they were safe. I explained that they had been given to me by Laura, he wouldn't have a bar of that theory, they were his and he treated them as if they were his most prized and valuable possessions.

I picked up a plastic rubbish bin in his room one Saturday to empty the contents as I tried to clean his room; the bin was attached to the carpet. On closer inspection I realized the bin was fused to the carpet. When I asked him later what happened, his reply "Oh I put wood on the fire and the hot coals came out so I swept them up and put them in the bin". Seemed logical to Fabian, he was unable to comprehend anything other than logical. I didn't say much, think I was too shocked, or did I explode, I can't remember. The fact a second fire could have resulted escaped him totally. He certainly would have been warm enough with two fires burning!

It was sad to watch him sliding down hill, I felt so helpless, unable to do anything to stop the progression and the inevitable.

Sometimes he managed to get sleeping tablets of some kind, whilst these were a blessing in some ways (particularly for me), it was horrific in others. I knew when I found him asleep. The bottle beside the bed; my life would be peaceful for at least a few hours or for the duration of that night. The down side - sooner rather than later, the symptoms of schizophrenia would worsen because of these very tablets.

I do not understand doctors who willingly prescribe medication to these kids, it is obvious to anyone these kids suffer from substance abuse of some description, so why add to the problem? Are they afraid of retaliation, or do they prefer the $$$$$$ these kids generate as a result of their dependence? Doctors with a social conscious deficit should not be permitted to continue to practice. The kids know which doctors fit this category and frequent their practices, for the sake of what used to be about $2.60 (at the time Fabian was ill that was the cost) they obtain their short term 'fix' for that night. Pharmacists must inevitably recognize these very same kids but again no action seems to have been undertaken to prevent them obtaining medication for fictitious ailments.

I hope by now 'the system' has something in place to lessen this particular problem within the medical profession, we have come so far in so many ways, yet as a society we are failing our children, what went wrong and how do we get back to where we should be?

I read about a group called Tough Love, so I summoned up the courage to attend my very first session. Unfortunately for me the first encounter wasn't overly great, the woman to whom I spoke informed me they prefer if you phone first - well terrific but how was I supposed to know that?

We were paired up with 'like' people, as in 'like' experiences. My pair: we identified with each other, both had sons with behavioural problems, mine just had the added bonus of mental illness.

She was wonderful, I would need to talk to her and before I could pick up the phone it would ring - there would be my new pair, she always ended up making me laugh, she was like a happy medicine, we coped with our sons, laughing and crying as we explained their latest exploits in detail. Sharing makes such a difference re mental balance within oneself, how or why people choose to cope alone is beyond my comprehension.

Thank you for being the wonderful person you are and for being there to help me when I most needed you. I hope you hear of my book and come find me.

Mental illness, severe behavioural problems, substance abuse, like domestic violence are not something to be undertaken alone, help, guidance, education is required by the truck loads. It is for this reason I continue to talk about my experiences, in the hope that occasionally, just maybe, I get through to someone who is in need, even if they don't acknowledge the fact.

One night around midnight I was woken by voices coming from my kitchen, I could hear cupboard doors opening and closing, the refrigerator door was next. I got up to see what was going on - I found three youths plus Fabian, the three were progressively going through my cupboards looking for anything/something to eat. Waiting for a taxi they informed me. I hate being woken at the best of times, only one thing worse and that is being woken on a week night when I have to get up for work next day.

You guessed it, it was a week night. I stood there all of 149cm tall in my dressing gown and slippers and said "Haven't you all got somewhere you need to be LIKE HOME" All three reversed out of the kitchen and headed for the back door apologizing as they went.

Imagine that, you wouldn't think it possible would you, seems these guys back down somewhat when people stand up to them. My thanks to all three for acting in this manner, had they become violent I would have been in real trouble. Laura slept through the whole situation and I lived to fight another day

CHAPTER TWENTY ONE

Somewhere during all of this I applied unsuccessfully for my position at work, I loved my job. The process wasn't overly great or as it should be in my opinion.

Nevertheless the process was sanctioned and a male from Canberra was appointed. My boss and I had loud arguments to the point where I had to get out of the section or do something I might regret, like run him down in the car park.

I had given 1000% to this position and I was having a hard time dealing with the loss, so were the staff with whom I had been dealing, they too couldn't understand why I hadn't been successful, my boss wasn't happy so our relationship deteriorated.

My boss had had to write a reference as my supervisor, I read the reference (hmmm certainly wasn't in line with what it was supposed to be, more like a deferral than a referral). It didn't make sense to me, I worked so hard yet he was pointing out faults I had never heard about, shortcomings which to me seemed more like his faults than mine. I showed the written work to others in hope of gaining some semblance of understanding. Their shocked reply was all the same "But these are his faults, not yours". Ok, now that didn't make any sense, how were his shortcomings appearing in my reference as me viewed by him?

Dr Counsellor to the rescue once again, I needed some serious assistance in sorting this one! He explained: you present a mirror to him; people like you who speak the truth are akin to a mirror; when he looks at you he is seeing himself and his problems.

My apologies to Dr Counsellor if I have remembered this slightly differently, either way you get the gist of what I was being presented with. I was a mirror?

…but having said the above, this particular supervisor had taught me much about the area in which I had been working. If I had to choose one person to have on my side during an emergency situation…it would be him. I respected his work, his work ethic and his commitment.

I was so disillusioned I offered myself up to see if any other section would take me on as I had had more than enough to cope with and needed some definite form of peace and order in my life. I knew I could not be able to continue working in this area in a lower capacity.

Another section took me up on my offer to transfer; here was my chance to start afresh. The first day in my new section, meeting with the personnel officer, only to be told some staff in that area was a little worried about my working with them because of my work ethic. Work ethic, me? Who had worked until midnight some nights just to keep my head above water, tears now welling up with me trying desperately to will them to cease and desist, I didn't want to appear this weak and weepy. Amazing, I worked my proverbial butt off in the property section, only a few office doors away how very different the perceived view was.

I have always loved being at work so I pretty much always had a smile on my face, I would jog, walk fast and be friendly with the majority of staff and their varied requests. I had thrived working in this particular section. I couldn't understand how another area could have questioned my work ethic. I commenced early of a morning and often worked late, took work home when absolutely necessary in order to keep up with the most pressing tasks. I followed through with any problems and where possible kept my clients satisfied with the services I was required to undertake.

I settled into work in this area, my previous 15 years experience meant absolutely nothing, this work was all new to me, I was starting from scratch.

My RADS obviously exacerbated because of my stress was causing me grief on a regular basis now. That wasn't helping anything.

During this time I was summoned for my biennial mammogram - no major problems so was allowed to leave as per previous visits.

A week or so later received a phone call at work to say they had discovered something in the mammogram which required further investigation. Ok, yes panic was a word which came to mind. I went into the clinic for further tests, fine needle biopsy I believe is the term, yes it did hurt somewhat, but wasn't too bad. The worst part was the not knowing and waiting to hear the results. At the end of the few hours I was absolutely drained, plus my breast was hurting thanks to those 'fine' needles. All clear given, no major drama, can't remember exactly what the verdict was - I think calcified milk may have been the culprit. Future visits are now tinged with an ever so slight feeling of dread and the 'wonder if?' factor.

Around this time I whilst still attending Tough Love sessions, one of the counsellors suggested I may need more intensive assistance, and suggested I make an appointment to talk to the counselors at Holyoake. Holyoake as most of you are probably aware, deal with people with dependency problems, drugs, alcohol, gambling etc and also counsel families/friends of the dependent person. Substance abuse as with gambling or any addictive behaviour becomes a whole of family problem. It never merely impacts on only one person. It is an illness which not only wears the user down but has a deep, draining effect on all family members, to the point where they can become ill themselves from the associated stress. You can't always help the person affected but you can take steps to help yourself to learn how to deal with certain behaviours and expectations.

1997 wasn't a good year for more reasons than one. Mind you I am still trying to locate a 'good' year and still hoping one will show up in the near future.

One day at work I began to feel extremely sick, it was close to lunch time so thought the best course of action would be to take an early lunch hour. I needed to escape 'whatever' had just bypassed the filters of the air conditioning system and was now threatening to cause an allergic reaction. I thought it best to leave whilst I still had the ability. My RADS was alive and doing well, I was reacting alright.

A longer than normal lunch sitting in the fresh air at Kingston Beach, came back into the building, thought to myself the 'whatever' should have now cleared by now. Not so, ten metres into the building and I had the worst allergic reaction I can remember - the onsite doctors were called, unfortunately that process seemed to take longer than normal. The world was going black. Where is oxygen when you need it?

A different doctor attended this time, I was lying on the examining table in the surgery and he says "This is it, I've had enough, you will never set foot in this building again". I'm lying there thinking he has had enough, could swear this is his first time, me? Well I was sort of used to it. I had had eighteen months of very minor to no reactions and now I was back to square one. Whatever had come into the air conditioning had caused some serious damage to my immune and detoxification system.

Turns out a temporary staff member in the mechanical work shop had spilled some paint (of the heavy duty variety) then used some type of thinners to clean it up. He was using a paint spray gun and hadn't put it together properly. The mixture of the two hit the air conditioning and well the rest was history. A vehicle was being prepped for Antarctica so the paint was extremely durable and toxic.

Two hours after this event, my vitals stabilized I was driven home. Not allowed back at work eh! So now what was going to happen?

I was still attending Holyoake sessions, this particular day I managed to reverse my car into a tree. Where did the tree come from? I was leaving Holyoake and took a wrong turn. I have no idea how and why I drove in the opposite direction, it wasn't as if the building had suddenly relocated. Seems the problem must have been in my brain maybe I needed a GPS. Realizing I was heading in the wrong direction, I reversed so I could turn in the direction I should have been going in the first instance. Where did that damn tree come from? I'm sure it wasn't there previously. Too late … crunch.

I can't remember whether or not I examined the damage, think I was too embarrassed at the time. The rest is a blur considering what happened next.

The news was on the car radio - a guy had been stabbed in the city that morning, it was beside an ATM - they supposed robbery was the motive. However, my brain and body were on a totally different thought process. I felt like I had been punched in the solar plexus all the wind went out of me. The feeling and pain couldn't have been worse if I had of been punched, the result was the same, except instead of angry I felt sad and sick. Add a dash of panic to that emotion and you may come close to understanding what was happening to me.

I knew it was Fabian, and I'm trying in vain to talk myself out of it, tell me how stupid I was. The news reader had said the guy got in a car and drove off. Fabian didn't have a car, probably couldn't even drive as far as I knew. I must be mad for thinking it could be Fabian, still I couldn't shake the feeling of dread that had overtaken my whole being.

Intuition is not only for good news I discovered, it covered bad news really well, right down to the emotional effect!

Fabian had been living with my mother at the time, so I had no idea where he was or with whom. I had had enough of his drug problem and had told him if he continued to take drugs he had to live elsewhere. (Tough love theory at play here). Elsewhere was with my mother, not my choice, I didn't want her to take him. Fabian and I had had argument after argument about mum, he couldn't see that his behaviour had turned her against him; he believed I had turned her against him. Against my better judgment mum agreed he could live with her then resented me for that decision… I felt like I couldn't win no matter what I did. Everything told me I needed to take a strong stance re the drug use in order to help him but it seemed that decision only created 'other' problems.

The rest of the day - well I have no idea what I was thinking. Confirmation came in the form of a phone call from my daughter about 5:30pm.

I think it was she who phoned to say they thought they had best tell me before I heard it on the news that night. My intuition had been correct. Oh geez.

Panic set in, unprovoked attack they called it. How? Why? Didn't make any sense. Nothing made sense anymore.

Someone called the doctor for me, I can't remember who was with me that night, the doctor came, I was shaking from end to end and back again. He gave me a sedative to calm me down and help me sleep. I can't remember where Fabian was that night, remand maybe, still being questioned, I had no idea. I may have known at the time but that has been stored somewhere along with a whole range of memories, stored deep in my brain, maybe one day it will emerge. Maybe after I employ that archivist to catalogue what she finds and install a contents page, maybe but maybe I might be ok again and remember things like normal people.

A couple of evenings later, I turned to tell Laura it was time for bed, she started to walk away. I turned off the television, turned to walk to the light switch and by this time she was folded up under a pot plant in the lounge room. Very neatly folded I might add.

I went over to her thinking she was playing with me. She was lights out folks. Then she began to shake and gradually come out of it, I suppose it was akin to an epileptic fit; at least that is what it reminded me of.

Father and doctor called. He was terrific, doctor that is. He made Laura undertake a series of tests to confirm she was totally coherent. He wanted to admit her to hospital but given the circumstances thought it best to leave her at home if at all possible. But tests would have to be carried out to try to determine the cause.

Oh my, what else could go wrong? Within the space of a week, I had potentially lost my job, Fabian had stabbed some guy and Laura went into an unconscious state. I felt like I had a target painted on me. The only unknown was which direction was the next missile coming from? Honestly, that is how I felt, like one huge target. Would the next missile take me out? Could I take anymore, at that point I didn't think so. Hey I could have undertaken advertisements for Target and made some money in the process!

Friends to the rescue! Funny but when the going gets tough that's when you really discover who your close friends are, people I used to talk to, be friendly to, but never classed as a close friend came to my rescue. This has been repeated time after time in my life. The ones you think you can lean on go AWOL; other acquaintances come to the fore and provide solutions.

A lady from work phoned me at home; she had heard my plight and wanted to let me know of a support group who may be able to assist. The group - a chemical trauma alliance - a group consisting of people like myself, innocent people who had been unfortunate to take onboard one dose of chemicals too many and whose life had taken on new challenges. Thanks you for taking the time to think of me.

The Chemical Trauma Alliance Group referred me to a GP who was experienced in dealing with people who were unable to tolerate their surroundings. So it was vitamin C and B injections, any vitamin I was lacking, acupuncture and lo and behold I was able to do about fifteen minutes of gardening. That was a bonus at long last!

This little episode guaranteed me nine months off work on compensation leave. I fought the "You are not stepping foot in the door again", I wanted to work, I needed to work. Not only did I have children to support and a mortgage to pay, I needed it for my sanity.

My new holistic GP asked the my work place to give me nine months; she firmly believed that following this period of intensive treatment I would be able to undertake my normal duties and return to work. I know they did not want me back at work but that was their problem not mine, they were of the mind that my severe allergic reactions put too much stress on the other staff. I felt sure that if I could cope with them, surely other people could to, it was a learning experience for all of us.

The major lesson 'do not use toxic chemicals' find alternatives, if toxic must be used then every precaution should be taken to ensure staff are not subjected unnecessarily. Lessen the amount of perfume/after shave worn, do not smoke in doorways, do not vent toxins to a location where they may be carried by a breeze to any nearby air intake. Minimise the risk factor, it should not be that difficult.

The above seemed the logical solution as far as I was concerned; it didn't seem a lot to ask. My attitude had always been "I am merely the early warning system; I get so ill I have to leave the building but other staff are still sitting in their seats inhaling whatever substance had just ensured my eviction from the building". I knew sooner or later they would have minor symptoms which would go unheeded by management. The symptoms may have been anything from a minor headache, slight brain fog to unexplained fatigue.

During this nine months I had to have my amalgam fillings removed from my teeth, a small fight with compensation ended with a letter from me saying "I am unsure as to your intentions but my intention is to return to work, in order for that to occur I need to lessen the total allergen load on my body". They agreed to the treatment.

It took two visits to a particular dentist who specialized in removal of amalgam (without it entering the body any further than it had already) for me to be free of this toxin. At the beginning of the process he tested each of my fillings with some type of meter, the majority of my fillings were leaching mercury. Following the second visit, I had three days of unbelievable withdrawal symptoms, seemed my body had become used to its daily dose of mercury poison and was getting cranky without it. The symptoms must have been similar to withdrawal from any major drug, can't say I expected that. It wasn't pleasant, like having severe flu like symptoms, every part of me ached, I drifted in and out of consciousness during that period before I finally emerged and felt so much healthier.

Dr B was the recommended dentist. Dr B was suggested by my holistic practitioner so he came highly recommended and I knew I could trust him to take good care of me. Visits to other dentists who had not taken my environmental disease seriously had not gone well, I always left feeling drained and stressed as I knew they were failing to monitor me for symptoms suggesting I was in allergic reaction mode. Bit difficult to tell a dentist that one is having an allergic reaction when one's mouth is full of implements. Dr B had treated my holistic GP who was also highly allergic to the world so I knew I was in safe and competent hands.

The days I visited the practice Dr B would arrange for a different disinfectant to be used for cleaning of the surgery, he would refrain from wearing after shave; latex free gloves would be worn. Wouldn't want too many patients like me if you were a dentist I bet? Dr B realized that the wearing of after shave was probably not in the best interests of his patients and applied that philosophy as a general rule after his experience with me. Have to admire a professional who is willing to see the bigger picture in the interests of keeping his clients happier and healthier. Every little gesture helps those of us who are sensitive to our surroundings. Thanks Dr B for being not only talented in the dental field but also for your ability to think outside the square and be prepared to act accordingly.

Coming out of the three day withdrawal period was akin to being kept in the dark for an extended period and then walking from the dark into the light. I felt as light as a feather, it was an amazing feeling. I felt human again.

Following this treatment, injections and other holistic treatment continuing I began daily walks, gradually the walks became longer and faster, my strength and health were returning. My sanity was still in question given all that was happening.

My holistic treatment consisted of regular vitamin B and C injections, B6 and B12 as my body seemed unable to retain any of them. Acupuncture and any other vitamin or mineral my body proved to be deficient of. I would be tested each visit to determine what I was lacking at that particular point in time.

Vitamins had to be of the very highest quality, vitamins made with natural products were all that my body could tolerate. Synthetic was definitely out.

I don't know how many Holyoake sessions I cried my way through, quite a few I must admit. On the first visit to the counsellor as opposed to a group session, I explained that I had had two failed marriages, lost a job which meant the world to me, had gained two serious diseases, the icing on the cake - not permitted back at my work place, Fabian's antics and Laura's subsequent unexplained illness.

The wonderful lady explained that I had had lots of losses in my life and I needed to grieve for each of them. I hadn't grieved. I had put my head down and got on with my life as best I could. I wasn't about to heal until I allowed myself to grieve.

I hadn't thought about any of the above learning experiences as individual losses nor the fact that for each major loss in our lives we need to grieve. This was all new to me. My first marriage I could deal with, my second was supposed to be my happy ever after and had failed after such a short time. I felt like a total failure. I knew I couldn't control or live with the domestic violence but that didn't make me feel any better. Society frowns on women who keep getting married and divorced. I felt like an outcast. A failed outcast!

I had given everything to the position in which I had been acting and to have that taken away was a major loss of great proportion in my mind. I had fought previously to have this position, I had been the successful candidate but the committee deemed I was unsuitable due to health concerns. At that time I had had to argue my case with the help of my doctors, now I had lost it again. My life was shattered after that, I felt totally and utterly useless. Self esteem and confidence shot to pieces. I knew I didn't perform overly well at the interview, cortisone takes a huge toll on the amount of stress one can deal with. But I also knew I performed well in the day to day tasks, of that I had no doubt. The before and after cortisone, has to be experienced to be fully appreciated. It isn't medication which should be administered without serious in-depth discussion and consideration. I felt like I had failed my children, I must have or Fabian wouldn't be in this situation. Laura? I felt like I should give up and hand her over to someone who could do a far better job at being a parent than me.

I had failed in everything I had tried. Failed in everything that meant anything to me! Was I being punished? I didn't know what to think. My friends tell me I haven't killed one proverbial China man I must have killed the whole bleedin' province. Why would one person want so many challenges in life? Perhaps I will have the answer for you in 'Beyond Description'.

Holyoake did me the world of good, as did Tough Love. Both helped me put the world into perspective, to a point anyway. I got to the stage where if I had heard one more "And how did you feel about that" I would have exploded. That is how I knew I had learned all I could from this particular brand of counseling. I needed to understand more so I could help myself.

I learned I had no more control over Fabian's addiction than I did over his schizophrenia, neither were my fault, he had choices just like each of us. His choice took him on a path of self destruction, what I didn't know at the time, it was a path for the good of many who were to follow in his footsteps.

Initial shock dealt with as best as could be expected from someone who was already a major mess. My life then managed to get ever messier - yes I know, as if it could!

Within hours of the stabbing hitting the air waves I began to receive phone calls from people, friends and acquaintances - all knew the supposed victim or I should say, knew of him. The surprise here being friends phoning were from totally different suburbs, different backgrounds, friends who had not met each other, I was the common denominator, yet the message in each was the same. "Did you know….?"

The mess kids can get themselves into without even trying seems intangible to me, how can they not see. Easy I suppose, the only thing on their collective minds at that stage is how to get the next fix, nothing else matters. Danger appears not to rate on the proverbial radar.

Fabian was released on bail, definitely not with our consent. As far as I was concerned my mother was pressured into allowing Fabian to remain living with her. Her stress levels were rather high by this stage. I am unable to recollect from whom she received the call, but firmly believe it should not have occurred under any circumstances. For Fabian's sake and for the community he should not have been released, he should have been in a hospital for the mentally ill, it was so obvious.

The knife used in the attack had been taken by Fabian from her house, this fact weighed heavily on her mind. Since the death of my father, mum had been attending the Salvation Army on a regular basis, so this event for her was extremely taxing on many fronts.

My mother's stress levels were already high, what she didn't need was more of the same from members of her church.

Mum received taunts from other members of the church when the 'Fabian' news hit the media. She had no part in this so why should she have to put up with feeling like a leper in her own religious environment? Hypocrites I would call people who behave in that manner, they profess to be Christians until they are put to the test. True Christians would have supported my mother, not made derogatory comments at her expense. These days I consider myself a Christian, spiritual certainly, but religious - no! One does not have to attend or belong to a Church to be spiritual and all it entails.

I find the most honest, respectful people are not found in the midst of professed Christians. Please don't think I apply this philosophy to all religious people, I don't. I know from personal experience that some are just that, others 'hide' behind the term and are certainly not as they appear. The expertise lies in recognising the difference between genuine and fake.

Fabian's mental state deteriorated at an alarming rate, the reason unknown to me at that stage.

Lots of events occurred within a short space of time. Fabian was challenged by the police one evening at Blackmans Bay for riding his skate board on the road. He told them at this point he had outstanding fines

- why? Why would he have willingly volunteered this information - the only reason I could fathom - he wanted to be arrested - but again why? What was going through his tormented mind?

A short time later he was arrested for suspected assault - again with a knife as the weapon. He had apparently slashed the arm of a friend, a friend who did not at any stage see his face, only heard a laugh as the attack occurred.

Fabian was arrested and this time placed in prison. Oooooooh! What else could happen?

A month or so prior to these latest events, my girlfriend and I were sitting in her car on the Eastern Shore having coffee - we were overlooking the prison, me and my mouth! I said, "Two things I would like, one is to leave work because I have had enough and the second, I would like to see through the prison one day, don't know why, just would".

Within a few weeks of that rather innocent comment, I had been thrown out the proverbial work door and was about to undertake my very first maiden voyage to the prison. Who would have thought, made me think about what I wish for these days. I didn't realize thoughts could manifest so quickly, if only I could manifest PEACE as easily!

That very first visit to the prison was daunting and that is a total understatement. Fabian's father took me given the state of my health at the time. Some nice person had pointed out to him that I shouldn't be alone on my first visit, someone should accompany me.

At first Fabian was placed in a 'normal' yard, I heard much later it was one of those very inmates who had pointed out to the custodial officers that this kid was obviously 'not normal' and should be in the hospital. I wasn't to learn until January 2000 the reason for this: Fabian believed a kid was being picked on by a larger, older inmate. He may have been off the planet but was still looking out for the underdog. He took a swing at the larger guy in question - had to jump to reach. I think from memory he did try to impart this information to me on one visit, he chuckled as he remembered how he had to take a flying leap to reach, but at the time trying to make sense and comprehend the meanings of his words was extremely difficult.

A few visits on, a man and lady approached me - they said our son is in the same yard as Fabian, he asked us to tell you Fabian is ok he is looking out for him and so are the others; they realize he has a problem. He wanted us to let you know he is alright because he thought you might be worried. Might be worried! That was an understatement to be sure.

How very kind of that beautiful soul to worry about me and ask his parents to relay that message. Life and some people never cease to amaze me. Fabian and he had progressed through some of the court proceedings on the same days, none of us knew each other but the faces were beginning to look more than a tad familiar.

Both boys had graduated from the Magistrates to the Supreme Court together - along with a whole group of others. I would say to my girlfriend sometimes, "See they look like normal parents just like me". These things happen to them too, not just me. I guess I was trying to reassure myself I wasn't all bad, other parents were experiencing the same nightmare voyage as me.

Both boys would make simultaneous court hearings, his parents and I became friends. One day his father said, "Sit down", there wasn't a lot of room, he said "Look 'stick insect' there is enough room for you". So yes I sat. Grateful to be amongst my new found friends and amused at his description of me, can't say I had ever been compared to a stick insect before.

My girlfriend would come to court with me when she could, Fabian's dad made the odd appearance, often late; Fabian would notice him come in and wouldn't be happy. So in retrospect it may have been a good thing it was usually just me.

It was explained to me that Fabian was devoid of emotion at this stage, he was unable to feel emotion in his current mental state. Emotion such as love and caring that is, anger he certainly understood. I hope he was unable to comprehend how much 'this' state hurt me, he was so loving under normal conditions, it would have torn him apart if he knew how much I was hurting.

I suppose the other parents realized I was mostly on my own and took me under their wing, many prospective clients for State Government lodgings came with heaps of family members. So I probably stood out being solo.

On another visit the mother I met initially handed me a small teddy bear, his name was 'Courtney' his inscription read:

> This is a special little bear.
> That you can always see
> The reason he's so special
> He's made for you from me.
> Whenever you are lonely
> Or ever feeling blue
> You only have to hold this bear
> And know I think of you
> You never can not want him
> Please leave his ribbon tied
> Just hold this bear close to your heart
> He's filled with love inside.

Inside the card read:

> I've named this little fellow "Courtney" as I've been putting him together on my way to and fro. He was made to absorb the heartache only mother's feel. He took mine while I was making him and if you just hold him awhile he'll take yours.

May God Bless and help you through this, I know just how you feel.

You are most likely correct in assuming that brought tears to my eyes. Some people are truly amazing; who would have thought one could find so much love within the judicial system.

One day outside the court room, my new friends were relaying what they had heard this parent saying to his kid during a visit that week - they were quite disgusted with the father's attitude. No prizes for guessing who the kid was and who the father was? Yep correct again, only Fabian's dad could speak those particular words to a kid with schizophrenia and one who was heading for a major court appearance. They were unaware it was his dad. He had relayed that very same conversation to me previously following his visit to Fabian geez! Where does this nightmare end?

Fabian was finally transferred to the prison hospital given his mental state. First step was to enter through the main gate, front up to the main reception area; they in turn phone the hospital and to advise them to expect incoming. Yes that is the simple version of events.

Once that is achieved it is quite a walking distance to the hospital gate, a lonely walk with no one in sight, press the button, gates open then shut with a metal clang - nerves really on edge now. Another buzzer/button - entry gained into the hospital, access only allowed into the first few metres of the building then more metal bars. My nervous system never did get used to the clang of the metal gate behind me.

The visitor area was rather small, certainly not user friendly but secure, no physical contact with the inmate is possible, they are in the opposite divided portion of the room, you can hear all the other conversations that take place, so if one couple raise their voices it drowns out the conversation of others. I was shaking so hard, wanted to look positive and happy - how on earth does one achieve that given the circumstances?

Fabian is brought out, his brain is so scrambled he has six topics in one sentence, where one subject began and ended was anyone's guess.

How does such a loving kid end up in this state! I was beside myself. Seeing my child locked away in what didn't appear to be very pleasant conditions is mind numbing and soul destroying, I just wanted to die.

Was I responsible for this? You can't even imagine the amount of guilt I felt.

Visits with Fabian's dad just didn't work; he and Fabian never were and never would be on the same wave length, it just wasn't possible in this life time. As much as I appreciated his coming with me on occasions it just wasn't working.

Fabian would be allowed to phone me, he would cry and ask me to come get him and take him home, he wanted out; he didn't understand and couldn't comprehend what was happening and why I couldn't come get him. It was so hard to handle, I just wanted to go and get him, give him a hug and take him out of that dreadful place, he didn't deserve to be there, he needed psychiatric care and understanding. He needed his mum.

On that very first visit, a rather huge, burly, unfriendly custodial officer (CO) said "You can't help him so you might as well help yourself - I've seen it all before" - well gee, thanks for that wonderfully positive piece of news, and just when I was thinking my day couldn't get any worse. Don't think this guy had been blessed with an emotional gene of any kind, if he had; it was akin to quarantine waste *deep buried,* access not possible in this lifetime.

My dearest, kindest, ever so thoughtful ex-husband then pointed out "Oh yes she is doing that"! She - doing that? Yep, well my going to counselling was certainly going to help him - that made sense didn't it – oh yeah to whom? I challenge any one to make sense of that comment. The CO must have thought - boy I can see why the kid's brain is scrambled.

I wasn't in a totally terrific mental state myself after that initial visit, time to regroup and compose ready for the next exciting episode. Numb probably best describes how I felt most of the time. My life certainly wasn't boring. Stressful definitely, boring no!

Next visit flying solo. Courage in hand and off I went. As I walked the laneway to the hospital I passed an inmate in the garden. His eyes looked familiar, like I had seen them before, face not familiar just the eyes, unnerving but I didn't know why. Nah couldn't see any officers in sight, just me and him; with a quick shudder I picked up the pace and made it to the dreaded gates.

When I arrived home I phoned my girlfriend to debrief, I discussed 'those eyes' with her, saying it was his eyes, they triggered some type of memory thing but still couldn't think what. Then it dawned on me - he had killed his wife and cut her into pieces. The press had been filming him in custody on one occasion and had zoomed in on his face and those very piercing dark eyes. Those eyes had been etched in my memory.

What friend's do best is to allay their friend's fears right? Her summing up of this, "Well he does the garden so he probably looks at you as his next lot of fertilizer". Well thanks for that it was hard to face the poor man again after that and still maintain some kind of composure. I would have to stifle a giggle at times, especially when Laura piped up one day and started to espouse her very words as we passed, "Is that the man who our friend says" … And I thought I needed to talk and think fast with my first child, this one was just as bad.

After I got over the initial shock I felt more relaxed. I used to stop and have a chat with him on occasions, never did ask if that was permitted, didn't really care to be honest. He always treated me with respect and was ever so polite. One day I said to him, "Isn't it a bit cold to be out here today?" his reply, "No not really; I would prefer to be outside in the garden in the cold than inside". Can't say I could blame him for that, I understood totally.

He absolutely loved his garden, he would say to me, "You have a nice long skirt on today, just what you need on a cold day". Or discuss his latest accomplishment in the garden. Brilliant mind at one time - so what happened? To me he was someone who loved gardening and treated me with respect, he in turned gained my respect. I didn't know or care what had happened to trigger what must have been a frenzied attack, it wasn't any of my business, it wasn't up to me to judge. I could only speak for how he treated me. I certainly didn't feel threatened in any way during those encounters.

One night I received a phone call from a young girl, she was Fabian's friend. She thought I might like to know the events leading up to his arrest and why his mind had become so scrambled. It appears 'someone' had given Fabian a considerable amount of drugs, some of which would have been damaging if taken over the period of a year let alone within a few weeks. No wonder his mental state had deteriorated to such a huge extent. I was forever in her debt after being given that information, the jigsaw was beginning to come together. The courage required to make that initial phone call would have been enormous. She had no idea what type of reception she might encounter upon volunteering this information. She will forever have my eternal thanks and gratitude. It was both thoughtful and caring to allow me to share that part of her life under the circumstances.

The information gained was invaluable both from the viewpoint of my sanity and for Fabian's medical history.

Fabian had been in the prison for quite a few weeks before I finally summoned up the courage to ask to discuss his condition with someone or anyone in authority. I was immediately ushered into an inner office, through the internal gates of the prison hospital. From memory four people were in the room, one or two were psychiatrists, unsure who the other two were, psychologists perhaps? Too much has happened since. Each firing questions one after the other. Seemed they had no idea of what they were dealing with, given Fabian's brain was so scrambled.

Obvious way to solve this would have been to ask me? Isn't that what you would do? I know that would have been my preferred chosen course of action, but only in the State Government could that initiative have escaped their attention.

I outlined Fabian's condition, what had happened to trigger the psychotic episodes, events leading up to the stabbing. Gave names of the doctors to whom he had been referred for treatment and assessment.

With that information they could now make an informed decision as to what path to take next re diagnosis and treatment.

Information downloaded and it was time for me to be dismissed, I'm sure they gained far more from that conversation than I did. Considering what happened next they were as shell-shocked as I. I was shown the door with a thank you. Except wait for it, no one thought to aide my escape. I had forgotten the way I came in. So here I am wondering which way was which, with only inmates insight, where was an officer when I needed one? I was locked in the hospital and had no idea which way to go to find someone to let me out. The funny side didn't hit me until a few hours later. I do have to wonder how far I would have got if I had taken off in the wrong direction. Mind you I might have got more than I bargained for!

Only *I* could get accidentally locked *in* a prison hospital.

Some visits an officer would say "Stay there when I take him back and I'll get someone to come and talk to you". On these occasions either an officer or medical staff would take me to the interview room and discuss his behaviour and progress or lack thereof.

I don't know if they ever realized how much those discussions meant to me, if not, I pray they read my book and understand how much respect and love I have for each and every one of them. I truly don't know how I would have got through this without them. So please accept my thanks and eternal gratitude for showing me such kindness. It could possibly have meant they themselves could have been in trouble with the powers that be. I had no idea at the time it wasn't a 'done thing' to discuss the inmates with families. Are you now as surprised as I? I hope so, because that type of thinking cannot be permitted to continue in this day and age.

I was told not to expect too much in the form of hope for a return to the child I knew. They believed he had done too much damage to his brain - the prognosis wasn't good.

Fabian was devoted to his friends so he was traumatized just thinking about his friend being stabbed. He had always admitted to the first stabbing but had always said he did not stab this guy. He would cry and say to me "Mum the courts will know I wouldn't stab my friend won't they, they will know it isn't true, they will understand I wouldn't do that". I couldn't destroy that illusion he clung to, I tried to appear positive for him, it was the least I could do. It just about broke my heart watching him suffer and wrestle with the whole stabbing incident. If he did do it he certainly hadn't been in any state to know or to acknowledge it. Given his vehement denial and grief over the incident I firmly believe he was innocent of that one but had been 'set' up by another party who had their own agenda.

Fabian had been in prison for about three months before he became coherent, his brain slowly regaining at least a small amount of comprehension, albeit for short periods.

One day I told him I had been shopping - he flashed his beautiful smile and said "Did they recognize you?" His statement confused me somewhat. He pulled at his jumper, seemed '*that*' jumper had belonged to *that* very store in which I had been shopping - he thought the store staff would make the connection. I merely shook my head. Yes you are correct in assuming no payment had taken place for what was obviously his prized and much loved jumper.

He said to me one day "You know mum, I never stole more than I or my friends needed to survive, we never ever took more than we needed". That was at least some consolation I suppose, in his eyes at least that made what he did acceptable in part. The child who had once been so distraught over having his wallet stolen at a shopping centre, his whole Christmas shopping money at that, now trying to say to me that he only took what he needed. How views change given different circumstances. The irony wasn't lost on me, just made me yearn for that beautiful, loving small child's return and the innocence which goes hand in hand with young children. That was probably the only moment in my life when I would have liked to 'turn the clock back' and return to a happier, less stressful time.

Following recent events I was convinced I would be able to undertake acting and be quite proficient, how I kept the tears from flowing on occasions I will never know. How I kept a positive expression is beyond me. I knew I didn't have a choice; the tears had to keep until I cleared the last of the prison gates. I would have excelled at NIDA.

Armed with the medical, emotional and behavioural advice, Fabian was diagnosed with hebephrenic schizophrenia. Treatment commenced and marked improvement in his behaviour noticed.

> *"Hebephrenic schizophrenia, a condition in which the patient's emotions are disturbed and confused to the point where, for example, news of the death of a close relation is met with howls of laughter or amused indifference".*

He would go to court time after time, I would attend every court hearing I knew about, take notes, discuss with his lawyer if possible so I understood what was happening. Visit Fabian then explain over and over, repeat the over and over then repeat again. Just when I thought he had it, it was time to repeat again a few minutes later. Following such visits he then gained a little understanding of what was taking place both in and out of the court room. Draining yes, but he was entitled to understand what would happen to him, and if that's what it took then that is what I had to do. If I didn't, no one else would.

How do kids get on if they are devoid of family or friends? That thought is enough to bring tears to my eyes and wonder why life appears to be so cruel to some and so kind to others. Some breeze through life seemingly without a care, others have lives filled with trauma after trauma.

The end result of his two stabbing incidents Fabian was sentenced to prison on a Hospital Order…which meant he remained in prison until such time as he could prove he was mentally stable.

How do I cope? I believe we are here on earth to develop our souls, to master our goals, to learn lessons which will ultimately assist others and leave the world in a better state spiritually.

For years I didn't understand what was happening to me, problem after problem, I mastered one and before I knew another approached from a different angle. All totally different, all challenged my faith and strength to the fullest extent possible. Each and every time when I thought I had experienced it all, along came the next, more difficult than the last.

I didn't understand how I came out the other end on some occasions, I took mental notes of the reaction of others (the human race and its individual traits fascinates me immensely) and filed them away for future reference.

> *None of these things made total sense until this year 2004 whilst I was so very sick and unable to undertake even minor tasks. I began to read books on numerology, not only wanted to but was compelled to by a force I have learned not to argue with. Numerology I have discovered is extremely addictive and helps one to understand many things including the behaviour of others.*
>
> *I was first introduced to numerology through Dr Counsellor, but it was the first time I had been guided/pushed to purchase books and read in some detail.*
>
> *There is a connection between the time, day, month, year we arrive on planet Earth, none of it is left to chance. Astronomy, numerology – all connected and has bearing on our Life Purpose. Our name /s is extremely important as you will understand if you choose to explore numerology.*
>
> *I have learned there is no better way for us to understand ourselves, our connection to others than numerology. Understanding our children, our partners, numerology is a must read for those who believe we are here for a purpose. There is more to life than we see at a first glimpse. Look deeper. Understanding will follow.*
>
> *'Discovering the Inner Self' by Dr David A Phillips is a wonderful tool as are many other books on the subject. Personally I defer to this book frequently for answers.*
>
> *Locate your ruling number and it will explain so much about who you are: life purpose, best expression, distinctive traits, nega-*

tive tendencies to be surmounted, recommended development, most suitable vocations - this is achieved by adding birth date numbers.

The day number you were born on also holds more detail.

The astrology numerology connection - your star sign gives so much information about you: characteristic expression, negative tendencies to be surmounted, health aspects, karmic lessons for this lifetime. For instance who would think or know that Capricorns are susceptible to weakened bones and tooth decay. True.

The health aspect I found extremely interesting as it points out your most likely health problems, also depicts preferable food which are highest in the vitamins and minerals particular star signs require. Amazing!

Another amazing feature of numerology is the description as to how best to understand your children through the 'arrows', again calculated using the birth date. Oh how I wish I had had access to this book when my children were young.

It gives the reader an understanding of where another person is coming from, an in depth understanding of their particular place in life. Of the lessons they are here to learn, where their deficiencies lie and what they need to overcome. Why they are like they are.

Understanding generates compassion, compassion translates to love. We can overcome challenges by first understanding they are there for a reason, then working toward overcoming them with love and grace.

Numerology will open doors of understanding for you, it not only helps you personally but will help you understand others which is crucial for sound relationships. Understand and soon judgment will be abolished as a thing of the past and you will wake to a whole new world.

CHAPTER TWENTY TWO

My holistic GP had removed herself from her practice (prior to Fabian going into prison), from memory I believe she went overseas for a period with her husband, she recommended another GP who specialized in holistic medicine. She had also recommended I take Fabian to a particular GP who was a counsellor and good with kids like Fabian. I knew I wouldn't get Fabian to go to counselling so I dismissed the idea as a nice idea but!

During this time I had to maintain my vitamin C regime as it kept my allergic reaction down to a dull roar and bought me some time so I could go pay bills, do any shopping in the city etc. Work I could cope with most of the time as far as my allergies went, the injections bought me time in the rest of the world, well at least 24 hours worth anyway which was better than nothing.

I fronted for injections one particular visit only to find a locum on duty. The locum turned out to be Dr Counsellor, the very doctor my initial holistic GP had told me about. Coincidence? I think not, the Universe had planned it this way. I was meant to meet Dr Counsellor one way or another. Injection given, Dr Counsellor explained that if I would like to find out more about why I had my ever growing collection of diseases to make an appointment to see him at his normal practice.

The first visit, Dr Counsellor explained so much to me, for the first time in my life the world I had found myself in was beginning to make sense. Here was someone who thought like I did, I was no longer so alone in this foreign land. I began little by little, visit by visit to understand more and more about myself, about the behaviour of others and the reason for certain patterns of behaviour.

Without Dr Counsellor in my life I doubt if I would have survived what was about to happen over the next few years. His counselling didn't consist of: "And how did you feel about that", it was so much more, so very much more. He explained about anger, frustration, self esteem, guilt. He explained how Fabian was on his own path and could I cope with the fact that I may not be able to save him. How the very people we can't help are those in our own family, as much as we want to, we cannot prevent them from living their own life and fulfilling their Life Purpose, whatever it may be.

Dr Counsellor was one very positive aspect of my life from the day I met him, he helped me see so much, to understand so much about human behaviour. So no I don't believe in coincidences, it was meant to be. If the Universe puts something in your path on at least two occasions it is a case of take note we are doing this for a reason. It may take three times to get your attention but you can be sure if it is really important they will ensure you take notice and obey the 'signpost'. It is a gift for the Universe.

The emotion of anger was probably one of the most difficult to comprehend. If you are angry with a particular person, ask yourself what it is about that person's behaviour that reminds you of your own behaviour. Why are you angry with yourself, yes correct, you are not really angry with them, you are angry with your own behaviour. Think about it the next time you feel anger, don't act on it, analyze it and see what you come up with.

Schizophrenia is one of the most cruel diseases I can imagine. At least with other diseases such as I have, I can read, go to support groups and at least talk about it. My brain has a chance of guiding me through. To have thoughts so confused that life ceases to make sense, paranoid thoughts, voices telling you what to or not to do - how scary must that be?

Fabian and I navigated our way through the maze of court appearances; at times he would scowl and mouth obscenities at me, hatred written all over his face. Other times he would smile with love, I never knew which way it would go. I tried not to take it personally, I had been told he was incapable of emotions in his state; I had to grin and bear it basically. Many occasions he would begin to laugh as the magistrate spoke (even considering his condition this never went down well in a court room). I wonder if the magistrates or judges ever took it into account, if they even knew why he reacted in this manner, if they knew it was merely symptomatic of the disease. Sadly I suspect not.

Fabian had a succession of legal aid lawyers; some so junior it was embarrassing. One day in court I could hear this girl speaking about one of her clients (it was Fabian) and it wasn't respectful, she obviously had no understanding of mental illness or his particular situation. She definitely needed to meet Thumper!

Solicitor Nightingale took over soon after the above episode; she was wonderful and will have my respect and love from now to eternity. She could handle him when all else failed, he respected her and given his state of mind that said so much about her, more than I could ever put to print. She respected his right to have optimum care as far as the legal system was concerned. Fabian liked her so much one day he said to me "Mum, when this is over I want to ask her to have a coffee with me", that made me smile, not sure how she would have felt about that. The statement was made with love and respect so I had to put my acting skills to the fore once again.

To save my sanity I would walk away from the court repeating over and over "Don't take it personally, he can't help it, it is the disease talking, don't take it personally, don't take it personally".

On some court appearances Laura would be with me, she would write in my note pad, she even drew a picture of Fabian behind bars with comments spoken by the judge, to this child going to court and to the prison was part of everyday life. Isn't that what other children did? She took it in her stride as well as anyone could expect. I don't believe the gravity of the situation was lost on her; she used to ask questions, I gave honest, positive answers. To her this was normal.

Fabian's mental state made slow but steady progress, this was more than I had dared hope for and far more than the medical profession thought possible or probable.

I would visit the prison hospital. If a delay occurred in Fabian's appearance I would hear an inmate say 'Mrs Long is here and Fabian hasn't been brought out yet". I would receive a hello; a friendly wave and a "Mrs Long how are you?" The other inmates were truly wonderful and considerate. I was always treated with respect and a greeted with a happy smile. The hello's and smiles received, made prison visits bearable, after awhile it felt like I was merely visiting friends. I didn't try to correct the Mrs Long thing; it was easier to let them believe that is what my name was. After all, Fabian was Fabian Long so it was a natural assumption to make.

Fabian had been in prison for approximately eight months when his behaviour and progress was deemed suitable for transfer to the Royal Derwent Hospital, he would still be retained on a 'Hospital Order' but merely relocated for rehabilitation purposes.

If this transfer proved positive he would eventually be permitted home on weekend visits and day release.

My girlfriend and I bought Fabian clothes in preparation for this major breakthrough. We arrived at the Royal Derwent Hospital in February of 1998 armed with positive thoughts, bucket load of love, the new clothes and everything he required that we could possibly think of.

The first thing he did was give me a huge hug, long time since I have been able to do that he said. I had tears in my eyes. You see, when his schizophrenia was in full flight he hated me to the max. When his condition stabilized he would return to the cheeky kid I knew and loved. I don't think Fabian understood 'contact visits' within the prison, visits with Fabian were always 'box visits' where the inmate is contained, no contact possible. Contact visits had to be arranged by the inmate and occurred during weekends, another of those things where it is extremely difficult for a schizophrenic kid to understand and act upon. Another example why people with mental illness should not be housed within the confines of a normal prison situation! They need to be housed with staff who can explain their rights and assist if necessary, where families are consulted on a regular basis.

We would visit, sitting on the lawn was heaven instead of enclosed behind metal bars, we would take him McDonalds or some treat. He met and fell in love with another mental health patient from another ward, it was funny to listen to them, they didn't have a fully functional brain between them, but it was still cute to listen to them making plans for their future.

Positive thoughts aren't sufficient when one has a child with a mental condition and into substance abuse. His condition improved so markedly that he had the duty psychiatrist well and truly hoodwinked. This proved to be not such a good thing.

He was permitted day and weekend release far, far too early - yes he abused both! A urine test proved positive - to marijuana. One of the staff had mistakenly told him what the punishment would be, or at least thought it would be. For some reason Fabian was again allowed into New Norfolk, he came back rather the worse for wear, I suppose his thinking was; if that was his last few hours of freedom he might as well make the most of it. Bad move!

He was relocated into the 'locked up' ward where life wasn't so normal. My girlfriend and I visited him close to my birthday. He said sorry I can't get you a present mum. Treatment in this ward wasn't very nice it seems. Different rules applied in this ward. Fabian said these words to me, words I shall never forget as long as I live. He was relaying whatever had happened that particular day between another mental health patient and a staff member and he wasn't impressed.

> *"Even we deserve to be treated with respect"*

Remember these words are from a kid with schizophrenia and subsequent scattered thoughts!

… How I retained my composure I will never know, I think I just about choked on sobs which were threatening to overtake me, somehow I got the strength to get through that visit intact. He believed the treatment that patient had received was disrespectful. Yes Fabian, I agree, even patients with mental illness deserve to be treated with respect as do each and every one of us….and they say 'out of the mouths of babes' I believe that quote said it all, just a pity we don't live by that eh?

That comment was so innocent, so passionate; it made an impression on me I know I shall never forget, I can hear it as if it was yesterday and it still brings tears to my eyes.

Following those misdemeanors he was once again returned to Risdon Prison hospital.

So it was back to a sort of 'normal' routine once again.

My first visit to him upon his return to prison was not one I choose to remember. I asked the officers at reception if I could bring Fabian's radio in to him. He had had this radio when he was here previously, had taken with him to Royal Derwent and now would need it again. I was told an emphatic 'no'. He would have to purchase a new one. I was fighting back tears now. He needed that radio when the voices in his head got all too much. I didn't have the money to give him and he sure as hell didn't have sufficient money. I explained the importance of the radio and left, fighting back tears which were threatening to over take me. Why, why is life so cruel? I understand the rules (well sort of), but there had to be exceptions given certain circumstances. Fabian was incapable of hiding drugs in that radio given his mental state. There had to be exceptions!

I didn't understand very much about the workings of the prison, Fabian was incapable of voicing much about anything at times, I didn't realize the inmates had to buy as much as they did just for normal day to day living. I had no comprehension about 'contact' visits. I only knew I could come and visit him however many times a week, even that seemed to be confused at times.

I gleaned that most inmates have previously had parents, friends or siblings in prison before them. This assumption appears to be taken for granted by officers and staff at the prison. Therefore, unfortunately information is not forthcoming, it seems to be taken for granted that 'you' know all this, either that or they just don't care one way or the other. A little of both, I suspect.

Education would go a long way in this situation but between 1997 and 2000 it certainly was not available as a matter of course. Mental health inmates were way out on their own proverbial limb without adequate means of comprehension and or assistance as were the families.

Trying to get information from staff wasn't easy, some were forthcoming some were not.

Within a matter of weeks of Fabian returning to the prison hospital, the schizophrenia returned, I telephoned (or at least tried to) the psychiatrist in charge, on a number of occasions over a two week period. When my call was finally returned he asked me what I thought. I stated that in my opinion the schizophrenia had returned. He agreed my thoughts were indeed correct, as he too had examined Fabian.

Medication was again commenced and in a short time the improvement in his behaviour and attitude had improved dramatically. He continued to improve to such an extent that the psychiatrist decided the Hospital Order was no longer required and once again it was back to the Supreme Court to have the Order lifted.

He was released in September 1998. Here began a whole new frightening chapter of our story.

CHAPTER TWENTY THREE

Fabian was released, from of all places, the Supreme Court in Hobart. A kid dealing with schizophrenia is allowed to walk out the door of the Supreme Court instead of from the prison hospital. What is the world coming to? Does anyone in the Judicial system have a functional brain which works on logic?

His medication, medical records, tiny amount of personal possessions all located at the prison hospital. It was a mammoth effort on its own just getting him back to the prison to collect these items and what little money he had owing to him. I think I aged another five years trying to undertake that mission.

That finally undertaken he was discharged, I was not given any instructions, advice, offers of assistance, help line - nothing! We were on our own!

Wouldn't it be prudent to release a mental health patient from the hospital? Wouldn't it be prudent to release them to a 'person' and give the 'person' instructions on what they might expect behaviour wise? Medication advice would have been useful given the circumstances. I said previously this kid should have come with an instruction manual; well the *advanced* section of the manual was definitely required from here on in, along with the *'troubleshooting section'*.

You can most likely guess what occurred next. He wanted to get dropped off in the city, he had no intention of coming straight home - my stomach felt like it had lead in it upon hearing that request. Fabian gave Laura $10 from his earnings and exited the car with a huge smile.

We headed home, me with a heavy heart and that familiar sinking feeling.

Later that evening a taxi driver knocked on my door, I was in bed, he said "I have a kid in the car who says he lives here but he can't get out of the car". Confused? Yes I was. Money in hand to pay, I headed outside to the taxi. Fabian was frozen, he had obviously bent down to pick up his cigarettes and had frozen in motion, I had not seen anything like this previously.

I believe the medical term for frozen is 'catatonic', I just didn't know it at the time.

I somehow managed to get him inside and into his bedroom. His eyes were wide open but there was no one home! That all too familiar panic feeling set in big time. I had no idea what to do. I phoned our local GP; he said he couldn't do anything, because he too had been asleep and that he didn't know what drugs Fabian may have taken. He didn't put the damn phone back on the cradle properly, which meant I wasn't able to call for an ambulance, couldn't call anyone. Damn him!

Midnight, me walking up the centre of the street looking for some poor unsuspecting person who might still be up and about, I picked on my next door neighbour, got her out of bed, the light only on because her husband was at work still. I asked if I could call an ambulance and Fabian's father. I offer apologies for my late night visit and a huge thank you for assistance.

That mission accomplished I headed back home to await arrival of Fabian's father, Ambulance and Laura's father, I needed him to stay with Laura whilst I went into hospital with Fabian.

Fabian screamed as they tried to put him into the ambulance, he hung onto both doors, he kept calling for me; don't let them take me back mum or words to that effect. It was horrible. His dad went with him in the ambulance to the hospital emergency department. Fabian hung on to me so tight when I got to the hospital his dad had to pry his hand off my arm, should have seen the bruise that left me with, he had some grip when he wanted. Hospital security staff notified, on alert and within reach. Fabian made me promise not to leave. He was given an injection and settled down, the hospital staff told me there was no point in my staying, he wouldn't wake until morning, best I go home and come back really early, that way he wouldn't know I had absconded.

From his screaming I deduced that in his mind he believed he was being taken back to the prison, he was beside himself, he wasn't in any state to know the difference.

Bright and early, back to the hospital, Fabian wasn't impressed; he was downright angry with me for taking him to the hospital in the first place. Oh isn't life wonderful?

Bought him cigarettes, or at least gave him the money from memory. We arrived home, Fabian went to have a bath, well at least some things hadn't changed he still liked his bath. Heard the bath water empty, then silence.

Lost him!

Believe it or not I lost him, couldn't find him anywhere. Finally looked out the back door and there he was frozen solid again on the back door step, he had gone to light a cigarette and obviously froze just as he was about to light. Seriously, he looked like someone had sprayed him with something which made him set in motion. I think you need to see this one to believe it. I certainly didn't have the 'Midas touch' if that is what you are thinking. If only! Oh geez! Now what do I do?

He came back to the land of the living and moving long enough for me to get him to his bedroom. Still not in good condition, I phoned and phoned the local doctor, phoned my eldest daughter to ask her to call their father as I needed help and needed it now. Sent my youngest daughter up to her sister (well at least I thought I did). Laura only had to walk up the street - only problem was she decided she wasn't going anywhere and waited and watched from the front garden. Think she believed I needed protection, don't know what she thought she would do but she wasn't going anywhere. Mild panic set in when I spoke to her sister on the phone only to learn Laura didn't arrive as per our earlier plan. Like my stress levels were not already high enough. Rather than angry I was so relieved when I located her hiding in the garden. My precious baby was once again trying to keep me safe. How could I be angry with her?

Fabian's dad arrived after what seemed like an eternity. I was on the phone to the doctor - I said to his dad go and check on Fabian he is choking. "No he isn't", came the 'know all' response, "He is asleep". I shouted "He is unable to sleep in this condition, please check because he is choking". I was getting impatient now; the morning's events were taking their toll on me. Yes choking he was, gosh I hate being right at times. Fabian went into the toilet, his dad? Well he decided he would shut the door for 'privacy' reasons. Shut the door, if he goes unconscious in there and falls behind the door we will be unable to get to him; open the door, like now! Were men given brains? Because if they were I was finding it really difficult to comprehend how an adult male can be so stupid! Why couldn't he have taken my words as truth and assisted me as I asked, I had been dealing with this condition and had learned the sequence through which it progressed. I learn fast given the circumstances.

By the time the local doctor finally managed to get to the house (at lunch time), Fabian was in a real state, he was turning somersaults on the bed and it was looking like any minute his head would go down the gap between the wall and the bed. Oh Mickey! Followed by choking only this time much worse, the doctor told me to get the ambulance and get it NOW! Ambulance dispatcher not impressed - he was doing the best he could but he needed details as well. Doctor now really in panic mode, if you thought I could panic, he surpassed anything I could manage. Difference was he was supposed to be trained to deal with medical emergencies; I had to try to logically make my way through them.

Ambulance arrived - thank God. They informed me next time, don't wait for the doctor just phone us, it seemed I had approximately two hours from onset of this 'deep freeze' before choking to death was a distinct possibility. Well at least I knew a little more this time around. Two ambulances in less than twenty four hours that wasn't bad for neighbourhood entertainment. I hope they all appreciated the effort that went into providing their brief detour from normal living routines.

Fabian's dad had once again taken the ambulance trip with Fabian, I had driven to the hospital, the ambulance guys had left their little bag of tricks in my house in all the confusion, so here I am lugging that up the street to emergency. Be handy if they were able to tailor it down to something sizeable to carry. It was almost as big as me.

Injection of cogentin given, three doctors advised me I could take him home. Take him home! They had to be out of their tiny collective minds, I wasn't taking him anywhere. I explained I had had no sleep for the last twenty four hours, I was supposed to be at work and believe me I wasn't taking this kid anywhere. He had frozen twice in twenty four hours; I wasn't going for a record three times, not right now anyway. They went away to confer. Back they came with a proposal. Their final offer, "Ok we will keep him tonight but you come back first thing (like 7:30am and collect him)". I agreed.

His dad and I were standing by Fabian's hospital bed, Fabian said "I love you Dad", his dad in his usual form, stood poker faced and said nothing. I would have kicked him had it not been so obvious to Fabian. When he finally spoke he said "If you loved me you wouldn't do this" - ok good, now that was a positive thing to say - like if you love me, don't freeze, or if you loved me, you wouldn't have schizophrenia - idiot! Like Fabian had any control over those minor details.

I could see the hurt on Fabian's face; it just about killed me inside. No doubt it did untold damage to Fabian. How could a father do that to their own child, isn't this where little white lies are supposed to be acceptable? A little white lie would have been preferable - but this was not to be, Fabian learned a harsh lesson that day.

Following that comment I wasn't expecting great things where Fabian's drug taking was concerned, I knew it would escalate; he would take drugs to mask the pain of that very comment. The love I gave him could and never would make up for the lack of love from his father – he needed both. He needed unconditional love and understanding.

That sinking feeling was taking over again.

My kind ex took me for a coffee when we left to go home. I asked him why he had not replied to Fabian when he told him he loved him. His reply, "Because I don't feel anything for him". Charming eh? Oh well, have to give him points for honesty at least.

I collected Fabian as per the agreed maintenance plan, Fabian once again extremely cross with me for taking him to the hospital yet again. Had he heard of the word compromise?

Apparently not!

Life didn't get any easier in case you were wondering. Each fortnight it was: leave work, go home collect Fabian, take him to Glenorchy (half hour drive away) for anti psychotic injections, stop in the city for a visit to the probation officer, drop Fabian off back home, return to work.

That's normal isn't it?

Normal would be - not having a full on fight during the half hour drive to Glenorchy, normal would be not to expect someone to exit the car whilst moving, normal would be going in the door to have injections in a civilized manner without the threat of him taking off in full flight just prior to. I felt like I should have been armed with a human size fish net so I could catch him should he decide to make a run for it before injection time. Normal would have been a God send.

Fabian obviously saw the injections as punishment so it was hell on wheels getting him there. Then arguments about we are/we are not going to probation on the way home. Probation or back to prison; didn't seem to phase Fabian, either way he didn't want to keep those appointments.

On the first occasion, whilst I put money in the meter, Fabian took off running so I couldn't see where he was going, if he was going, he was going alone. Well at least that was his theory. Me? I had different ideas. I'm quite fit all things considered so I took off as fast as my two vertically challenged legs would take me. Saw him enter the building, well at least I had the building in my sights, then up the stairs; please don't let it be the top floor I'm thinking. Still had him in my sights as he entered the correct floor, yes, cornered - just have to not lose him in the last few metres and doorways. Yes, victory. Quite proud of me I was. I was running up the street thinking 'rotten little shit!'

Probation visit a reasonable success - well as much as it could be with a schizophrenic kid. Deposited Fabian back home then headed off back to work, by this time they must have almost forgotten I worked there, between court appearances, prison visits, now this.

Got back into work and started laughing at the thought and sight of me tearing up the street trying to keep this kid in my sights, followed the by saga of the stairwell and the offices. It must have looked odd to anyone who was watching the event unfold.

Thank heavens for a sense of humour!

By the time we reached home he would say "Thanks for taking me to the doctor mum", his mood would be a total contradiction. What an about face, it was great once those injections hit the spot.

One day I do remember; he was a right royal pain in the butt on the way there; it was close to Christmas time - memory a little hazy. After he had had his injections and we were walking back to the car he said "Mum I can't remember ever being this happy, and I don't know how to handle it". Ok, confused now, if I wasn't mistaken there was both good and really bad in that statement. Am unable to recall my reply but in true Fabian fashion when you don't know what else to do - take the drugs /alcohol numbing solution, if insufficient, repeat dose. Schizophrenia now exacerbated again.

The episodes outlined above were repeated over and over. Finally I had had enough. My Crohn's disease had sky rocketed from 5cm to now 25cms in a matter of weeks, he was slowly but surely wreaking havoc on my already sick body.

Some occasions I would insist he get his father to drive him. You know, like take turns. Well those occasions were a huge success. Fabian so stressed from the experience always went and bought drugs and/or alcohol afterwards in order to de-stress. He told me he did it and why it was necessary. Seriously, life is terrific isn't it? Yes I know, sarcasm doesn't become me, I apologize.

I said to the psychiatrist "I can't do this anymore", he will have to find his own way here. On the way he had threatened to jump from my moving car - he just didn't want to go. The pains in my stomach were excruciating, driving was dangerous, I couldn't continue with this every two weeks and stay with my inside pieces intact, something had to give and I was afraid it was my body. I still had Laura to consider.

That particular visit proved almost fatal for me. I gave him some money from the ATM and said "You will have to find your own way home I have had enough". I began to walk back to my car, pressed the button at the traffic light and waited. The 'walk' light and I set off, for some reason I glanced to my right, a car was coming through the red light and straight for me, I had absolutely no where to go, didn't even have time to jump either forward or backwards. I literally stopped and waited for the impact, the lady managed to brake just as the car touched me, boy that was close. I got back to work then shock set in and I started to cry, the feeling of waiting for the thud on top of everything else was way too much on this occasion. I was again saved for another day. (I must be a like a cat with nine lives because that was three times I had had near misses with oncoming vehicles, so three down how many more to go?)

The day after I came out of hospital from yet another colonoscopy I was so very ill and in bed. Fabian wanted drugs, he wanted money. In retrospect my being sick was another stress factor his schizophrenia could have done without, so as usual drugs provided the solution. He absolutely terrified the poor dog when he was unable to move me from the bed. Poor Sally she was outside shivering with fear, I couldn't do a thing to help.

Prior to going to prison, Fabian could at least prepare food and help himself, when he came out all that was impossible. Even simple meals eluded him, life really was hard work. He would have the injections early in the week, sometimes by the Sunday they were already beginning to wear off and his behaviour would markedly deteriorate.

One Sunday morning I was outside talking to my neighbour, I said "Do you have a smoke detector? After a few seconds discussion we realized, with alarm, it was my smoke detector. Remember I said I could run fast? Well that included that particular morning. Fabian had decided to cook chicken breasts, only he forgot to use a cooking tray, the juices were dripping merrily on to the hot elements of the oven. Smoke filled the kitchen and family room. Well at least that is all it was, it could have been a whole lot worse, thank heaven I was in ear shot at the time.

Each day when I went to work or went out, I wondered whether or not I was coming back to a home or a smouldering mess that used to be my home. I was stressed most of the time.

At work I tried to concentrate wholly on work, at home I concentrated on problems at home or just daily living. To keep the two elements separate was basically my only survival mechanism. If I worried too much about home at work and vice versa I would have been six feet under by now. The mind can take on many tasks when there is a requirement to do so. Very complex set up, thankfully.

If Fabian took drugs and/or alcohol within hours of the anti-psychotic medication I could guarantee a 'freeze' episode and emergency here we come.

The ambulance officers decided one night Fabian needed privacy to get dressed; he was usually if not always naked when they were called. So they politely closed the door so he could get dressed. I advised, he is unable to dress himself in this condition, next thing I hear "Muuuuuuum, I need help", needed help alright, he sure did, poor kid. I would dress him and off we would go again, with the paramedic in the back saying, stay with me Fabian, stay with me, as he drifted in and out of consciousness.

We would walk through the emergency room; Fabian would have his hands on both my cheeks telling me how much he loved me. You see in this state he reverted back to a toddler and all accompanying mannerisms. The emergency staff said on one night, "We recognize you more quickly now than we do your son". Terrific, first the court staff get to know my face, I was such a familiar sight, now I have graduated to emergency, oh well at least I spread me around!

One night we arrived home, Laura and I that is. Laura made straight for the toilet. I walked up the hallway only to find her bouncing around outside the closed door. She had assumed 'someone' was behind the closed door. I opened the door thinking Fabian may have left it closed accidentally.

Ok, not so vacant on this occasion, Fabian naked and frozen yet again. Terrific, as if I didn't have enough to do already, still had to go buy some groceries from the supermarket, visit mum, and that was before I started preparations for dinner. I was livid, he had had injections again and I knew exactly what had occurred.

By this time I was now armed with medication, tablets, if I caught him in time and could get two tablets in without choking him to death, I had bought myself some time before the emergency dash. This night I wasn't happy, shoved two tablets down his throat then headed off to vent my anger.

A couple (people Fabian mistakenly called friends) living in a unit in our street often phoned him the minute they knew he was in possession of his Centrelink cheque. Sure as little green apples grew on trees, the phone calls would commence and not end until they were assured all his money for the fortnight had definitely expired.

I marched up to their front door - not happy Jan! that was me. I proceeded to inform them that if Fabian died that night I would have them charged with manslaughter, as they were fully aware of the implications of him having drugs and/or alcohol on top of his anti psychotic injections. It was a 'duty of care' obligation. An obligation of which they were fully conversant!

Well it wasn't received too well, the guy threatened to rearrange my face, he staggered toward me (yes staggered, see I knew he had been on a bender with Fabian's money) they had most likely mixed sleeping tablets with alcohol so he was probably seeing two of me anyway. Brave me then stated "I am not scared of you, I have dealt with worse than you" as

I made my retreat. I got back to the car, there was Laura cheering me on hanging out the car window. Not scared of you, have dealt with worse, where in God's name did that come from?

I made a fast drive to my mother's house, collected what I had to and headed back home. Fabian was with it by now, the tablets had taken affect and there was no need for a trip to hospital, this time!

To say he was livid was another major understatement, when the guy up the street told him what I had said, boy did I wear it. This guy had Fabian's permission to rearrange my face it seemed, would serve me right for interfering, Fabian advised me. Suppose in their world I asked for that one.

That night in bed, shock set in, the danger I had placed myself in was unbelievable, how stupid was I? No, please don't answer that, leave me with some dignity! I was finding it difficult to believe I could have been so stupid or brave not sure which term is the most appropriate for the occasion. I was a mum and I was mad, I was fighting to keep my son alive. I was a force to be reckoned with at that moment; luckily they are few and far between. Only happened once previously and that one had a good result. Might not be so lucky next time, so best quit whilst I am ahead eh? Hmmm that's four lives used up!

The following Saturday morning I was out mowing my back lawn, I looked up and here comes the guy walking toward me, oh no, here he is, rearrange face time? Oh dear! No way out I was trapped in my own back yard this time.

He walked up to me; wonder he didn't hear my heart pounding, sure as hell seemed louder than the lawn mower engine. He apologized, boy was that a relief, he wanted to apologize for the way he acted and spoke the other night. Relief plus. It took quite some time for my heart rate to settle back to normal. Adrenalin rush definitely in 'peak hour' on that occasion.

One of Fabian's more lucid moments once again brought my acting skills to the fore. We were going through his work from high school. He turned to me and said "I wasted my time in high school, didn't I mum?" He looked scared, forlorn and so very dejected. He had tried to give college a re-run but this too failed due to substance abuse. At that moment I felt so very scared for him! So very scared for me! I didn't want to lose this precious child but his look of despair spoke volumes.

My girlfriend decided somewhere in this I should have a mini rest so she arranged for us to go to Scamander for a few nights during a long weekend. Mum agreed to have Fabian for the weekend. We returned on the Sunday night, got to mum's, Fabian said his arm was hurting. Hurting, now why would that be the case? If you could only have seen what I had to look at! Think I nearly fainted on the spot whilst still swearing at him. He had a black swollen spot, it was as if an egg (duck egg that would have to be) had been placed under his skin, it was probably a third or slightly more of the way up his inner arm from the wrist. Black? Yes you read correctly. It was really "caning" unquote. So welcome home Denise, hope you had a nice short holiday because now it is back to the emergency department of the hospital. Forget the washing, ironing and dinner for tonight.

The things this kid managed to do to himself were unbelievable! See what I mean when I say some of my experiences were choices others made and I was merely an unwilling participant - well unwilling participant I sure was.

How he coped with that level of pain is beyond my comprehension, it must have been something else.

When we arrived in emergency, he tried in vain to get me to sit in the waiting area and not listen to his explanation of the cause of this 'black egg'. Think he would have learned by now, I can't be rid of that easily. Funny, you will never guess. He had been injecting temazepam, the oil from the capsule. Seems substance abusers inject the contents into their blood steam, gives them quite a buzz. Problem factor: oil and blood do not mix; the result was this revolting obviously infected swollen mass. These capsules were readily available upon prescription during this time. Thankfully, this is no longer the case. I thank the pharmaceutical industry for recognition and resolution of this problem.

The mass had to be lanced, all without an anaesthetic of any kind. Don't know whether they refused him medication given the circumstances or whether it was a punishment thing, either way how Fabian withstood the pain is beyond me. My guess was it didn't stop him from undertaking the same injecting. Luckily though, he didn't have a repeat reappearance of the 'black egg'. The hole left behind in his arm was something else you sure don't want to experience. Oh man, the things these kids do to themselves. How any drug and/or high would be worth that risk is also beyond my comprehension! Suppose that doesn't even come into the equation for them.

On another occasion I came home and discovered him catatonic. Intermittently he would come out of the 'frozen state' then go into repetitive behaviour, such as scratching himself in one spot until he would bleed, usually on the hands. Other times he would get stuck doing something else. This particular night he started going around and around under a circular light shade, here I am two feet firmly planted on the floor trying to stop him from turning and turning, he was picking up pace and I needed to get him to the stop position. If he only came equipped with batteries it would have been so much easier, at least the batteries would have worn out or I could have extracted them. This kid was 'ever ready' charged. So ok, trying to call ambulance but needed girlfriend here to help out until the ambulance came or I at least got to speak to them in between the "Mum", "Help me" and the "I love yous" . He would repeat these words over and over. By this time I realized how fruitless it was phoning either his dad or Laura's father, both excelled on the useless scale. Girlfriend at least used common sense and followed any request I asked. When she walked in the door, this would or could also act as a trigger for return to normal for at least two minutes (or less, or not). He would come out of his catatonic state, say "Hi" then within seconds revert to the original status.

That was another of the examples I explained about earlier where his behaviour became obsessive, where he seemed unable to stop either a thought or a particular behaviour pattern. He would be set in a pattern of doing or thinking 'something'.

In hospital I had to hold his hands, one hand was now bleeding and he just kept on and on with the scratching. The duty doctor walked in and said, "He is fine, nothing wrong with him". I said "Hang on, stand here for a couple of minutes and he will return to his pattern" - sure enough he did, he had momentarily come out of the 'whatever stage' upon her arrival. Two minutes later he had relapsed again. Don't think she quite believed it but gave him the required injection anyway. Whether she believed or not, to me her opinion was totally irrelevant. Injection in his body, he was discharged and we were on our way home.

Biggest problem was; following these injections he was wide awake, so the night was then taken up with pacing, pacing and more pacing, consequently sleep eluded me on those nights. Fabian got to sleep next day but I had to go to work, no rest for the wicked. I used to wish those injections came complete with a sleeping tablet, if not for him then at least for me so I wasn't kept awake with Fabian pacing the floor, or worst still heading out the door to goodness knows where.

There were times when I would think, "I come home from work to a frozen child, take preventative action, call ambulance, phone girlfriend to mind Laura, accompany ambulance to hospital, wait at hospital until whatever occurs, come home". Food? Yes have some if at all possible. Go to bed, get up go to work. What do other people do? Coming home to the above was normal for me, normal for other people would be; cook dinner, watch television, go to bed. Oh for the 'other version of norm'. I probably wouldn't have known what to do with myself for a whole week!

CHAPTER TWENTY FOUR

Upon deciding I had had enough and all I could possibly take for a while, Fabian once again moved in with mum, much to her disgust and my dissatisfaction. He found work with a friend at a working nursery (flower nursery that is). Am unsure how successful or otherwise this proved, they most likely were not aware of what they were dealing with. Keeping him working would have been close to impossible, his comprehension of what/how jobs needed to be done would have been limited, his attention span would have been negligible. I still have the scribbled notes he made as to what to do with the bulbs and other instructions he had been given re their care, another part of him I cannot part with.

Prior to moving out he came home so excited one day; he had met this beautiful girl on the bus coming home. He couldn't stop talking about her. She was the only female I can ever remember him even being partly interested in; he was more interested in his skate board and surf boarding. This girl had him captivated. In his eyes she was so beautiful; it was so good to see him this happy again. I had hope again. Maybe this female wizard could perform small miracles? Maybe this is what he needed?

Not to be, unfortunately. One Friday night he returned to mum's a bunch of flowers in hand he had picked for his lady (compliments of the nursery where he was working I suspect). She never received them, drugs and/or alcohol, or both took him over for the whole weekend. Life can be a bitch at times.

When I knew of her existence and the fact that I knew her parents I said to Fabian "Don't you ever do drugs in front of her, will you?" he flashed me his 'as if I would' look, quite disgusted that I should even think such a thing. He gave me his word he wouldn't. Thank you Fabian, for keeping your word on that score, she didn't deserve to see that and thankfully she never did.

Fabian loved her with all the emotion his thought processes could muster under the circumstances. If only she could have met when he was ok, free from his mental illness. If only she could have known the beautiful soul I knew and loved. Fabian wanted her to know how much he loved her, who knows maybe one day they will be together ….in another time and place.

One of the most difficult things in life to deal with is kicking your own child out of home, Fabian had his choice on way too many occasions and he kept choosing drugs and alcohol. I chose not to tolerate this behaviour so he had to leave.

He would return home periodically for a change of clothes, I was desperately trying to follow some of the Tough Love theories by sticking to my guns. Malcolm Fraser didn't know what he started when he said "Life wasn't meant to be easy". It sure wasn't meant to be this hard either; at least I hoped it wasn't. One night I made him change on the doorstep. If you think I have erased that one from the memory banks, forget it, mission impossible. I feel physically sick even thinking of it now and it is six years later. I was desperately trying to illustrate to him that he had to make a choice. He made his choice but it wasn't the one I was hoping for. The sacrifices we make in the hope of keeping our children alive and in one piece. Sacrifice? Yes, it is, there are occasions where it is necessary to make a really tough decision in the name of Hope. In order to make a point I had to sacrifice my own feelings and stand my ground. I hated myself for that decision and the resultant images I continually carry of that evening.

His lack of medication and most likely increase in drug use exacerbated his schizophrenia; he committed another two offences whilst psychotic and was returned to the prison hospital on 20 May 1999 for three months.

One of the above mentioned offences he committed whilst residing in Flint House - for some inexplicable reason he ran at a car and kicked the door, smashed the side mirror, the lady was merely driving her car up a small, reasonably quiet street. I can only assume Fabian misconstrued some glance - maybe he thought she was thinking something she knew nothing about. Either way this behaviour should have been sufficient for the police to acknowledge he had a major mental condition which by now was way out of control. Surprise, surprise, they obviously noticed very little, because he was released once the interview re the incident was terminated. Defies gravity!

Fabian's behaviour on this day was another one of those in the 'unbelievable' category, My girlfriend and I had gone to Flint House during our lunch hour. Had briefly spoken to Fabian, he had just been kicked out of this establishment due to this incident. Appears the lady with the car, was a friend of the gentlemen who owned and ran Flint House.

Flint House - it was 2004 before I could drive past without tears welling in my eyes. It is the most depressing, sad boarding house I have ever had to enter.

Whilst I applaud the actions and aims of the owner, have the utmost respect and admiration for him, can understand why its very existence is necessary, this does not detract from the depressing state of the building and its residents.

I found it sad, run down, demoralizing substitute accommodation for people who are mentally ill or for those who would otherwise be homeless for a variety of reasons. I suppose the residents are grateful for having somewhere to call home and I thank God someone cares enough to provide this accommodation. Heaven knows the Governments do very little in this regard.

The building was in a state of disrepair but for the fifty or so residents it's a home they otherwise would not have with two hot meals prepared daily. So they eat and sleep within the confines of four walls in lieu of streets, park benches or under bridges.

To me these residents are the 'people the world forgot about' or worse still 'don't want to know about'. If only Government heard Fabian's words from the Royal Derwent Hospital "Even we deserve to be treated with respect". Maybe someone would care enough to ensure adequate funding was forthcoming for people like the owner of this establishment. That way he could improve on the care he gives to these people who depend on him. Their lives are virtually in his hands, if not for him and people like him where would they be? I doubt they would be at all, in fact.

The second offence I was unable to comprehend any more than the first. Fabian had hit an Asian boy over the head with a skate board. Why? He wasn't brought up to be racist, like everything else this didn't make any sense either. Trying to make sense of the world sometimes is a losing battle; this particular occasion proved to be no exception. Fabian never judged anyone or anything, he was first to reprimand anyone who did. So why this?

Later I read a report of the psychiatrist's interview with Fabian. For days he had been hearing Asian voices coming out of the walls. I have no idea what the voices were saying, can only presume it wasn't positive or friendly, this poor kid wore whatever frustration had been building up in Fabian's tormented mind. I pray he found it in his heart to forgive Fabian.

I later discovered (whilst sitting at yet another court hearing), that during this three month period in prison Fabian spent most of his time in solitary confinement due to behavioural problems. Now why would a kid with schizophrenia and no medication have behavioural problems? Hmm nothing comes to mind! Obviously didn't for the resident psychiatrist either. Sarcasm is warranted and justified on some occasions, so I feel I can be excused on this occasion.

During this period he was not permitted treatment for schizophrenia. In between prison visits there had been a changing of the guard so to speak. The psychiatrist no longer held the same position. The new psychiatrist decided that Fabian did not have schizophrenia, his diagnosis:

anti-social personality disorder. In order for a patient to be diagnosed with this disorder they must fulfil four different criteria, these criteria could be applied to any person with chemical substance dependence, especially if this dependence is acute.

I really do wonder why God didn't give some men a functional brain. Guess I shouldn't generalize eh? But there are times I just can't help myself.

You see, personality disorders fall outside the umbrella of 'mental illness' so I suppose if you wish to lower your case load, re-categorize and hey presto, work load reduced - don't even have to extract water, instant reduction. I shouldn't be so cynical but again, there are some times my cynicism can be justified.

What other reason could be given for such a reassessment? Fabian's original diagnosis had been made collaboratively between psychiatrists with years of experience; here was a 'new kid on the block' deferring to his own judgment in lieu of the experience of his colleagues. Was he trying to prove a point? No one will ever know the answer to that one, not even the psychiatrist in question I suspect.

He had a right to disagree; I am not disputing that point. However, he should have kept an open mind. Withdraw medication, monitor results, if condition deteriorates, reinstate medication - again monitor results. If he had chosen this approach in lieu of his own arrogance he would have realized how incorrect and foolish his assessment had been. Any psychiatrist who has the arrogance to believe that he, and only inexperienced he, is correct should not be placed in a prison hospital situation where the consequences can be so devastating for so many. This psychiatrist should not have been allowed to be in charge of a chook pen let alone be responsible for forensic mental health.

Fabian was excluded from counselling of any kind. This was especially devastating considering his alcohol and drug addiction; again these were orders from the same psychiatrist. To hear this in the Supreme Court made me ashamed to be classed as a member of the human race; one human wouldn't do this to another human, would they? It is criminal and immoral to think medication and counselling were withheld when it would have been obvious both were mandatory requirements, sometimes I don't like the world very much or being part of it when it is reduced to this.

If I could have asked to be 'beamed up' at that point I would have. I was so very ashamed of what we as humans are capable of. Power becomes abuse in the wrong hands.

This revelation, combined with his physical and mental state, rendered me into tears for a couple of days. I was unable to return to work that afternoon, tears wouldn't abate. His appearance was unkempt, his behaviour in court really bad, his eyes were dark and sunken and he was pathetically thin. I would not have expected to see him in this state given he had been in custody for a period of time. His appearance and behaviour mimicked that of a wild animal. This wasn't my child, what had they done to him? The range of emotions I felt was truly unbelievable.

I had not been able to visit Fabian for much of this period. When his schizophrenia was in full volume he wouldn't have a bar of me. Everything was my fault, he would have been difficult enough to control during this period without my insisting on seeing him and making life for the prison staff even more difficult.

I did visit Fabian just prior to another inmate committing suicide. One of the custodial officers asked me if I thought Fabian should be in the main section of the prison. My reply was an emphatic no! They agreed wholeheartedly. I discovered much later on that most of the inmates believed that the main prison was not the place for Fabian.

In retrospect, I should have known something wasn't right. Once medication was commenced and his illness contained I would receive a call asking me to come and visit him - that fact alone should have rung more alarm bells than it obviously did. Hindsight is a wonderful thing.

On the August 13, 1999 I received a call from probation advising that Fabian would be released from prison in the coming days. What in God's name were they thinking? Now I was worried sick, wondering what would happen next.

Fabian ended up in Devonport somehow. There he went to a shelter for accommodation. The staff at this shelter were so concerned re his mental state they contacted probation in Hobart. Seems Fabian had been having bath upon bath and slashing himself continually. Staff from the shelter put him on a bus and two probation officers met the bus upon arrival in Hobart. He was then accommodated at Bethlehem House until the next court hearing.

My girlfriend and I were on our way to the Supreme Court when we heard someone shouting behind us. It was Fabian, also on his way to court, mouthing obscenities. I suggested we keep walking right past the street and not act as though we, too, were heading in the same direction. Once I ensured he was no longer aware of our presence we again headed for our original destination.

Consequently, second and third of September saw Fabian not only back in court but back in prison.

Probation officers, his solicitor and myself were so concerned with regard to Fabian's mental state we had joined forces to have him put back in prison where hopefully he would receive treatment before he ended up harming himself or doing harm to some other innocent person. Ironic when I consider the final outcome.

So great was our concern with the lack of acknowledgement of his condition and lack of treatment, she managed to convince a Supreme Court judge to order an independent psychiatric report, with the aim that he might once again receive treatment. It was our only hope. Crazy, but true unfortunately!

Seems 1999 passed in a sea of: go to work, go to counsellor, go to have injections. I read my diary for that year and I honestly have to wonder how I coped. It was a full-on year on all fronts, from my health not being good, trips to hospital for tests, Laura sick on quite a few separate occasions. Fabian! Laura's dad was still being extremely difficult; guess there was nothing unusual in that. How I got through my working days I will never know, how I got through the year I will never know, only know I must be a whole lot stronger than I gave myself credit for.

Thanks to the Supreme Court judge another psychiatrist saw Fabian on September 20, 1999, he stated in his report that Fabian's mental state was clearly abnormal and was clearly psychotic at the time. He disagreed with the new diagnosis and stated that due to his level of distress Fabian had received a 'depot' anti psychotic injection. This psychiatrist disagreed with the conclusions of the current psychiatrist and also stated that his own conclusions had been derived from frequent contact plus an interview with myself. He believed his level of medication should be increased.

You see, the level of medication Fabian was receiving was akin to my gynaecologist putting a bandaid on my caesarean cut (a cut which extended from one side of my body to the other) - in lieu of stitches. The result would have been the same. I hope this analogy puts it into perspective for you.

Fabian's behaviour as at November 12 1999 had modified significantly; was still not good but definitely an improvement. He had ceased slashing himself (which he did during times of distress due to auditory hallucinations).

In a report dated November 18 1999, it was stated Fabian would need continuing anti psychotic medication. A report totally disregarded by our user friendly psychiatrist.

On Thursday October 21, I wrote in my work diary - Public Holiday, under this in large letters - Thank goodness, I needed it!!! Guess that said it all.

On October 29, I received a call from probation to say Fabian had two full days in a normal yard instead of the prison hospital. I had no idea what to make of that. Unsure if it was good or bad.

By November 12, probation was discussing supervision and a residential program upon release. Release, now that was a scary thought, especially if Fabian had not been reinstated to normal levels of medication.

My level of concern was so great I wrote a four page submission to the then Ombudsman, I chose my words carefully as I need someone to pay attention and help me to help my son.

I outlined Fabian's mental history, prison history and subsequent lack of medication and the consequences of same. This letter was dated November 25, 1999.

I later learned during a 'butt' covering exercise on his part - my submission, my plea for help, was *filed* - not actioned; merely seen as a submission and filed as part of an enquiry into the prison. How could anyone have interpreted my plea as merely a 'submission to be considered?' I shall elaborate more fully in the next book. Life really can be the pits at times. Might also interest you to learn this same guy was also Commissioner for Health Complaints - quite ironic eh? All things considered. He actually got paid to be this useless and incompetent! The State Government has a lot to answer for at times. Accountability non-existent!

Schizophrenia, I had absolutely no knowledge of or experience with. When Fabian was diagnosed I knew I had to educate myself if I was to help him. I discovered ARAFMI. This group provides support, counselling and information regarding mental illness. I don't know what I would have done without them and their co-workers, they were all fantastic. ARAFMI support not only the mentally ill but also support members of their families and anyone who happen along to their meetings.

Not only did I not know anything about schizophrenia, I didn't know anything about drugs at that time. Fabian taught me (from watching his behaviour change) that when on speed one could jump the back fence in a single bound, when on marijuana or not on anything one needed one's mum to drive them to the shop for cigarettes. Fabian taught me that when on morphine or prescribed drugs one slept for extended periods and gave one's mum a much needed break. I began to learn the signs of each and the frightening signs of withdrawal and the obsession to have the next fix at any cost.

I learned that kids on drugs with mental health issues fell through the cracks of the medical profession. Drugs and alcohol would send the kids to mental health, mental health would send them to drugs and alcohol - there was a rather large void in between the two. It didn't seem to occur to them that they should maybe ….hmm I don't know - WORK

TOGETHER! Combine resources so these kids could have a one stop shop where they could have counselling, where they could receive help. Instead many fell through the cracks alright, straight into the judicial system; there was nowhere else they could go given their mental state. They would end up committing a crime whether from the perspective of wanting money to buy drugs or committing a crime due to their paranoia as in Fabian's case with some of his convictions.

A series of four deaths rocked the prison from August through to October 1999. Three were by suicide, hanging to be precise, the fourth remains unexplained. Each and every one of these deaths affected me deeply. The possibility of its happening was way too close for comfort given Fabian's mental state and lack of adequate treatment.

What did affect me deeply was knowledge of Fabian's fight with one of them two days prior to their particular death. Fabian had been under investigation for that incident, but was cleared of any wrong doing. Two youths with schizophrenia so acute mixing together, was a recipe for disaster even under optimum conditions; if Fabian's medication was insufficient any glance could be misinterpreted because of paranoia. Heavens, didn't even have to be a glance, it would have been highly probable Fabian could have imagined those thoughts.

Probation staff was kind enough to keep this piece of news from me until they knew the outcome of the investigations. They didn't believe I needed more stress at that time.

When I spoke to Fabian about this or vice versa he said "He got into a fight, they were arguing as to who had the best body", I kid you not, he couldn't believe the audacity of this guy to voice that he had the best body when Fabian obviously thought he had. Sad isn't it? Two kids with a serious mental illness fighting to ascertain who had the best body. Inconceivable to you and I but a sad reality to them, given their mental state.

I would like to take this opportunity to point out how many wonderful people work in this environment. Prison staff and in particular hospital staff has gained absolute admiration from me. When Fabian was in prison for the **first** (you see everything changed after that unfortunately) time, nursing staff, doctors would all ask me to wait after visitation, explain how Fabian was going and ask if I had any concerns about my visit. When he wanted to return to the main prison someone would phone me, discuss and explain why they had agreed and that he could return to the hospital whenever he requested or required. If a visit only lasted seconds because of Fabian's mental state, by the time I got home my phone would be ringing to see what had happened. So you can see why I think so highly of the staff.

Probation staff was absolutely magnificent (no other word would suffice). The amount of time they put into their clients and associated families is certainly appreciated. They did not have enough time to bless themselves with, case load versus time availability, way out of proportion, but somehow they managed. Probation staff was sometimes my only means of ascertaining how Fabian was doing whilst he was in prison, particularly during his worst periods, schizophrenia-wise. These two beautiful souls have my undying respect and love.

The custodial officers at the prison have my love and respect for life. The work these guys do, well you wouldn't do it unless you wanted to make a difference. In some cases I do believe we have the occasional 'power tripper' but on the whole they are a fantastic group undertaking a remarkable job in extremely difficult and sometimes volatile circumstances.

Staff at both the Magistrate and Supreme Courts grew to recognize me. I would be scanning the notice boards and would hear a voice behind me say "Fabian is in Court Eight today" or "Court has already started early, hurry". Thank you to those very kind gentlemen, thank you so very much.

Medical staff at the Royal Hobart Hospital Emergency Department - what can I say? Again another fantastic group of people, I was always treated with respect and Fabian's condition stabilized as fast as humanly possible. And I should add - without judgment.

Ambulance officers, up to and including the plain clothes police officer who accompanied them on a few occasions, have my undying love and respect for the work they do and the way in which they helped Fabian and myself.

The Kingston police, each and every time they landed on my doorstep, same as above, I was always treated with the utmost respect. They listened and offered assistance if I so required. The Commanding officer has every right to be extremely proud of his group of staff. I walked into the police station one day - what can I say? Another place I was recognized by name, like I said, I spread myself around, unintentionally that is!

Early December 1999 I received a phone call from a nurse, he was a wonderful, caring psychiatric nurse at Risdon Prison. "Gut wrenching stuff" to quote him. Fabian was on a low dose tranquilizer, thanks to him, at least the psychiatrist had agreed to this much. He wanted a total 100% review of Fabian's case. He had been trying to organize some activities for Fabian, behavioural difficulties needed to be challenged and he wanted to undertake with Fabian. He encouraged me to phone him anytime.

He had referred Fabian to a senior forensic psychologist for psychological testing and this action had not made him very popular with the psychiatrist. He requested a battery of different tests. He hoped to use the results to verify whether or not the psychiatrist in question had indeed made an incorrect diagnosis.

He advised that if all else failed he could ask for a second opinion but it would in fact be a recommendation only - and it was still up to the attending psychiatrist to agree or not. The impending release time was a problem - the big question; what state would Fabian be in mentally at that time?

CHAPTER TWENTY FIVE

Christmas 1999 isn't a time I really wish to focus on. Laura was sick most of the time, pre and post Christmas. Continual visits to the doctor, all without resolution. I suspect she was nervous. Her dad would 'steal' her on occasions and force her to go to Launceston with him to visit his relatives. Laura hated those visits when she was young and each Christmas and Easter the same symptoms would reappear only to disappear as soon as the 'danger' period had lapsed.

I drove to the local shopping centre on this day, bought pens and paper for Fabian, believing if he had his drawing then all was not lost, he at least had something to do to fill in his long days and nights. Mostly in the vain hope it may save his sanity, yes, and ease mine!

Christmas time without my children was always bad regardless, but the fact that it was also his birthday made it even worse, it's my teary time. No one should be in prison for Christmas and/or birthday, let alone someone who is seriously mentally ill.

I was not permitted to give him that small gift, not even given the circumstances. Laura was in the car lying down, me praying she would not vomit again until I at least returned to the car, hot day, me at the prison reception trying not to dissolve into tears and make a total dork of myself. Thoughts of Fabian in prison for yet another Christmas and birthday all too much to bear at that moment. Would life ever improve? I defy anyone to find 'positive' under those circumstances.

December 28 1999. My girlfriend, Laura and I visited Fabian for his birthday. If I believed I couldn't feel any worse than I already was, I was about to get a rude shock. Fabian's mental state was atrocious. The poor kid was an absolute mess.

He had pierced his nipple with a safety pin, he had burn marks over his body (self inflicted), he was responding to voices the whole time we were with him, he asked if I could hear what he was thinking (now a common question, even on good days).

The piece of news to end all "I tried to hang myself but fell on the bed" he laughed as he imparted this piece of information. Hebephrenic schizophrenia will cause this type of reaction - laughter at the most inappropriate times was becoming predictable, not acceptable just a sad, predictable fact of life for Fabian. This laughter was a marked symptom of this hideous disease, a symptom not fully understood by the very staff who were tasked with his care.

The laughter compounded what I can only describe as a mind numbing statement. The impact freezing my frazzled brain to such an extent that the next sentence he uttered failed to register on the radar at all. Even to this day I cannot recall what he said next.

During this visit he told me he had killed another mental health inmate, I stated that I was aware of the incident and that no, he had not been the cause of his death. He said "Mum, what did he die of?" I had to say I had no idea, just knew he wasn't to blame. The look of absolute despair and disbelief on his pained face made my heart sink to an unbelievable depth. I knew this lack of explanation was insufficient and I had failed in my attempt to convince him. He wanted the truth and I didn't have any facts to justify innocence in his mind. The look on his face I shall never ever forget.......... I had felt helpless before was I had just entered a whole new depth of helpless, one so low I wasn't even aware it existed.

I try not to dwell as to how much this must have played on his already tormented mind. He was a child who never judged others, loved his mates, believed everyone was born equal, never hurt anything deliberately (well except for the mouse he decided looked like a helicopter as he dropped it). He was absolutely distraught at the fact he may have harmed another, it was written all over his precious face.

I prayed that night; no parent should see their child in the state in which I had to leave Fabian that day and not be able to do a single thing about it. He was in the hands of the State Government, two different departments in fact, neither taking responsibility for his well-being. I prayed for God to take him if there wasn't any hope of recovery, no one deserves to live in that state of mind, or lack of it. No one!

Other inmates present at that visit couldn't help but notice Fabian's mental state, one inmate closer than the other kept shaking his head, saying he should be in the hospital. It wouldn't have taken a rocket scientist to make that deduction, yet no one at the prison acknowledged this fact; I should qualify that by saying - no one with the power to take assertive action.

As I stated earlier, the amount of medication Fabian had been receiving for schizophrenia would have been an equivalent of my gynaecologist putting a bandaid on my open caesarian wound - the likelihood of success … negligible. The evidence of the analogy was only too obvious that particular day.

On a visit with Dr Counsellor, evening I might add, visits I needed so badly at this period, I was leaving his room and said "See you next visit", his reply "Oh if the baby hasn't been born before then". Visits with Dr Counsellor were always set up months in advance. As I was walking out the door these words came into my mind "The baby won't be born by then". I got into my car and thought, how did I know that, how did I know his baby won't be born by my next visit? Confused I drove home.

There were times throughout the periods of schizophrenia I would pray Fabian be taken rather than prolong his suffering. As a mother there are times when being selfish isn't good, for my sake I wanted him with me but what kind of life did he have, one controlled by voices and drug addiction, what kind of life is that for a twenty one year old? The long term prognosis by the treating psychiatrists was viewed as extremely poor.

I Make Mark

What happened to my precious little boy? By now I was acknowledging I had absolutely no hope of getting him back.

Those words spoken to me in 1979 were coming back loud and clear, I assume I was learning the meaning of the voice's words: "Make the most of him because you only have him for a short time"?

I have no idea why I didn't make it back to the prison - maybe I wasn't meant to, maybe the pain of that day was a little too much to bear and I needed some time to get my head around it.

January 10, 2000

Laura, then 9 years old was still experiencing all the same symptoms as previously, stomach cramps, nausea, the hot weather certainly not helping in the slightest. I remember having to go into the city, remember thinking I would have liked to visit Fabian, but all things considered, believed driving out to the prison in a hot car was not going to be in Laura's best interest. I decided to shelve that idea for a more suitable day, if only I had known, I was not meant to visit that day.

All afternoon I was restless, couldn't sit or focus on one thing for more than a few minutes at a time. Couldn't even begin to understand why, didn't make any sense. My neck hurt, ached, I couldn't get comfortable no matter how I sat. I tried lying down in the hope it may relieve the discomfort. No, didn't work. Back to pacing around the house wishing my aching neck would return to normal.

I remember cooking dinner for Laura and myself, remember not feeling hungry but going through the motions. Interest in anything? Well that left me sometime late afternoon; again any hope of an imminent return or explanation had deserted me.

Nine fifteen a loud knock shattered my restlessness. I wasn't impressed by a visit at that hour, it was loud and insistent enough to be my ex husband, a visit from him at that time wasn't something I relished; it usually meant an argument ensued.

One of us reluctantly answered the door - the gentleman explained he was … from the Kingston police, funny how when you hear those words the brain hits panic mode, time freezes and input and comprehension stop dead in its tracks.

He was sorry to say … my son Fabian had been found dead in his prison cell at approximately 6:30pm. He had apparently hanged himself.

I remember stating I knew it was coming, just didn't know when. I explained what had transpired at our last visit on his birthday.

Laura came out of the bedroom, I explained what had happened, remember saying there was only the two of us at home now, that Fabian had found peace at last and we should be grateful for that.

The detective was reluctant to leave us alone under the circumstances and wanted the name of a friend or relative who would be available to come and stay with us. He explained I would need to contact the Coroner's office tomorrow……what did I know about the Coroner's office? Should have seen the trouble I had just trying to locate it in the phone book, let alone phone and ask what? Didn't even know what I was phoning them for. It all seemed to happen so fast and the poor brain had to try to keep pace whilst still slightly frozen.

I phoned my girlfriend, when she answered I started crying, couldn't say a word - I heard …I'm on my way…I put the receiver down much to a startled police officer trying to grab the phone before I managed to put it down completely. Quite an athletic attempt but he failed. I explained through my tears she was on her way.

I remember crying uncontrollably that evening once alone, crying from both relief and pain. A beautiful son I would not see develop into an adult and all the happiness and joy that can bring, a son with a cheeky grin, a smile never to be seen again except in my memory. How he would stir me until I would spin around to have a say back, to find him standing in front of the fire place with his trademark grin, knowing he had once again managed to set me up beautifully. He had a knack of being able to reel me in hook, line and sinker.

Relief, I loved him as any mother does, but how could I be selfish enough to wish him back to a life tormented by voices, voices which were sometimes friendly, but mostly menacing. Tormented by a drug addiction which took over his young life, I couldn't do that, I loved him too much to watch him suffer anymore. Watching him suffer and self destruct was soul destroying, the feeling of desperation and frustration knowing that it was all going to end sooner or later and unable to do anything to stop the inevitable.

Ok, momentum took over at this point, everything happens so fast. Funeral to arrange - ooops no money, now that could be a problem. A continuous stream of phone calls and visitors took over what was a normally a relatively quiet time of the year for me.

The attending psychiatrist telephoned me on his way home from the prison, now that was definitely a first, nice of him to phone 'after the fact'. I shouldn't be so unkind, I am unable to recall the conversation but I am sure he probably meant well.

I somehow managed to telephone a friend – the auntie of one of the boys who too had taken his life in prison. I wanted her to hear this news from me, her nephew's death had only occurred in August; hearing of Fabian's death in the news would have been a major shock, one she didn't need. I figured if I could lessen the blow a little I would.

January 11, 2000

I managed to finally obtain a number for the Coroner's office - death by neck compression, results of a toxicology test wouldn't be known for a few weeks. Seems they were concerned re the number of deaths occurring at the prison and were about to launch a full scale task force into Fabian's death in the hope of preventing any further deaths. I didn't know what a full scale task force consisted of or meant, but I was pleased they were taking assertive action.

Funeral service had to be arranged. Like now!

Phone calls from far and wide, continuous stream of visitors once again. My girlfriend and I worked on a system - one manned the phone, the other manned the door, it worked reasonably well. Either way we had a system of sorts to help us cope.

January 12, 2000

Made an appointment to view his body at 3pm - mixed reactions now, driving into the city I didn't know what to expect or how I would feel, the closer we got, the more peace I found. Strange!

I realized that my peace of mind came from the fact that this was only Fabian's earthly body, a body he no longer required. His soul had found peace and he was happy at last. I had to be happy for him, how could I not be? *That day he gave me a minor insight into what was to come. How my life was to take a new turn, any pre-existing perceptions challenged, how my soul development was to be accelerated. All I had to do was be open to what I was about to experience.*

Having Dr Counsellor in my life as a counsellor had been invaluable, he had assisted me in gaining understanding and to make sense of the foreign land I had found myself in. Thanks to him, I realized Fabian had fulfilled his 'Life Purpose' and had found peace. He had prepared me as much as was humanly possible. It was Fabian's journey and he had had a right to end it as he thought best - in Divine Time as per his contract. At this point the 'big picture' as to why, was only just beginning to take shape.

Laura had written Fabian a letter, this we placed in the coffin with him. I spoke to Fabian, explained I was happy for him, not happy with him for leaving us like he did. No preparation, no written note of explanation, no good bye - one minute he was with us, the next he was gone. Life is like that I guess. If there is a moral to be had here it has to be, treat every day like it is your last, tell that person you love them, don't send them off angry. Appreciate every person in your life and don't ever take them for granted.

Hey I didn't say it would be easy, I know for a fact it isn't and I speak from experience, I am just asking you to think about that aspect and try to make a difference in your life and those closest to you. Some things you will be unable to change; as much as you wish otherwise, not everything is within your control, but some things are, it is those I ask you to challenge yourself on. The rewards will far exceed your expectations.

And for the record ... Dr Counsellor's baby was born on the 10 January 2000, either just before or just after Fabian took his own life. Why? I don't have an answer for you...well not at the moment anyway. Hopefully by the time I write Beyond Description it may clear. I shall keep you posted; again I don't believe it was a coincidence. In my mind it was the universe letting me know I had a 'connection' to Dr Counsellor in some way. A connection which would be revealed in Divine Time.

As I write this particular piece it is now January 21 2005, five years since Fabian's death. I had been writing of his death at the time of his death five years ago (same dates). It seems as though it were yesterday. I have cried and cried this year. Each year I remember his death but try not to dwell on it, try to keep busy is my guess. This year for the first time I allowed myself to feel everything, every day seemed as if this were the day of...his death...his funeral...the prison service...and it was as if I was living through it all again, only this time I knew what the next day would bring. Honestly needed wind screen wipers as I wrote, some days I could only write for a short time before it all got too much, I would go to bed absolutely drained with red, swollen eyes.

This year I allowed myself time to feel the pain, to grieve for the son I lost, five years it took me but looks as if I finally got there. On January 10, the date of his death, I cried most of the day. I sat at my back window and just sobbed and sobbed, at the time it didn't make a lot of sense. At 6:25pm I was watching the news and burst into uncontrollable tears, that was the time he would have been setting himself free five years ago. Is it only as bad this year because I am writing this book and the dates coincide? In retrospect I suppose it does make sense, allowing myself time to feel the emotions and go with it. Will this mean 2006 won't be anywhere near as bad? Will writing this book and this period of grief allow closure for me? Guess only time will tell.

The one thing or I should say person who has kept me going through this very trying, albeit short period is a very special man whom I met at ballroom dancing during November. He and Fabian share the same birth date, only the year varies, coincidence? I think not. He understands and although we don't always speak about Fabian he is giving me the strength to get through this period and to continue writing. For that I am most grateful and also for the gentle, loving way in which he holds me when we are together. Without him I don't know how I would have managed to continue writing when it was altogether too painful. Thank you, thank you so very much. Also thanks to another person from dancing - he would phone, hear my voice and say "you working on your book again?" he could tell I had been crying. Thank you for understanding.

> *Prior to Christmas 1999 Laura and I had purchased a 'pound pup'; she was approximately two years old. She was purchased as a companion for Sally. The pound had named her Shelley. Shelley had come complete with an extremely bad dose of kennel cough so had been housed indoors since her arrival. Night two or three following Fabian's death Shelley woke me by her incessant barking, something she never did. She was barking at 'something' in the hallway, but I couldn't see anything that would have caused this type of panicked reaction from her.*
>
> *It took me a few days of 'other things' happening before I realized she was merely announcing Fabian's arrival home. His spirit, now free, was back home to let me know he was now happy and healthy again, free of his tormented thoughts. Shelley had not met Fabian so to her he was a stranger invading our home, spirit or not she was letting me know of his arrival.*
>
> *The first noticeable sign was a photograph of my two grandsons, it was housed on a bookshelf just inside the front door, it was the first thing I saw as I walked into my home. The photograph would be turned around, thinking it may have been accidently left in the wrong position by 'someone' doing the dusting for me, I would return it to the rightful position with only a brief thought as to why it may be happening more than once.*
>
> *This happened a few times, by the next time not only was it turned around but the corner was also bent down (like a bookmark dog*

eared effect). I broached this subject with Dr Counsellor on my next visit and he said "What do you think it is trying to tell you?" I replied "It's Fabian trying to let me know he is free and happy, the dog eared effect was his way of saying take note, it is me mum". With a beaming smile Dr Counsellor agreed, he said he is wanting you to know he is ok again. Some souls are stronger than others, he believed Fabian was a strong soul.

Even from beyond the veil Fabian was still teaching me, he was and is still my greatest teacher and for that I love and appreciate him so very much.

Following this realization other things kept happening, I shall elaborate further in Beyond Description. All I ask is that you keep an open mind in your own life following the death of any loved ones. Picture frames which are constantly being moved from straight to crooked, small items going missing only to be found days later in a different location, light taps on the shoulder, items come crashing out of the cupboard...the list goes on. They have a myriad of ways in which they try to gain your attention. It is the most beautiful experience should you be open to it and it certainly helps one to understand that our Souls continue beyond our Earthly experience.

These experiences are a beautiful, heavenly gift from our dearly departed, they are not meant to be feared, they merely want us to know how much we are loved and that they are and shall remain with us.

You could say they are 'dying to be heard'.

January 13, 2000

Funeral service at 10:30am today, how am I going to get through that? The funeral director had been absolutely wonderful. Fabian's dad came around the day after Fabian's death. When we were speaking to the funeral director about what type of service, his dad was saying yes we want this. Hang on, no we don't I'm thinking. Fabian would have wanted it said as it was, he didn't lie (well unless drugs and money came into it), Fabian would have wanted the truth. I asked for the service to be conducted by a member of the Prison Support Service and thankfully they agreed.

The service was so Fabian, he would have been proud. The inmates were mentioned, as too, was the mother of another inmate for her thoughtfulness in giving me Courtney the bear. Words were said that spoke the truth, even down to the fact that when I viewed Fabian's body I knew his soul had already departed. I couldn't have asked for more.

I am also grateful for the many wonderful family and friends who made the effort to come and say their last goodbye to Fabian, thank you for your kindness and support, he certainly touched the lives of many people. Thankful to Fabian's dad for paying for the funeral service, I kept costs as low as I possibly could.

Following the service, a group of us headed off to the prison (all female that is), no, it wasn't planned. I wanted the flowers from the service to be placed in the prison so they too felt a part of the proceedings, he was their friend too, but they were unable to be there for him or for them.

I was on a mum mission venturing into unknown territory - only this time I had company.

I was fortunate enough to speak with the Accommodation Manager, think we took the prison reception by surprise, they didn't quite know what to do with us. We were handballed to him. He was absolutely magnificent, he too, amongst others have my respect and love forever for the kindness and respect he showed us on that and other visits. If reception staff had had time to think and handballed us to senior management, the day's outcome would have been vastly different, senior management were definitely not in the user friendly category as I was about to learn. Thank you for being the beautiful soul you are, don't ever change.

He held the inmates from E Yard over in the mess whilst he showed us Fabian's cell, Laura too was included in the visit. I needed to see where he committed suicide; I needed to make sense of his death.

I Make Mark

He understood my need to see Fabian's cell, he explained as much to us as we could comprehend, he sat me down and spoke with me at length about Fabian. About the reaction of other inmates to Fabian's death and the toll it had taken on everyone. He shared some of his Fabian stories with me and for that I will be eternally grateful.

It seemed Fabian had made an impact on many, both inmates and staff alike. They were all feeling the impact of his death to varying degrees. The I MAKE MARK statement was alive and well it appeared.

The cell was a small, cold concrete room, rectangular in size, not a place any person would willingly wish to take up residence, let alone someone with a severe mental illness. As difficult as it was, I had had to make that journey for my own peace of mind.

I couldn't picture Fabian's body tied to the hanging point he had found, I just couldn't go there. I had to be positive and believe like never before he had found peace the only way he knew how. I had to be happy for him, and for the moment leave my feelings aside.

I needed to understand what it was like in this dreadful place, how they coped with their surroundings, I need to understand so I would know how to help others. I wanted positive change to come out of this dreadful situation, in order for that to occur I had to make the most of every learning occasion.

One call I received from an ex-inmate said to me "Your dog would have better living conditions Denise" seemed N Division (punishment division) was far worse. Hard to believe given what I had just witnessed.

The Accommodation Manager also explained that E Yard was to hold their personal service for Fabian the next day, and I would be most welcome to attend should I wish. Should I wish? I was most humbled and grateful for the opportunity and the invitation? Of course I wished.

My girlfriend, Laura and I left the prison and went to The Mercury newspaper, I had written an article I wished them to publish, I wanted the truth told about Fabian's schizophrenia. The original press release from the prison stated he was suffering from depression, his death described as an 'unfortunate tragedy'. How could they? Doesn't speaking the truth mean anything anymore? This child had been diagnosed with schizophrenia whilst under a Hospital Order - depression? Please! I wanted the truth told.

I was told the editor couldn't see me - too busy - oh, can I tell him what it is about? Guess what? I explained I was Fabian Long's mother and I had an article I wished them to publish stating the facts about Fabian's death. This busy editor became less busy - funny that! I was taken to an office where he explained this was far too important for a small article, he wanted a feature article and that his journalist would be in touch.

I thank the staff at the Mercury newspaper, up to and including the editor, I fully understand his reluctance to meet with a myriad of people who must ask. I thank them for their support and for their honesty and integrity in the reporting of Fabian's death.

As if all this wasn't enough, I had a date with a dental surgeon at the end of the day, root canal work required. I kept this appointment, they wouldn't do the surgery on that day - you have had more than enough for one day they explained as they packed me off out the door. Thanks Dr B for being so understanding and compassionate.

January 14, 2000

CIB Bellerive Police Station - 10am-12noon - had to be interviewed by the detectives about Fabian's death. I walked in the door rather nervous, they were expecting it would take all of fifteen minutes unquote, they asked me a couple of questions and I said "I think you had better read this". They read my four page submission to the Ombudsman outlining Fabian's history and decided this was going to take way longer than he originally anticipated. I obviously knew and had deduced way more than he had suspected, I explained I needed to be at the prison by 12noon. I wasn't going to miss the service for Fabian held by E yard, it was way too important to me.

After reading the submission, the coroner was telephoned, the detectives wanted Fabian's death incorporated into the Deaths in Custody - five deaths in a six month period!

I was pinpointing the prison psychiatric services as the cause of the deaths of these five inmates and in particular the attending forensic psychiatrist, I was also pointing out that unless something was done there would be more deaths, little did I know it would be my son. Yes they were interested. My, the power of the written word, and I thought when I painstakingly wrote this submission it was only going to be viewed by the Ombudsman, now it was going to be included as evidence at the Deaths in Custody Hearing. Two hours of taped interview ensued.

Twelve noon - made it to the prison in time. I was fortunate enough to attend Fabian's funeral service in Risdon Prison, E Yard. I met each of the inmates in this yard, a privilege and a pleasure. The sea of red eyes, a considerable number Fabian's age and younger - they too were having trouble dealing with yet another death in their yard.

Following the service I asked if I could speak to the inmates, me, who hated public speaking of any kind, I didn't have any idea what I wanted to say, I hadn't planned anything. I only knew I wanted them to be aware of how much I appreciated their friendship and for making my visits pleasant instead of horrific. I outlined my experiences from the very first visit, how they had helped me tremendously, some by saying hello, by helping lookout for Fabian, by a friendly wave of the hand. I wanted them to know how much they meant to me. I wanted them to know how much they meant to Fabian, his mates meant the world to him and I needed to give them that message, Fabian would have wanted that.

I explained that Fabian had died amongst friends and who could ask for more. They were not to feel guilty but grateful for the fact that he did not die alone. It was his choice to end his life at that time, I felt it was important for them to understand and hear those words. I didn't want them to carry guilt for something which was out of their control.

I met all the inmates in turn and spoke to most of them - one inmate had recently lost his son, another had lost both parents since incarceration. One was in the shower with Fabian on the 10th, realized how bad he was and gave him a hug. One inmate had written a piece for the service but was too upset to read it. One inmate only received one visit per year because his parents were in Northern Tasmania - he wanted to take over the role as Laura's big brother.

One inmate said "It should have been me not him!" They were overwhelmed with grief but still had an infinite amount of compassion for Laura and myself.

It really was an experience I shall always treasure. Nothing but nothing could surpass that. *I left the prison feeling like the richest person in the world.* They gave me so much on that day when I most needed it. Thanks guys for being the best!

The strength gained from that experience got me through the rest of the afternoon - yes CIB yet again for another two hours of taped interview. I must have had a lot to say given I took up four hours of tape ... or the Police had many questions????

We arrived back home at whatever time. The reporter phoned from The Mercury, could they come and interview me tonight? As you can probably imagine I was feeling pretty washed out, ecstatic and overwhelmed with the prison service, disgusted but pleased with my experience at CIB. Disgusted as they were ready to dismiss me as just another mother of an inmate who had committed suicide, pleased that because of my ability to write I had been give the opportunity of being taken seriously, thank heaven for my submission to the Ombudsman. But why should it have taken that?

I explained to her - if you can take me as you find me then you are most welcome tonight, I outlined my day's itinerary and the fact that I was exhausted and far from my best.

From 9-10pm, both reporter and photographer listened with interest as I outlined Fabian's history and the events of the day. I felt as though it had gone well, now I had to put my faith and trust in her like my life depended upon it. I wanted the truth spoken and I hoped she would follow through for me.

One of the inmates I had met at the service really stuck in my mind, I could feel the warmth of his hand as he held mine, I was unable to recall his facial features, remembered how very shy and upset he appeared, his head downcast as he spoke to me. He was brought over and introduced by another inmate, introduced as the person who had written the words for the service. He was the yard representative. Why he had made such an impression I didn't know, but the warmth of our joined hands stayed with me. It was as if the imprint had been set permanently and felt familiar. I couldn't get him out of my mind; I should say I couldn't get the feeling out of my mind.

The written words for the service

> *On behalf of all E yard inmates:*
>
> *Fabian was one of the family, well liked by all, some knew him better than others. To some he was a brother. Our words and prayers cannot change whats happened but in our hearts he will never be forgotten. He will be sadly missed by in E yard and all other inmates he knew. 6 months ago we lost another family member which broke our hearts, now to lose another, our lives shattered forever.*
>
> *Fabian you will forever be in our thoughts and hearts, memories of you are ours to treasure not today but forever and ever.*
>
> *To Mr and Mrs Long and family our deepest sympathy*
>
> *Written by E Yard Rep.*

Was the warmth and memory of his hand a signpost?

January 15/16, 2000

Weekend at last, exhaustion caught up with me on occasions and I fell into a sleep even an explosion would not have woken me from.

Received news on the January 16, an inmate had attempted suicide, tried to hang himself. Oh dear God when will this madness end. The inmate was also housed in E Yard.

January 17, 2000

The Mercury headlines today, our story the feature article alright, front page to be precise. At 7am I had a visit from a psychiatric nurse; he had read the newspaper early and felt he had to call on me. How very kind, this blew me away entirely. This gentleman had been working at the Royal Derwent hospital when Fabian was there, he had also worked at the prison hospital. He was disgusted at the lack of caring by hospital staff. He wanted me to know how very sorry he was. People never cease to amaze me. I have not had any more contact with this particular man. I hope he too reads my story and understands from this how very much his visit meant to me. Thank you so very much for your kindness and for taking the time to come and visit me. I shall never forget you. I have that image of opening the door that morning permanently imprinted on my brain, can still recall his features.

Phone calls in abundance today, one from a guy whom I met through work many, many years previously. He, too, was upset when he read the newspaper article. He had been in prison and he advised had he known, he may have been able to have people look after Fabian. If I ever wanted to talk to him all I had to do was phone. He told me I had been kind to him when he needed it and now he wanted to give some of that back. Like I said, people never cease to amaze me.

I had been informed by the Coroner's Office that I needed a lawyer. Geez, like I could afford that minor luxury! I figured I owed this to Fabian, what choice did I have? Accordingly, I made an appointment with the lawyer who represented Fabian during his last court appearances. I didn't know what else to do, at least she knew his history; what I would do if this company refused to represent Fabian I had no idea, courage required for this appointment, I didn't have money but I needed representation for my son.

At 1pm, interview with journalist for Australasian Post Magazine - he had previously written an article on Risdon Prison - he wanted to follow up with *our* story. I felt propelled into another dimension, so much was happening. It was a chance to get my message 'out there' a chance to improve understanding of mental illness, in particular care of the mentally ill within the judicial system. To hopefully help people to understand that everyone including inmates deserve to be treated with respect.

Received phone call to advise that an inmate from the infamous N Division (punishment division) had been taken to see the psychiatrist for depression; consultation lasted for approximately 93 seconds ... and I bet you thought 15 minutes for a routine consultation with a GP was insufficient, how would you feel if you had a mental problem and you were in and out in less than 2 minutes?

I received a phone call from a mother who had a son taking drugs, was about to face his first court appearance. He had attempted suicide a number of times; she would take him to hospital only to have him sent straight back home. He had been in street fights, he was eighteen. His mother was now suffering panic attacks; they came from nowhere she explained. Her son had been diagnosed with ASPD - she was told to go home, no treatment for this. I referred her to a couple of doctors whom I knew would help her and her son, if only she could get an appointment.

January 17 proved quite a day all up, information coming in from all sources, people apologizing for contacting me at such a time, but they needed help and they had no idea where to turn. They had read my story and figured if anyone could point them in the right direction, I could. Or at least they knew or hoped I would listen and offer assistance if at all possible, seems I was their last hope. What a sad indictment on our society when the only person who can help them is a mother of a child (a child who had just committed suicide under the most trying and sad circumstances). If I couldn't help my own child what hope did they think I could offer them? I will never know the answer to that, I pray I did help them in some small way.

As I said, my life took on momentum like you wouldn't believe; the telephone unrelenting. Not a negative unrelenting, a rewarding unrelenting if that makes sense. Each and everyone a challenge of a different kind.

January 18, 2000

I packed Fabian's clothes into bags to give to Dr Counsellor for distribution to those who needed them. Today was definitely the pits. Getting rid of Fabian's clothes meant I had to admit I would never see him again and that this time he was definitely not coming back. *It was the most difficult task I have ever had to undertake in my life.* Even now thinking of this has tears streaming down my face, by now I should have the cleanest face (if not the saltiest) in the world, I have cried so much over the last two weeks. If it were good for the complexion I would look a million dollars by now. If only eh?

Fabian's clothes deposited with Dr Counsellor, now it was time to go to my grandson's birthday party, like I really felt in the mood for that one. Brave face, emotions in check; off I went.

By night time I was absolutely exhausted, that feeling was becoming all too familiar!

At night I would feel totally spent, particularly if the day had been full with visitors and phone calls, I would get into bed, usually extremely late, Laura would begin to cry and scream, just what I needed. Why she couldn't get it out of her system during daylight hours I will never understand. Sometimes I tried talking quietly to her, some nights I actually got angry with her (yes, I know I shouldn't and I didn't like myself very much when I did become agitated), but in my own defence, exhaustion and grief do funny things to people. I was in danger of losing my sanity and dealing with this amount of screaming late at night was beginning to be akin to the straw that breaks the camel's proverbial back.

January 19, 2000

A friend phoned, his daughter had run into Fabian one day, he was red in the face and going in circles screaming (like he was possessed by the Devil - her words), sad so very sad. Mental illness doesn't have to be like this does it? He and I arranged to have lunch, he probably figured I could use lunch with a friend.

The messages I continued to receive keep blowing me away, letters from people I knew fourteen years ago, twenty years ago and they still cared enough to write - unreal! I received letters from inmates, written by one and signed by many. Letters from different parts of the prison, remand, the hospital, the staff! Each one brought tears to my eyes, happy tears. Each one reminding me of the son I had lost, but more importantly letting me know **the mark he had made on so many**! They all cared enough to write to me for that I thank each and every one of them from the bottom of my heart.

An ex inmate from Canberra telephoned - he was in E Yard with Fabian, had at that time written a submission to the Ombudsman, not mentioning Fabian by name but using him as an example. He thanked me for the article in the newspaper, he was going to send copies of his two submissions he wrote. Seems Monday's article has prompted him into writing a second. Good for him, we need people to push for change. He believed his submissions as an ex-inmate wouldn't count for much and hoped mine would receive due attention; I suspect his view was correct, sad, but correct.

My sincere thanks and appreciation to the reporter for keeping her word on positive reporting and not manipulating anything of which we had spoken. My thanks to the photographer for a wonderful photo which certainly depicted how I was feeling.

Fabian's probation officer phoned, one year to the day since she met Fabian, she was quite upset. Seems my son had made quite a big impression on quite a few people. I never realized the impact he had had on so many lives.

The one thing that did stand out following Fabian's death is the amount of people caught up in the incident. I can only describe it as 'a ripple effect' - I never realized one death could encompass so many people from different walks of life. Each person, with their own story, their own grief, guilt, this was a personal experience for so so many.

When Fabian wrote 'I MAKE MARK' I didn't comprehend the meaning of those three words. Following his death I understood. Fabian touched many people, from shop owners, sales people, policemen, custodial officers, probation officers, doctors, psychiatrists, nursing staff the list goes on. I have not had one person say a bad word, they all relate their various experiences of Fabian, his infectious smile and pleasant and always friendly manner usually rates a mention - I thank all of those people for sharing their stories with me, like me, they were left totally perplexed how a happy child with his trademark grin could have been misdiagnosed with a personality disorder when nothing could have been further from the truth. I think each and everyone of us will be left with those words *"can you hear what I am thinking?"* firmly implanted in our minds and know in our hearts he is now in a far better place.

I found it was necessary for me to be the comforter, I found it necessary to console a number of people, weird when you consider I was probably the one who needed the TLC. It was not to be. I received phone calls from people with whom he had dealings legally, they were feeling the guilt factor, it was they (along with me) who ensured Fabian went back to prison where we firmly believed he would receive much needed treatment. This was not merely one person from one department but a variety. Persons from organizations which were in a position to help Fabian, didn't do enough they said - yes they were correct, but then we are only human and humans have failings. Friends of mine who felt they were in a position to help - but didn't, correct again but same philosophy applies. I found I was comforting people who were carrying varying degrees of guilt for whatever their individual reasons.

I didn't understand, it didn't make any sense. Were they looking for my understanding, forgiveness, to alleviate their guilt or merely to express and reiterate the fact that we as humans have a long way to go as far as taking care of those less fortunate. I held person after person as they cried because their actions had been insufficient - insufficient on a variety of levels. I thank you all as it made life appear less senseless and reiterated the fact that change needed to occur, I needed to advocate for change.

Some had tried everything possible to gain and secure adequate medication for Fabian, everything possible 'within the system' that is. Everything possible outside of sticking their proverbial necks out so far they found themselves unemployed as a result.

As far as I was concerned - they tried - I couldn't ask for more than that - they did the best they could at the time. I was grateful for the fact they cared enough for Fabian to try. I couldn't condemn them for what they didn't do, merely thank them for what they did do.

I believe Fabian's life had purpose; unfortunately five inmates had to die in a six month period for changes to occur in the Tasmanian prison system. I am proud of my son and what his short life helped to accomplish. Hopefully other inmates in the future may have better living conditions and a chance at a 'life' once released instead of returning to that horrid place. The average person on the street may now have a better understanding of 'mental health', realize that the popular misconception that all inmates are 'born bad' is incorrect, that it can happen to any family given certain conditions and view inmates in a different light. If any of these theories I choose to believe in are even partly true, then Fabian's death wasn't in vain.

Fabian's death was incorporated in the *Deaths in Custody Coroner's Hearing - a story in itself and contained in Beyond Description - a story of grief, disbelief and insight.*

CHAPTER TWENTY SIX

PLEASE try to keep an open mind and discuss a taboo subject. Discover for yourself how rewarding it can be to share your story knowing by voicing your experience; you are now in a position to impart your new found knowledge/experience on to someone who may be desperate.

Who else best to pass on detailed knowledge of how it felt? Required resources? professional assistance? What happens? How it happens? How you survived the experience? No one but you, go ahead, free yourself of society's *'don't go there attitude'* and share, who knows, it may save a life; it may help someone feel they are no longer alone - *dare to be an individual.*

> *Too many of life's challenges are taboo subjects, age, bowel disease, domestic violence, mental illness, substance abuse, sexually transmitted infections to name a few, don't keep these subjects behind closed doors any longer, give yourself permission to speak out.*

We can survive life changing traumatic experiences/lessons by learning, living, laughing and crying together. Together we survive, alone we disintegrate brought down by the pain of our experience - I am totally in favour and a great believer of the 'together and share' theory.

Please don't think I dwell only on the negative happenings in my life, the aspects I have outlined are there for a purpose, my main aim for writing my story was to let the reader know nothing is insurmountable if one seeks assistance.

Many of my experiences made me feel so alone, if you have chosen to read my book I hope you feel 'connected' to me in some small way.

Know that we are all 'one' and are here for each other, no matter how large or small the problem. Know you are on a journey, only you can decide the outcome, you have choices. Make your choice count for the Greater Good.

Trust your intuition, love and acknowledge your personal challenges, they make you who you are.

'Know yourself, then thou shalt know the Universe and God' … Pythagoras.

Thank you to every person who assisted us on our journey. Please know i truly thank and appreciate you for who you are and the difference you made to our lives.

… and for the record, when I met with Fabian's solicitor I learned that her work colleagues were outraged at what was happening within the prison, it wasn't only my perception. They too wanted the deaths to stop. Enough was enough. They agreed to allow her to represent Fabian's interests (as I stated earlier this wasn't my death, I wasn't the one requiring representation). I advised them of my financial situation and agreed to pay a certain amount each and every fortnight. They promised me they would NEVER put pressure on me to pay the amount in full, small payments would suffice. I have never forgotten that moment, without their help I don't know what I would have done or how I would have coped. I shall elaborate further in my next book as to events which occurred. Suffice to say you can surmise how highly I think of these two wonderful people. If only the world had more of them we would be in a far better condition.

A huge heartfelt thank you to those two beautiful souls, two very devoted, compassionate lawyers I shall never forget. Solicitor J's compassion brought tears to my eyes that day, he didn't hesitate in offering the services of his firm to represent Fabian, the look on his face when he told me they would never put pressure on me for the money was so genuine, honest, heartfelt, I knew I could trust his words. I knew they would never let me down!

So many people gave me words of encouragement following the newspaper articles, they too voiced their concerns re the mentally ill housed within the prison system, like me they wanted positive change and helped me in the only way they knew how. The words of encouragement combined with the love and support I received from both staff and inmates from the prison and the judicial system gave me the strength to continue in my quest for positive change.

I read Dr Wayne Dyer's book 'Change Your Thoughts - Change Your Life' Living the Wisdom of the Tao. It is Wayne's translation of Lao Tze's 81 verses of the Tao Te Ching. Lao Tze is purported to be the greatest philosopher who ever walked on Earth. Lao's writings are simple yet powerful and give us a blue print for how to live our lives. When you read this book you will understand who Lao was and how much he is respected and loved. 'A Journey of a thousand miles begins with a single step' Lao Tze wrote, this is so very true; and true for your journey also. Start with a single step today.

One of the things I learned from reading this magnificent book is that *you don't have to know the Tao to live the Tao*. We actually incorporate it into our daily lives and if we were all to live the Tao, life would be so, so much better than the life we have come to know.

It is a must read for anyone wishing to live a richer, happier life, so when you have a chance, please avail yourself of the opportunity and tune into the Tao compliments of Wayne Dyer.

I have a few selected banners hanging in my lounge room above my spiritual table; they each remind me of the Tao and a way of life to which I aspire. I find it comforting to have these sayings around me where I can glance and be reminded of how the world could and should be.

I knew I had oceans of love and support behind me on the next part of my journey; it will be elaborated upon in Beyond Description.

In the meantime …

I Make Mark

The *Holistic Wheel Theory* I believe to be of value to all of us, especially in this day and age if we are to survive all that is thrown at us. I was going to incorporate this Wheel in Beyond Description but I was incorrect, a line went through that idea in my mind and I knew 'Upstairs' wanted it in this one.

Early one morning (well, early for me), whilst still in my dressing gown I had to go find a piece of paper and on it went the Holistic Wheel Theory, the idea was obviously channeled to me, all I had to do was add the spokes as I saw them, spokes which will be different for all each of us.

Balance is the key to most things in life, this is merely another aspect for you to consider.

Imagine if you will, a *wheel*, like you would see on a wagon from days of old. It has 3 major components.

The outer rim is the *framework* which holds everything together.

The centre or hub - the *pivotal* point.

The individual *spokes*

Living the **Tao** is the *fundamental framework* or rim for living as one, working as one and moving forward as one. Without a sturdy framework the wheel cannot function.

The *centre or pivotal point* is spirituality and your role in the Divine Plan. I am not speaking religion, I am speaking spiritual awareness.

> *Spiritual growth assists to make our everyday life work and brings harmony, clarity, compassion and love into every area of our lives.*
>
> *Growing spiritually enables the bigger picture of our life to emerge. We gain more awareness of humanity's evolution and our part in it. We discover our life's work, our purpose and gain the insight and knowledge to undertake this mission with passion. Our individual work has the ability to make a meaningful contribution to people, to Mother Earth, to our planet in general and to our precious flora and fauna. Our Life Purpose has purpose - gain the required insight you require and* **Make Your Mark.**
>
> *What many of us are looking for in another - compassion, understanding, love, happiness, we will find first in our connection to our Higher Self. What we are truly seeking is our own inner wisdom. When we find this space in ourselves we find true unconditional love - where anything and everything is possible.*

The spokes are another mandatory element of the wheel. If the spokes are not balanced moving forward will not be smooth.

The **spokes** as I see them include:

Chemical free - avoid use of 'external' toxins ie. make-up, perfume, hair dyes, cleaning products, toxic paint, herbicides, pesticides … and the list goes on.

Whole foods - return to whole foods in lieu of processed food, eat organic, chemical free food, hormone free meats, avoid genetically modified food, eliminate preservatives and additives from your diet. Eat less sugary foods. Balance your diet and rotate foods.

Exercise - whether it by yoga, Tai Chi, walking, gym work, ballroom dancing. Exercise is extremely important to your health and mental state.

Dental care - maintain your teeth to the best of your financial ability, I believe dental care should be incorporated into Medicare - it is the only viable option for everyone to have access to this important care.

Rest, relaxation, sufficient sleep, stress free (well as free as possible)

Happiness, love, compassion, respect, forgiveness, honesty, do unto others as you would have them do unto you. These elements do way more good than, hate, resentment and anger. Apply them to yourself, not just to others. Forgive yourself, love yourself.

GP who also understands the value of holistic treatments, realizes the value of the body's signals and values the opinion of the individual who knows how to read their body's signals. Pain is a warning that something is out of order! The body needs to heal on three levels, body, mind and soul. The aim is to find the balance.

Holistic therapies: Kinesiology, Chiropractic, Naturopath, Massage Therapy, Reflexology, Reiki, Acupuncture, Aura-Soma, Crystal Therapy, Chakra Balance/Cleansing…. and the list goes on.

Counselling - in particular 'guided' counseling or any other which happens to suit your needs.

Meditation supports the mind, body and soul.

Vitamin and mineral supplements: which you are unable to retain naturally or are unable to gain from your diet. As advised by a naturopathic practitioner preferably. Chinese herbs have the ability to assist the body in a natural capacity, I thoroughly recommend them especially if one's body is unable to absorb by other means.

Respect Mother Earth - take care of the environment, if you take from the environment then please give something back in return. If you buy or build a house and land needs to be cleared, plant trees, shrubs, native where possible so the native birds, bees and the balance of the world is restored. Strive to make the word pollution redundant.

We have beautiful Mother Earth - so please treat her with love and respect.

Build your wheel. Read, learn and continue growing in accordance with the Tao philosophies and you world will change not only you but for those around you.

Select the spokes which would help to support your life, your body, your soul. I select my holistic therapists by intuition, I allow my Higher Self to guide me first of all. If I walk into a practice and they have a Buddha or Feng Shui applied I know I am on the correct path. If they tell me they are 'guided' with their method of healing, I know I am home and where I am meant to be. Intuition has never failed me in my quest to seek assistance with my mind, body and soul therapies. Trust your intuition to guide you to your correct path.

What better gift could you give to yourself, see the Light and the way to a better life?

Remember, trust *your* intuition.

Talk to 'someone' should a problem appear insurmountable - there is a solution to your problem; you just need to search for it.

I hope you have gained something from reading my book, my son Fabian was and is my greatest teacher. I believe I was meant to pay it forward.

I hope this helps you gain some perspective in your own life.

Nourish your *soul* daily and remember to love yourself and give thanks for all that you are, remember you are a *soul* having a *human* experience, not a *human* having a *soul* experience. Have faith in the Universe, it will provide what you need, when you need it, and in the way you need it all in Divine Time.

This book was written with words woven from love.

Take care of you, you are very special.

Until next time …

With much love and light

Dee

About the Author

I was born in Tasmania and grew up in the picturesque Huon Valley, the youngest of three children.

The experiences outlined in my books are based on a true account of my life and how I viewed life from my perspective.

"In my life, fact is often stranger than fiction" and this will become evident throughout the journey I take you on, as I travel through time recounting my life.

Writing was not on my radar until my son died in tragic circumstances when he took his life whilst in Risdon Prison. He had a severe mental illness and was only receiving minimal medication, it would be sufficient to bring any parent to the brink let alone the many other events I have endured throughout my 66 years. Five deaths in a six month period rocked the Tasmanian Prison System from 1999-2000, I had written a four page submission to the then Ombudsman outlining my son's case and my final words of the submission stated "Unless something is done there will be more deaths" there was ... that of my son a short time later.

Discover how I coped and survived my many and varied experiences and My Recipe for Survival.

I am spiritual and believe in the power of positivity.

In 2009 I fully opened to channel Spirit and with it came a whole new realm of possibility, one which enriched my life but also left me feeling isolated to some extent.

I MAKE MARK the title of my first book, a dedication to my son's short tormented life, BEYOND DESCRIPTION, *a story of Grief, Disbelief and Insight* is book two in the series of my life.

I completed High School with what was then a Schools Board A Certificate in 1967 and then my life really commenced. I had had no writing experience until I MAKE MARK came into my life and words flooded onto the pages. It became a passion and a way in which I could help change the lives of others. A doctor/counsellor had literally 'changed my life' with his method of counselling and for the first time in my life … life according to me finally made sense.

So … whilst life had to be lived and I had to keep on keeping on … never far from my mind was my ultimate aim … to be in a position to help others to help themselves.

These books are my first steps in fulfilling my dream of witnessing and walking around a Holistic Centre where every aspect of a person is considered, a holistic approach in every sense of the word. A centre where the emotionally disadvantaged and those like myself who have been challenged beyond belief can be taught the skills to make their lives work for them instead of against them.

I have a self confessed 'warped sense of humour' so don't for one minute think my books will be gloomy, hopefully I will have you laughing and crying with me along the way.

My hope and aim is to help others feel not so alone … so if you are experiencing your own challenge … take it from me … you are not alone … and you can come out the other side … bigger and better. I am living proof, I may be small on the outside but I am a giant on the inside where it most counts. Once you locate your inner giant you too can come out the other side stronger, more confident and a whole lot wiser as a result.

Acknowledgement

Acknowledgement and well deserved thanks to:

Julie-Ann Harper and her team at the Pickawoowoo Publishing Group.

Intuitive Artist: Cover Design: Laila Savolainen (Pickawoowoo).

Logo Concept & Layout: Ben Reali.

Publishing Imprint Logo: Laila Savolainen (Pickawoowoo).

This book would not have been possible without the invaluable assistance of these wonderful humans.

Julie-Ann has demonstrated the patience of a saint in dealing with my maiden voyage in to the publishing world, apologies and a huge heartfelt thank you. I promise next time will be easier!

I fell in love with the cover the minute I saw it on my computer screen, a huge thank you also – it is truly beautiful and the colours are so perfect, so me!

Ben, you are definitely one of a kind, please don't ever change, you are amazing.

Although I have not met most of you in person, I love and treasure the contribution you have made toward the dedication of this book in memory of my son.

I think you are all amazingly beautiful souls.

Much love and thanks.

www.ingramcontent.com/pod-product-compliance
Lightning Source LLC
Chambersburg PA
CBHW071857290426
44110CB00013B/1181